MY LIFE IN DOHA

MY LIFE IN DOHA:

BETWEEN DREAM AND REALITY

By Rachel Hajar, M.D.

Œ

Strategic Book Group

Durham, Connecticut

Strategic Book Group
P. O. Box 333
Durham, CT 06422
http://www.strategicbookclub.com

ISBN: 978-1-60976-591-0

Book Design by Julius Kiskis

Printed in the United States of America
19 18 17 16 15 14 13 12 11   1 2 3 4 5

DEDICATION

To my loving husband; Children: Alia, Tami, Haifa, Salma,
and Asma; Grandchildren: Aziz and Saud

"We are such stuff as dreams are made on, and our little life is rounded with a sleep."

–Shakespeare, *The Tempest*

CONTENTS

Introduction.. ix

Part One-Landing In My New World

1. The Arrival 3
2. Standing at the Gate 6

Part Two-Beyond the Gate

3. A City by The Sea..13
4. A House for Dreaming......................................27

Part Three: Living Adventure

5. The Black Veil 39
6. The Majilis: A lesson in Culture 55
7. Abui 68
8. Ummi 88
9. War on Evil Weed 103
10. Driving in Doha...119
11. It's Time for Fish...126
12. The Adhan...133
13. Romancing the Souk 143
14. Footsteps of Morning: Eid and Christmas...................167
15. Ramadan: A Special Month 178
16. It Makes Sense to Burn Incense 196
17. Looking for Mother Pearls 203
18. Love the Child That Holds Your Hand 220

Part Four-Life Is an Ocean

19. Arab Love Song..237
20. Dancing with Flowers 274

INTRODUCTION

Many of our dreams are elusive fantasies; they fade and melt away into thin air. But life itself is like a dream and we create our own reality—or illusion. When I left my homeland to pursue further medical training in the U.S.A., I never dreamed I would marry an Arab cardiologist from Qatar; neither did I dream of living in Qatar, a country I had never heard of before I met my husband.

When I came to live in Qatar in 1978, my knowledge of the customs and culture of Qatar and the Arab world in general was almost non-existent. I was born in the Philippines and grew up a Catholic. I found that the social customs and traditions in my new world were vastly different from what I was used to and I had to learn a different way of life. In my early years in Qatar, my husband directed me to books written by European travelers in Arabia, to gain insight into my new society. One of the books he gave me was Thesiger's *Arabian Sands*, which I read with fascination. Thesiger wrote about his life among the nomadic Bedouin Arabs—the Bedu, "a people whose spirit once lit the desert." He wrote: "While I was with the Arabs, I wished only to live as they lived . . . No man can live this life and emerge unchanged. He will carry, however faint, the imprint of the desert, the brand that marks the nomad; and he will have within him the yearning to return, weak or insistent according to his nature. For this cruel land can cast a spell which no temperate clime can hope to match."

Unlike Thesiger, I am an "insider" being married to a Qatari, enjoying a civilized life in a city at a time of economic prosperity; but I found his descriptions of life in the desert and Arab social customs extremely helpful in understanding my new world. I found that although the circumstances of the modern Gulf Arabs have changed, they still carry within them and in their ways what Thesiger called the "imprint of the desert." I have felt, as Thesiger did, the magnetism, the spell. He wrote at the end of his second journey through the sands, "This was the Journey's End that I had no desire to reach." Through marriage, my life's journey has brought me here in Qatar and I live within that spell alluded to by Thesiger.

This book is about my personal experience and narrates how I met my husband and came to live in Qatar; getting to know my in-laws; recollections of my early experiences, impressions, observations, and insights into another culture; how that world is different from the world I have been brought up in; what it is like to live within the heart of a culture not your own; the social changes I have witnessed; and the evolution of my perspective about the region and its people.

I have written articles about some aspects of Gulf Arab culture, which have been published in magazines. I am also an intermittent diarist, and I write to my friends about my experiences and observations in my new world. My articles, diary, and correspondence were valuable sources for the book.

I would like to thank my husband, Dr. Hajar Ahmed Hajar Albinali, for his support, encouragement, valuable comments, and suggestions. I would like to extend my special thanks and appreciation to Dr. Floyd D. Loop, former CEO of Cleveland Clinic Foundation, for suggesting to me the idea of writing this book and for encouraging me.

Part One

LANDING IN
MY NEW WORLD

CHAPTER 1

The Arrival

There are unforgettable moments in our life. A scent. A sound. A scene. My first glimpse of Doha was one of those moments. It was from the air on a July summer day at high noon in the summer of 1978.

My husband and I had finished our postgraduate medical training in the U.S.A. and my husband was bringing me and our two young children—a daughter, two and a half, and a son, ten months—to live in Doha, Qatar for good. We were arriving aboard a Gulf Air flight from London. I remember the pilot announcing the plane was "descending . . . Doha can be seen nicely through your window . . ." I felt rather than saw passengers position themselves for a good view. I remember the hush that followed—and no wonder. Doha from the air was flat and beige. It shimmered and trembled in the heat like a mirage. Peering through the plane's window, I scanned the terrain anxiously for spots of green or elevation. There were none. Butterflies quivered in my stomach . . . I wondered what life would be like in a beige city.

As I gazed at the monochromatic landscape, the plane seemed to veer slightly as though making an arc, and the clear water hugging the city's shoreline came into view. The green surface rippled and sparkled, like emeralds. "Fasten your seatbelts, ladies and gentlemen," the pilot announced. The plane continued its descent, and then hovered, before landing. I could see rocks and undulating algae at the bottom of the water as far as ten meters from the shore. The sea, the water, was reassuring. It was real . . . it had substance. The quivering butterflies in my stomach took flight.

The plane landed smoothly, taxied, and came to a full stop on the runway. It felt like we landed in the middle of nowhere. The army of men with tools who usually greets and swarms around an arriving plane, like bees, was absent. Through the plane's window, I saw two or three planes parked a hundred meters away. The airport was small and not busy. The main airport building was one-story and rectangular, with a forlorn look, but emblazoned bravely on top was a sign that read DOHA INTERNATIONAL AIRPORT in English and beside it in Arabic. I watched as men in overalls brought a portable stairway towards the door. Two airport buses also arrived, stopped a few meters away, and waited for passengers with an expectant air.

"Ismael must be waiting for us now." Hajar, my husband, said in a low voice as we waited for the seatbelt sign to go off.

"Who's Ismael?" I asked.

"The driver," he replied as he got our passports ready. Over the microphone the pilot thanked us for flying with Gulf Air and wished us a good rest of our journey and a pleasant stay in Doha. Gathering our two young children and our hand-carry bags, we lined up to disembark. The line moved slowly. The temperature seemed to rise as we approached the exit door. As we stepped out from the plane onto the stairway platform, hot air met and surrounded us, overwhelming us with its intensity. Some passengers hurriedly descended the stairway to get into the waiting buses.

"It's 40°C (104°F) and humid. Let us get in the bus quickly,"

Hajar said as he guided me towards one of the buses. He held our daughter's hand while I carried our infant son in my arms. The sky was deeply blue and cloudless. Our dark glasses protected us from the intense, blinding light. The sun's heat penetrated the tops of our heads, encircling us. Little beads of perspiration formed on my forehead and upper lip, collapsed, and dribbled down along the sides of my face as we walked the few meters from the plane to the bus. Little watery droplets trickled down my back, like prickly needles. My dress clung to my body.

On boarding the bus, I was relieved to see vacant seats. The cool air in the bus was soothing, a pocket of relief from the ferocity of the desert sun. The bus stopped in front of the airport building and we got off. A shaded veranda flanked the runway building's façade, providing momentary reprieve from the relentless heat.

My husband pushed open the glass door. We entered a room cooled with window air conditioners that rhythmically sent off whirring vibrations. The room, plain and matter of fact, had two glass-fronted cubicles. A sign in front of the cubicles proclaimed Customs in Arabic and English. We did not have to stand in line. There was no need. There were only a few arrivals, mainly men.

Behind each cubicle sat two bearded and mustachioed men in white floor-length shirts and white flowing headdresses. I was entering another world.

CHAPTER 2

Standing at the Gate

"I see Ismael," my husband whispered as we emerged from the airport entrance. A man dressed in a white floor-length shirt and wearing a small white head cap advanced to meet us. I felt, without knowing what it was, that there was something missing from his costume. He looked rather incomplete, as though he had not quite finished dressing. Later I realized that he was not wearing a white flowing head cover. Hajar had told me that only Gulf Arabs wore the complete Gulf costume with flowing headgear. Non Gulf Arabs wore western style clothes but non Gulf Arabs who were employed as drivers or cooks in private homes sometimes wore the Gulf Arab costume minus the flowing head cover. Ismael was Egyptian.

Ismael greeted my husband with deference and an affection that made him grab Hajar and try to kiss him on his head. My husband, resisting the kiss on the head, sheepishly glanced sideways at me. In his culture, the recipient of a kiss on the head signifies an older person or someone greatly esteemed. But Ismael would not be denied and prevailed in planting the head kiss. Then the glow of jubilation on his face slowly ebbed as he became aware of another presence—mine. I seemed to present a complication, a snag to an otherwise happy and smooth Gulf Arab homecoming.

"Salaam alaykum, Madame," he murmured, turning hesitantly in my direction, smiling but keeping his eyes averted. He was polite and respectful but his discomfort was acute and palpable. Ismael acknowledged my presence and valiantly overcame his embarrassment. He picked up our luggage and arranged it on the curb, telling my husband he would bring the car around.

In turn, Ismael's demeanor had stirred my dormant angst. I thought, *is something wrong with me?* But the question I whispered to my husband was, "What's wrong with him?"

"Huh?" Then comprehending the situation Hajar whispered back that, in general, men in the Arabian Gulf were not used to meeting unveiled women and Ismael's behavior was typical.

"He's just shy," Hajar said. I learned later that in Arab Gulf society, women should be veiled in public. Apart from mentioning once that women in his country veiled themselves, my husband never once mentioned to me the unique male/female dynamic in his society, before our marriage or in the early years of our marriage. I have wondered many times since why he was silent on the issue, but there were times when I thought that it was just as well that I had been kept blissfully in the dark. It is almost impossible to understand a culture by just looking in from outside, which is like peeking through a window at events happening on the street. You see an ice-pick view. With the wisdom of hindsight, I realize now that one has to live the life within a culture to fully comprehend its perceived mysteries.

But on that summer day, when I first set foot in the state of Qatar, I was unaware of the implications of being unveiled in public. I suppose my being unveiled must have been an affront to the existing social order. In retrospect, it must have been shocking since my husband's father was also the Islamic judge of Qatar. No wonder Ismael had been acutely embarrassed. My husband, however, did not blink an eye. He seemed to consider the situation amusing, and taking my cue from him, I relaxed. All would be well. I had no inkling at the time how different life would be. Unknown to me many new sights, sounds, and experiences awaited.

Part Two

BEYOND THE GATE

CHAPTER 3
City by the Sea

The car that Ismael had brought around was an American sedan, a white Buick with plush red velvet seats. Hajar, sitting in front next to Ismael, commented that American cars were "very nice and comfortable but, with a peak performance of only two years, didn't last long." The car he had in the U.S.A. was a sports car, a hard top Chevy Camaro, and incredibly roomy for a young family with two small children. He had bought the car while still a bachelor, when he used to love sports cars. He used to drive fast and was given speeding tickets. But old habits never die. Recently, he was very surprised to receive a speeding ticket. "I was not driving fast," he had exclaimed in disbelief. Radar, equipped with a camera, had caught him driving at a 100 km/h (62 mph) on a road with a speed limit of 80 (49 mph). He loved telling the story of how, when he was a medical intern in the U.S.A., a judge had once tried to scare him by making him watch a video of car accident victims.

He had kept the Camaro after our marriage. It had never occurred to him to change it to a sedan. When it was time to leave the U.S.A., for good, he sold the car. It never crossed his mind to ship the car to Doha. The buyer had offered to buy it for $5,000 and my husband had accepted the offer without hesitation. He had shaken his head with amazement when he told me the news.

13

He had bought the car new for $3,500, six years before he sold it. The buyer had told him that Chevrolet had ceased producing Camaros. He said the buyer had been "taken with the car," which was "hugger orange," a hot color that always managed to look cool on the road.

Compared to the sporty Camaro, the Buick was more comfortable; it was pleasant and cool inside. The extra springs of the American car gently cushioned us over road bumps and occasional potholes.

"We will take you on a short tour around Doha before heading for home, just a few minutes. Doha is small." My husband said adding, "You can drive from the south to the north of Qatar in one hour and fifteen minutes. Qatar is very small."

"What is the population of Qatar?" I asked.

"Uh, I'm not sure exactly. Total maybe around 200,000; Qataris maybe 50,000. Qataris are the minority and foreigners are the majority." With a little laugh, he added that the exact number of Qataris was a "closely guarded secret." Since then, however, the total population in Qatar has increased yearly and significantly in recent years due to the influx of foreign labor but the exact number of Qataris is still "classified" information.

Sitting in the backseat, cradling our sleeping son on my lap and our daughter snuggling next to me, her head resting on my arm, I settled back, relaxing in the oasis of coolness. In the heat, the coolness in the car was thrillingly pleasurable.

While my husband and Ismael conversed in Arabic, with Ismael filling him in on domestic happenings, I took in the local scenery through the closed car window. There was only one major road that led to a network of medium and small side streets. There were no crisscrossing highways or bridges and very few traffic lights. There were plenty of roundabouts, which automatically controlled traffic with the quirky rule: Give way to traffic on your left.

An island of date-palm trees divided the main road into two one-way streets. The palm trees were magnificent with their graceful pinnate leaves casting cool and inviting shadows on the ground in the noonday heat. Amber, elongated fruits dangled from them. Men dressed in baggy pants and loose over shirts rested in their shade. Palm tree leaves peeped out from fences. It seemed to be the favored tree in Doha. The date palm originated in the Arabian Gulf, with scientists and archaeologists claiming Bahrain as the specific place. It went to Europe in the seventh century, when the Arabs conquered Spain. Spanish missionaries carried the tree to the New World in the eighteenth and early nineteenth centuries. Hundreds of varieties exist today, and the tree has become a favorite decorative element in Arab and Mediterranean countries. In Doha, it was the ornamental tree of choice.

"This is the Corniche," Hajar informed me as we neared the waterfront. He told Ismael to slow down. Doha Corniche even then, before its development into a first class Corniche, like the one in Cannes, France, was appealing. Date-palm trees lined the sea promenade. The deep, blue topaz sea lapped gently. Gazing at the smooth blue expanse at midday through the closed car window, I heard soft sleepy rhythmic swishing in my mind, conjuring up lazy afternoons. Cities by lakes, rivers, and seas are pleasing. The water imparts an aura of romance and glamour to a city. What would Venice be without its canals, Paris without the Seine or London without the Thames—and Doha without the sea?

Doha is the capital of Qatar, a tiny peninsula in the Arabian Gulf. I read later that Qatar is nicknamed "thumb of Arabia" because it protrudes from Arabia's eastern coast into the Arabian Gulf. The deep, blue waters of the Arabian Gulf surround it on three sides. From the airplane, I had marveled at how clear and pristine the water was and admired how the shimmering blue water hugged the beige-white coastline like a necklace. Water shapes the history, culture, and lifestyle of its inhabitants. Riverfront settlements blossomed into great civilizations along the Tigris and Euphrates Rivers and the River Nile. Qatar, with its long tradition of fishing and pearling, has strong historical and cultural ties to the sea. Archaeological digs have unearthed settlements scattered along its coast dating back to bygone eras, hundreds and thousands of years old.

As we leisurely drove along the Corniche, my husband fed me with some historical tidbits about his habitat.

"Arabia," he said, "is nine-tenths desert. Before the discovery of oil, the inhabitants were mainly Bedouins, Arabic-speaking desert nomads. Settled folks called Hadhr tilled the soil oasis or worked along the coast as fishermen or pearl divers."

I gathered from his talk that before oil, life was as hard and relentless as the desert itself. The Arabian Peninsula had been relatively unknown to the world. And then "black gold"—oil—was discovered in the middle of the twentieth century, and the region changed forever. In just a few decades, barren wastes and clusters of small fishing and pearling settlements were transformed into modern metropolises. No other nations have experienced such profound changes in circumstance and lifestyle so rapidly. It was as though the people woke up one morning to find gleaming buildings . . . paved roads . . . highways . . . shiny cars . . . sparkling fountains . . . beautiful mosques . . . pleasant green gardens . . . air-conditioned houses . . . nights illumined with electric lights. It was a metamorphosis straight out of the *Arabian Nights*.

"The old ways of life—nomadism, pearl diving and seafaring—are irrevocably gone," Hajar continued with nostalgia. "But over there on the harbor, you see ships," he said pointing in the direction of the harbor. "Remnants of Qatar's seafaring and pearling past are embodied in those ships."

I was enchanted upon seeing the cluster of ships in the harbor. They evoked romance and nostalgia, unlike the huge modern cruise liners.

"What charming ships," I exclaimed.

"Those are called dhows," my husband said. "They are fishing boats. In the old days, they were also used for pearling. The big ones used to sail to India and Africa for trade." He instructed Ismael to get closer to the harbor and stop the car a few moments, so we could admire the sleek lines of the dhows.

The dhows, rocked gently by the sea, looked dreamy, longing for the solitude of a sunset at sea, for the endless immensity of the sea. They were as graceful as gazelles. Made entirely of wood and burnished in red mahogany stain, they were as glossy and lustrous as scimitars. The shaded rear end was high, sweeping low towards the bow, then tapering, rising and jutting at the prow. I could not see them up close but some, I found later, had beautiful carved wooden panels attached to the hull. Wondering if such exquisite carvings had a protective function since seafaring was a dangerous occupation, I recalled reading that Vikings decorated the prow of their warships with a fearsome dragon's head for protection.

Contemplating the polished silhouette of the dhows, I imagined ships at sea, sails unfurled, on voyages of exploration, military expeditions, or trade. Men sail in search of romance and adventure, and in so doing make history. Alexander's epic expedition in 326 BC was both a military campaign and a journey of exploration. His expedition not only opened Mediterranean Europe to the East—Central Asia and India, but he left behind illustrated travelogues full of exotic flora and fauna and information about the fabulous inhabitants of the remote lands of the East: men without heads; dangerous animal-headed beasts;

Cyclops, beings with one foot; and exotic monsters, like griffins
and dragons. Whether the writers actually thought they saw such
hybrid creatures, or merely heard about them or saw them in their
dreams and believed them real, we shall never know. Stories
of such implausible creatures abounded and were circulated by
travelers and sailors who had been to the orient. These stories,
compiled in classical antiquity as facts about the world's regions
and wonders, were passed on through the centuries, with new
details and motifs being added as they circulated.

Watching the languid to and fro bobbing of the dhows, I
imagined a solitary ship, motionless in the middle of the wide
blue sea, waiting for favorable wind, its sailors sitting around at
night under starry skies, swapping stories of monsters and beasts
inhabiting and guarding treasures in a far away land, somewhere,
beyond the deep blue sea. A gentle breeze rustled through my
mind with whisperings and murmurings about a bird, a large
bird —the rukh, whose wings hid the sun. The rukh (griffin), an
enormous bird with the head, shoulders, and legs of an eagle and
the body of a lion, appears several times in the *Arabian Nights*
as a guardian of treasure and plays a leading role in the story of
Sinbad the Sailor: "Behold the sun was suddenly hidden from me
. . . an enormous bird flew through the air, [and] veiled the sun."

Of course, such imaginary beings only existed in the human
imagination. But these tales were told at a time when people
believed such provoking and unsettling creatures existed in
the exotic East. Nowadays, it may seem incredible that people
used to believe in their existence; yet, even in our scientific and
highly technical world, stories of monsters and hybrid creatures
still occasionally surface in the media as reported "sightings":
the Loch Ness monster, described as a long-necked aquatic
reptile inhabiting Scotland's Loch Ness lake; Bigfoot, a large
bipedal apelike creature standing between seven and ten feet

tall and said to inhabit remote forests of North America; and the Yeti, the apelike animal of Nepal and Tibet. Several years ago, Hollywood even made a movie of Big Foot. Among the young, photos of fantastic creatures circulate on the Internet. One of my daughters recently emailed a picture of a "fish with legs and hands," and a note saying, "Hey, I don't know whether this is real or played around by Photoshop." As a child of the digital age, she did not dismiss the existence of such a creature as impossible. In her mind, a "fish with legs and hands" just might exist, somewhere.

Images and stories of imaginary beings will live on as long as we humans are around, for the human imagination is preoccupied with monsters, dwelling in the labyrinths of our unconscious minds and revealing themselves to us in our dreams. They live on in mythology, breathing life into art, for art stands midway between what is perceived and what is believed. Many imaginary-being legends survive in the Alexander romance, a collection of well-known legends that developed around the heroic figure of Alexander the Great. Although shrouded with magic and enchantment, Alexander's historic voyage changed the world —and so did oil—fuel that fuels dreams of prosperity; fuel that spins our modern world; fuel so vital that world economy and international politics revolve around it like planets orbiting the sun.

The dhows, languorously swaying in the midday sun, excited my imagination. Beyond dreams of discovery, military dominion, and power quests, ships have other splendid pursuits and allures—love and romance, carried on the rays of the sun. Who can forget Cleopatra's famous barge, that ship of seduction, sailing from Egypt to the city of Tarsus (in modern-day Turkey) to seduce Mark Antony? "The barge she sat in, like a burnish'd throne, / Burn'd on the water: the poop was beaten gold / Purple the sails, and so perfumed that / The winds were love-sick with them; the oars were silver / Which to the tune of flutes kept stroke and made / The water which they beat to follow faster, / As amorous of their strokes."

Gazing dreamily at the anchored dhows gleaming in the sun, I fancied that Cleopatra's celebrated barge must have been related to the big dhows.

"No. The Egyptian ships, Mediterranean ships, were different" my husband said firmly, smashing my fancy. "Dhows have triangular sails whereas ancient Mediterranean ships had small square sails." I wished to see a dhow at sea, sailing into the sunset, triangular sails billowing in the wind. Admiring the sleek silhouette of the dhows, I asked Hajar if dhow was the Arabic word for ship.

"The Arabic word for ship is *markab* or *safinah*. Dhow comes from an African word, *daw*, Swahili, I think. Swahili refers to the language of East Africa. The construction type of the boat itself is probably Indian. Some are made in India, some locally, but the wood is imported from India. A dhow, called locally as boom, is identified as Arab, Gulf Arab."

"They are shiny, like new," I remarked. "It's quite amazing how the varnish stays glossy in this heat and humidity."

"Shipbuilders and sailors use fish oil as varnish. The ships are varnished every year."

"Fish oil! They must use a lot of fish. And uh, how did it smell?"

"Very bad, but only in the beginning. The unpleasant smell is burned by the sun," my husband said, laughing softly. "Oil is extracted from shark liver and sardines by heating and pressure. This has been the method used for centuries. The oil is water and heat resistant. That's why the ships look glossy."

Compared to me, my husband is an expert on ships, Gulf ships. Growing up at a time when seafaring played an important role in the life and economy of the people, he frequently told me stories from his childhood, before oil brought prosperity to the region. His father used to own a large sailing ship used for trade called Sinbook, a type of ship that sailed to Africa or India. As a child, he eagerly awaited the return of the ship, anticipating the gifts of toys, candies, and clothes the ship's captain would bring him. Once, the captain had brought him a large flashlight from India. He had loved that flashlight, considering it his most prized possession. With it, he overcame his fear of the dark. On dark nights, he would flash it everywhere. One night, curious to see how far he could see with it, he had gone to the seashore near their house, pointing the light towards the sky and admiring the shaft of light slicing through the darkness. Moisture and particles in the air had reflected the light, creating a strong and clearly demarcated laser-like beam. An old man had ruined his fun by asking, "Are you looking for angels in the sky?"

"You know, I told you once that my father had night blindness when I was seven years old," my husband continued. "He was cured with fish liver." He narrated how a local folk healer had advised his father to apply fish liver oil on the eyes. The oil was prepared by cooking the fish livers on a tin over hot charcoal. When oil oozed out, it was collected and cooled. Then *merwud*, "a thin piece of stick made of silver or mother-of-pearl" and used by women to apply kohl around their eyes, was soaked in the oil. The oil-soaked merwud was then placed between the upper and lower eyelid like applying eye ointment, and when the patient closed his eyes over the merwud, it was slowly pulled out from the side. After the oil application the patient usually ate the cooked livers, just because it was cooked food and liver was considered quite tasty. His father had eaten the cooked livers during his treatment. Within one week, his father had regained his night vision. The people, not knowing that eating the liver did the curing, believed that applying fish oil to the eyes cured the disease,. The practice of curing night blindness with fish liver oil originated from the Babylonians who had been treating night blindness with animal liver as early as 2000 BC. The ancient Egyptians and Greeks followed and transmitted the Babylonian practice. Night blindness is caused by a deficiency in vitamin A. When vitamin A was discovered in 1906, it was found that animal and fish livers were rich in vitamin A.

As Ismael continued the leisurely drive along the Corniche, my husband pointed to a white building with serrated walls.

"That is the Qatar National Museum," he said. "It used to be the residence of a past Amir." He instructed Ismael to drive closer to the building. Ismael, driving slowly, made a few turns and then stopped in front of the museum. Through the car window, I admired the entrance, a big heavy gate made of teakwood decorated with black iron bars and copper knobs. The door was set within a striking pointed arch with delicate stucco ornamentation. Museums are repositories of cultural heritage, memories of a society. Through their artwork and artifacts, we learn about a people's collective human experience, their aspirations, their hopes, and their dreams. Memory and identity lie within museums, as in the mind. I longed to go inside—a wish fulfilled a few days later.

"Shall we go?" My husband asked, his voice intruding through my reverie. There's really not much more to see."

Ismael drove us back towards the Corniche, making an uninterrupted U-turn at a roundabout, our bodies swaying and bending to one side, like willows in the wind. My daughter Alia giggled as I exclaimed "Oops," grabbing the back of the front seat to abort a fall. "Corniche Roundabout" my husband said. "I don't know why they don't just install traffic lights," he muttered. But I liked the roundabouts. Going round a roundabout was fun, easygoing, and less intimidating than traffic lights. Traffic lights leave no room for doubt and are straightforward. Red: Stop. Green: Go. Missing a turn required driving until the next traffic light—very boring, or a detour through a maze of little streets— very frustrating. At a roundabout, you just go round and round, spinning, like a top, 'til you get your bearings, that is, if you don't get dizzy.

The roundabout is a remnant of British presence in the region. Traffic, however, drives on the right, but according to my husband, it used to be on the left before 1966. Qatar used to be a British protectorate like the rest of the Arabian Peninsula. In return for oil concessions or the right to oil exploration for companies appointed by the British government, the British promised to protect Arabia and the coastal states against attack by an external power.

We passed clusters of little shops that were closed because it was midday, some scruffy-looking, before coming to an impressive-looking building several meters off the road and fronted with spacious parking and landscaped walkways. "The Amiri Diwan," he said. "It is the official workplace of the Amir of Qatar." Qatar is a monarchy with an Amir.

"Oh, what's that?" I asked excitedly, on seeing a pink and white tower with a clock several meters from the Amiri Diwan. Beyond, the dome and minaret of the Grand Mosque could be seen.

"Huh, that? The Clock Tower. You like it? What's so exciting about it?" he asked, puzzled, shaking his head.

"Oh, I don't know. I like it. A pink and white clock right in the middle of traffic, dusty buildings, and a mosque; it is so unexpected. You know, like Alice in Wonderland . . ." my voice trailed as the image of the White Rabbit with pink eyes taking a watch from its waistcoat darted through my mind. But of course he didn't know. He was brought up on *jinni* (genie) stories, told on hot, dark, summer nights, under starlit skies. I had read the book, *Alice's Adventures in Wonderland,* by Lewis Carroll, as a young girl and had started reading parts of it to my daughter at bedtime.

"Alia knows the Rabbit story in Alice. What did the Rabbit say, Alia?"

"Oh dear, oh dear, I'm late, I'm late." Alia said laughing. Then in a singsong voice, she began, "Once upon a time there were four little rabbits, and their names were Flopsy, Mopsy, Cotton-tail, and Peter." It was the opening line in Beatrix Potter's *The Tale of Peter Rabbit,* one of her favorite bedtime stories.

"Alia knows a lot of stories," I said. "She loves stories."

"I know. I made up a bedtime story for her, *The Little Red Hen.* Alia, you remember the story don't you?" He had made up the story while putting Alia to sleep one night. He had been reading from a children's storybook, but it was taking Alia a long time to fall asleep. Getting tired, he had closed the book, turned the lights off, and just made up a story in the dark. Alia had fallen asleep before the end of the story. The next time he told Alia the same story, he didn't remember the details and had adlibbed; but Alia had corrected him, "No Daddy. That's not how it was." So, the story had developed over time, with Alia correcting him on details here and there, while he spun episode after episode.

I had admired his story-telling prowess. He narrated that one summer, while still a high school student he had been hospitalized for mumps. While he had been recovering in the hospital, he had amused and entertained himself by writing a short social story, a tragic one about love and a young man and woman falling in love. But the girl's father had betrothed her against her wish to the son of a rich man, an event that brought the girl much unhappiness. The young man left town but on her wedding night, she received a note from him bidding her "goodbye forever." And that had been the title of his short story, *Goodbye Forever*. The story had won first prize in a student literary contest. While a student in high school, he had read the works of famous writers such as Tolstoy, Gorky, Victor Hugo, and Ernest Hemingway. He had even read *Gone With The Wind*.

"Your grandmother will tell you plenty of stories Alia," my husband said. "We'll go home now."

We left the Corniche and passed walled, one-story houses, large and small, as the car detoured into side streets and alleys. Qatar, like the rest of the Arabian Gulf states, imposed restrictions on the height of residential houses to safeguard the privacy of the women. Although there were two-story houses, those did not have neighboring houses close by. The women must have freedom to move about their houses without being seen by neighbors. Nowadays, however, two-story residential houses are quite common.

The houses were fenced and their exteriors plain. The roofs were flat and straight because rain was scarce. According to my husband, residents used to sleep on the flat roofs during the hot summer months, in the days when there was no electricity. Houses now are made of concrete and cement, but before oil, houses were made from sun-dried mud bricks or stones of either limestone or coral mixed with clay. In a region where summer temperatures often soared above 45°C (113°F) and humidity made clothing cling to the wearer, resourceful and creative uses for available materials evolved to help make life tolerable. Mud, an excellent material for insulation, was commonly used, as it was abundant, easy to use, and ideal for hot climates.

Some of the houses we passed had magnificent, ornately decorated wooden gates outfitted with a little door—a door within a door—that had intrigued and fascinated me. "It is called a *farkha*, which means a small girl," Hajar had informed me. It was an endearing description that I had thought charming. These doors, used for daily access, were up to three meters tall, made of teakwood, and decorated with iron or copper bars, and studded with one-inch, copper-headed nails and finely carved geometric shapes. The doors, imbued with exotic charm, gave off an aura of romance that enthralled me. They were either made locally or imported from India, East Africa, or Basra in Iraq. The beautiful wooden gates are disappearing and being replaced with metal that echoes the style and decoration of the old wood doors.

Minarets seemed to rise from every block. Mosques—big, small, old, and new—festooned the landscape, tangible testaments to the country's Islamic persona. I had not expected so many mosques. The small or old mosques had little or no decoration. The biggermosques were more beautiful and invoked traditional Islamic architecture from different regions and time periods. Ornamentation was simple, understated, and elegant. Graceful arches, rounded, pointed, or lotus shaped with exquisitely pierced screens in wood or plaster, decorated the exterior façade. Window grilles featured delicate woodwork and beautiful gypsum and stucco panels designed with arabesque or geometric designs. Under the glare of the desert sun, in the midst of flat-topped roofs, the mosques with their distinctive dome and spire silhouettes stood cool, calm, and collected.

A place of worship, a church, or a mosque, maps intimate human needs. I always loved the feeling of peace and rest emanating from churches. I shall always treasure the memory of attending mass with my family on Sundays, Christmas, and Easter. People go to church for many reasons: prayers, supplications, blessings, thanksgiving but most of all, for consolation. I have always thought of churches as self-contained, brimming with quiet life and yet isolated, life of a different dimension,. The mosques had an air of enduring dignity and quiet majesty that I admired.

CHAPTER 4
A House for Dreaming

"We're home," my husband announced as Ismael slowed the car and stopped in front of an iron gate. The gate had a farkha, like many gates we had passed. Although the farkha was partly open I could not see the house from outside.

Holding Alia's hand and carrying Tami, I followed my husband through the little door. There were a couple of date-palm trees along the inside of the concrete fence, and the house was situated about three meters from the front gate. The one-story house, freestanding and rectangular, had no plants or grass in the space between the fence and the front of the house. Three steps led to a porch that extended alongside the front façade. Above the stairs was a wooden lattice through which vines wove and entwined. My husband stood under its shade, squinting up.

"I was hoping it would be bearing fruits," he said with some disappointment.

"What is it?" I asked.

"Grapes."

"Grapes! You can grow grapes in the desert?"

"Oh, yes."

"And the fruits are sweet?"

"Sometimes. But we grow this mainly for its shade," he said. "In the winter, the leaves are very green." The grapevine was not luxuriant; its leaves were yellowish and sparse, like a sickly old woman. It was in the middle of summer in the desert. I had been surprised that the grapevine was still surviving.

We passed through the porch and entrance hallway and into an inner open-air courtyard. Around the courtyard, *al-liwan* (shades or covered patio) added protection from the sun's merciless rays in summer. All the rooms opened onto the liwan, in the manner of interior courtyard houses.

In my mind a courtyard conjures up beautiful tiles or marble floors, green plants, flowers, and fountains. But that courtyard was very different that summer. There were no blooming flowers, no green plants, and no fountain. The flooring of the open-air section was not marble but mother earth herself. The liwan was tiled. A mango tree and a couple of young date-palm trees provided shade. Surrounding the perimeter of the rectangular courtyard was a bench-high concrete wall with supporting liwan columns that resembled a colonnaded walkway. Resting along the low concrete wall were some disconsolate-looking flowering plants that must have bloomed once, as gorgeous women did in the summer of their youth and beauty. In the cruel desert summer, plants wither and perish. Although the mango and date-palm trees retained their green leaves, they were powerless to give succor to the sorrowing plants. The plants and flowers needed more than shade and water; they needed invigorating cool air.

In the days before air conditioning, the open courtyard and surrounding colonnade provided shade and moving air, which offered the best natural relief from the extreme heat. When the sun reached the interior court, convection currents set up an airflow that ventilated the house and kept it cool. Trees and plants enhanced the coolness. Besides providing coolness, the open courtyard also served as light wells, as windows were kept small to reduce the intense, blinding light. But the wind tower was the most sophisticated and successful method of channeling air into building interiors for ventilation. It is locally known as *badgeer*, which is not Arabic but a Persian word meaning "opening for air." Often rising to 15 meters (49 feet) and placed high above roof terraces where wind velocity was greatest, cleaner, and less dusty, the wind tower caught and trapped the wind and by its unique construction forced breezes entering it downward into the room below. Wind towers no longer dot the landscape but they used to be a characteristic feature of buildings before air conditioning.

The courtyard was usually where I encountered other members of the family. It was inevitable since all the rooms opened into it. It was where visiting relatives gravitated. Sisters, brothers, aunts, nieces, nephews, and children gathered informally in the courtyard to chat and exchange news and gossip while children ran and played. I remember how safe and secure I felt seeing my children run around and play in the courtyard. Besides air and light, the courtyard provided privacy, security, and tranquility. In the winter, when the weather was good, it was very pleasant to sit in the courtyard. Regrettably, the courtyard house is fast disappearing as air-conditioning increases and people maximize their interior living spaces.

The courtyard house plan, with its interlocking combination of indoor and outdoor spaces that together make up the house, was a novelty for me. I grew up in a house with a front lawn and a backyard. In my mind, a house clearly demarcated "indoor" (inside the house) and "outdoor" (outside the house) space

The lack of grass and the scarcity of plants and flowers in my husband's family house made me remember with nostalgia the lawn of my childhood. It was covered with Bermuda grass, sturdy and bearing invasiveness and competitiveness deep

inside its genes. It frequently attacked our flowerbeds much
to my mother's irritation. She futilely schemed to annihilate
the creeping weed. Green shrubbery and multicolored flowers
adorned the wooden fence. Yellow roses and white orchids
were my mother's favorites. Rain was abundant and kept the
grass, shrubs, flowers, and trees happy, except during the dry
hot months of April and May. The flowers—jasmine, roses,
hibiscus, and some orchids—were cared for by my mother and
they blossom perennially in my memory. How green were the
leaves . . . moist and sparkling with morning dew; how sweet
the flowers . . . delicate and radiant; what a pleasure to behold,
soothing and comforting to the spirit.

I remembered the hibiscus, joyful in red, yellow, orange
and pink blossoms, waking up to kisses by the morning sun
and trembling with pleasure. Fragrant flowery notes floated
in my mind and a star-shaped blossom—small, white, and
dainty—blooming all year round, rose up from the depths of
my memory. *Sampaguita* we called it, but the world knows it as
jasmine, Arabian jasmine. While the vivacious hibiscus flaunted
its charms and unashamedly flirted with the sun all day long,
timid and pure jasmine slept, its petals curled. But at dusk, a
rich delicious scent filled the air; sampaguita was waking up,
announced by evening breezes. I still see myself sitting on the
porch, at twilight, sniffing the air, delighting in the heady scent,
and watching fireflies flitting about. Such golden moments never
will come again, but whenever a whiff of jasmine comes my
way, I recall those fragrant evenings, instantly, for the scent of
sampaguita is imprinted in my mind, like a genetic code.

A garden . . . scents of jasmine . . . me sitting on a porch . .
. a house. We dream in our houses. While my husband dreamed
his dreams in a house with an interior courtyard, I dreamed mine
in a different kind of house. It was not glamorous–just a two-

story wooden house with a porch and a canopy between the first and second floors. The living room, dining room, and kitchen were downstairs and the bedrooms upstairs. With the windows open, white crocheted curtains, crafted by my mother's loving hands, fluttered in the breeze. The house, simple but fresh and airy, had a one-story kitchen with a sloping roof and an awning. I used to climb out a window and walk over the canopy to the kitchen roof. The kitchen roof was where I used to spin dreams. The upper floor of the house and trees that surrounded the house provided shade over the kitchen roof; and it was cool, pleasant and quiet there. During siesta (that magically sacred time of day when every living creature pauses and suspends the day's activities) I used to go to the kitchen roof and read or lie down and watch the clouds change shape. They were never still but moved restlessly this way or that, in search of the perfect form, the impossible dream. I loved watching the clouds, listening to the rustling of the leaves—and dreaming; but not of the desert or Arabia. Arabia was unknown and lay in the future.

That future came, however, the way time has of catching up and I found myself, that summer, standing and musing in the courtyard patio of my husband's family home—in Qatar, a tiny state in the Arabian Peninsula. I lived in that house with my husband and two small children for about a month before moving to a rented Western-style house. We moved twice after that before we finally moved to our permanent house, which we built according to our needs.

I still recall clearly the night when Hajar informed me that a house had been found for us. Hajar and I had decided early on that we should get settled first before I started working. It was around 11 p.m., and with the children already asleep, and the commotion of the day over, it was a time when a husband and wife with young children take a breather. I lay on the big floor mattress in our room in the courtyard house, feeling tired and tracing shadows on the walls and ceiling with my eyes.

"The Department of Housing called me today. They found a temporary accommodation for us, a villa," Hajar said quietly. That perked me up and I half got up excitedly, supporting myself sideways on one elbow. A villa! My astonishment had been great. In my mind a villa implied the residence of a rich person. I could not believe it. But the villa turned out to be an ordinary house with a garden. Puzzled, I had looked up the word villa in Merriam Webster's Dictionary. It read: "a country estate; the rural or suburban residence of a wealthy person; British: a detached or semi-detached urban residence with yard and garden space." In Qatar, a house, even now, is still popularly referred to as villa. Qatar was a British protectorate, which most likely explained the persistent grand habit of referring to a house as villa, just as the way the British still refer to their country as Great Britain.

Looking for suitable accommodation in a new city is one of the frustrations of modern life. Qatar provides housing for its senior employees and in those days the housing department in the Ministry of Civil Service and Social Affairs allocated housing for all government employees. That being so my husband had completed the necessary forms. Where there is paperwork, there is bureaucracy and so it was in the housing sector. The process of acquiring a residence was like jogging with iron shackles tied to your feet and could take as long as six months or longer. My husband had told me that it was usual for expatriate senior government employees and their families to live in a hotel for several months at the expense of the government while the housing department conducted its business at snail speed. Upon learning this, I had fantasized about moving to a fancy five-star hotel for our temporary residence. After becoming accustomed to sleeping on a floor mattress, sitting on floor cushions, and getting used to my father-in-law's 5 a.m. rap on our bedroom door to wake up my husband for dawn prayer, we were fairly comfortable in my in-law's courtyard house. Nevertheless, living in a hotel had seemed appealing.

When I raised the subject with my husband, he had considered it but said that his parents would feel insulted. Furthermore, he was not aware of any Qatari who had ever left a parent's house to reside in a hotel. Such cultural perspective had arrested my attention, making me pause and reflect. After being welcomed with warmth and affection, moving to a hotel at my request would have been insensitive and barbaric, akin to being like a bull in a china shop. Therefore, I focused on the hidden exasperations of hotel life, musing that I probably would get sick of greeting the same doorman every morning or of seeing the same hotel staff day in and day out or worse becoming the auditory victim of the chamber maid's laments of misfortunes and body ailments. Hotel life would have been foreign and artificial and so the thought of living in a hotel lost its appeal. Moreover, in the courtyard house our two small children had more space to play in and run around with their cousins who came to visit daily. It was infinitely more pleasing to live with my in-laws until we found a house, getting to know them, and learning their customs and traditions in their native setting.

Even so, there is nothing more frustrating than waiting for an abode. The myriad ironies of life are thrown in relief. Two weeks after submitting the housing application, my husband was dismayed to find that his papers were still sitting in the clerk's office. He was told that the papers needed the signature of the director who was reportedly so busy he frequently was not in his office. The director was an expatriate Arab whose idea of work apparently was being absent from the office. When my husband was finally able to speak to him on the phone, he complained of suffering from chest pains. My husband had advised him to go to the hospital emergency room where he would see him. The director had replied, "*In sha'allah*" (God willing). He showed up, a week later, in the emergency room—dead! The guy had had a massive heart attack and had died on arrival.

Despite such setbacks, the bureaucratic process did not blink an eye; it traveled inexorably, albeit with glacial speed. A week later, my husband told me that there was an available house for us, and we moved from the courtyard house to the villa, the first of three villas we were to occupy before finally moving to our own home. The villa was fairly comfortable and one of several guesthouses owned by the Ministry of Health for locum consultant physicians. The two-story, concrete house — three-bedrooms and two-and-a-half bathrooms—was spacious and modestly furnished with bland and boring furniture, and equipped with tableware, kitchenware, and cutlery. I had liked the kitchen; it was bigger than the kitchen of the house we had rented when we lived in the United States of America.

That first villa, in the manner of Western style houses, did not have a *majilis* (male reception room), which, I found out later, was a fundamental feature of houses in the Arabian Gulf. Besides shelter and refuge, the style and construction of houses expresses the lifestyle and social customs of the people. In Qatar, as in the rest of the Arabian Gulf, maximum privacy for women is of utmost importance. Surrounded by a concrete fence, the inner courtyard house ideally fulfilled this social need with its high, windowless walls that were interrupted only by a single door. The main door of the house never opened directly into the family quarters. The majilis was usually placed close to the entrance hall and accessed only through a doorway. Respect for privacy, especially that accorded to women and family is a feature of the society that I appreciated from the beginning. Etiquette requires that friends and acquaintances inform you of a forthcoming casual visit. This allows the host or hostess to prepare tea, coffee, fruits, and sweets to serve. The ability to offer adequate refreshment and food to guests is an essential aspect of Arab hospitality.

Nowadays, in some houses, the majilis is a completely separate building from the main house. The majilis is a symbol of the economic status of the household. It is often the most richly decorated room in the house. Size and ornamentation varies according to the economic means and taste of the owner.

The first time I had entered my husband's home, we had passed through a hallway with two rooms, one on each side, before coming into the open-air inner courtyard with the desolate-looking flowers. Later, my husband had shown me those two rooms by the hallway, explaining that they were the majilis, and that only male visitors were received in those rooms. I suppose it was his way of warning me not to stray into those rooms, and from that time on the majilis held a certain mystery and fascination for me.

Part Three

LIVING ADVENTURE

CHAPTER 5

The Black Veil

The first woman I met wearing a face veil was my mother-in-law. When I saw her standing in the courtyard, completely veiled, I felt as though I had entered the heart of the house, as though I had penetrated an inner sanctum.

When we arrived, that summer day, she had come out from her room to greet us in the *liwan* (patio). She was dressed in an Arab shift dress and had on a black face cover. I was not shocked at seeing her veiled because one weekend, several months into our marriage, while showing me slides of Qatar, my husband had flashed a photo of a woman wearing a black face veil. "My mother," he had said. "She wears a veil. Women in my country are veiled." He also informed me that women in the Gulf, especially the generation of his mother, do not want to have their picture taken. I had thought amusedly then, that he probably cajoled his mother since he succeeded in snapping a photo. Besides priding himself on being a superb photographer, his powers of persuasion are quite considerable.

But I shall never forget that picture. It burned itself into my subconscious, occasionally coming into my dreams. The woman in the picture had been dressed in a black, floor length, loose, and shapeless garment. Her face was covered with what looked

39

to me like a black mask, with two slits for the eyes. Hajar had referred to the face cover as "veil," which had puzzled me. At that time, the word "veil" implied, for me, a transparent sheer delicate cloth such as chiffon, lace or netting worn over the head or face. I had thought of it merely as ladies clothing accessory used primarily for religious service, official functions, and social events. Movies and literature have portrayed the veil as a coy object that can be used as a tool for flirtation and seduction. In dance the veil is used to enhance fluid movement and makes the dance come alive. The sight of a female dancer gracefully twisting skillfully and creatively while twirling a veil around her is beguiling and pleasurable. In fiction, when authors want to impart an aura of mystery, they create a character, usually a veiled woman. The veil, for me then, had romantic connotations. I had never before seen a face veil that was mask-like such as the one in the picture. To me, the idea conveyed with the words "veil" and "mask" was different, and the images that floated in my mind were not identical even though both words meant "concealment." When I looked up the origin of the word "veil" in the dictionary, it stated: "from Latin vela, plural of velum, sail, awning, curtain" and it was defined as "a concealing curtain or cover of cloth."

I had been very curious about the veil in the photo, but Hajar had quickly changed the projected image, while brushing aside my questions and stating merely that in his country, women of his mother's generation wore that particular kind of veil. "It is the custom," he said. Because of his reticence on the topic, courtesy and politeness mandated that I abstained from being too inquisitive.

It was one thing, however, to see a photo of a woman wearing a face veil and quite another to meet a woman whose face was totally shielded by an opaque veil. When I first met my mother-in-law, the only part of her visage that I could see were her eyes—"window to the soul"—but eyes alone are not enough to convey the breadth of human emotions. I could not see my mother-in-law's facial expression. How did she feel, I had wondered fleetingly, meeting unveiled me, the wife of her son? For my part, my brain had already formed a template of her external appearance since that weekend long ago, so I was not shocked at seeing her hidden behind a veil. Still, I had felt bewildered.

I was not a stranger to the concept of veiling. I used to see nuns wearing veils but their faces were exposed. Traditionally, the Roman Catholic Church mandated that in church, women should cover their heads as a mark of modesty and as a sign of respect for the sanctity of the church. Catholic women used to cover their heads with a veil when attending mass. In the early 1980s, however, the Catholic Church no longer enforced the veil directive and, consequently, the practice was abandoned. I remember that in 1992, when we traveled to Spain, I had looked for a lady's church veil in Madrid as a memento. I was referred to one specialty boutique after another but none of the stores sold them anymore. The stores, however, still sold the fancy and elaborate Spanish mantilla worn over a high comb. Interestingly, I read that the mantilla originated in Andalusia, Southern Spain. Andalusian ladies used to wear translucent veils to cover themselves when they went out in public, for modesty and privacy. The practice spread throughout Spain. The lace mantillas were worn not only for attending church but also for occasions when an aristocratic lady went out in public. This practice was attributed to the Arab influence in the region. The Arabs invaded Spain in the eighth century and established the mighty kingdom of Al Andalus, Hispanicize to Andalusia. *Al Andalus* means "to become green at the end of the summer."

Spain has strong Catholic roots spanning centuries, and

Catholicism has always preached that women should dress modestly. Whatever its origins, the mantilla, a lightweight lace scarf worn over the head and shoulders, fulfilled this religious function., It became fashionable among ladies at court to wear the lace mantilla, and over time eventually evolved as part of traditional Spanish costume. Its use later declined and it was worn only on special occasions such as Holy week, bullfights, and weddings. It also became traditional for ladies to wear a mantilla or veil when received by the Pope.

The Spaniards brought Catholicism to my country the Philippines, and therefore Spanish style Catholicism is strongly embedded in the lifestyle of the people. Growing up Roman Catholic, I used to wear a veil made of black lace over my hair when I went to church. It was a lightweight rectangle that fell over the shoulders and gathered in front under the elbows, like a shawl. There was also a shorter veil but I favored the longer version. The sheer veils with their delicate designs in petal, leaf, garland, and sometimes-elegant fleur-de-lis enthralled me. The patterns were spread out generously along the entire edge and the same design was scantily spread over the veil's surface. The edge was frequently scalloped. Sometimes, white- or grey-colored lace was used sparingly to outline the veil motif. No other color was used. When the ladies donned their veils in church, with the lace cascading to their elbows and framing their faces, they radiated charm and mystery; and I used to marvel at how the veil seemed to flatter their appearance. The veil was used to cover the head only, never the face.

So the kind of veiling I was familiar with was transparent and made of lace and was used only for head cover, hence, the type of face veil that my mother-in-law was wearing when I first met her was incomprehensible to me. I found the mask-like contraption she wore bizarre and alien, an anomaly. I did not understand why women should wear such an item.

I recalled that while we were in the U.S.A., I had met a female student from Kuwait but she had not worn a veil or any head cover. I remembered her sitting in our living room, resting comfortably on a big cushion, conversing easily, smiling, and saying she liked the "pleasant vibes" in our house. Not once did she mention the topic of veiling or discuss the custom of veiling in the Arabian Gulf. When she and the other guests left, I had wondered aloud to Hajar why she had no head cover since she was Muslim and from the Gulf. "Kuwaiti women consider themselves liberated," he said, "so, some don't veil themselves or wear a head cover." He narrated with relish that when he was a high school student in Kuwait in 1960, three Kuwaiti women participating in a parade during a cultural festival in an open stadium had removed their veils and stamped on them in front of the grandstand. "It was a historic moment," he said with exhilaration.

Unfortunately, I did not have many opportunities to meet and socialize with Muslim ladies when my husband and I were living in the U.S.A. and hence, when I came to live in Qatar, I did not know much about veiling in Islam and in the Arabian Gulf. My husband also never once discussed the status of women and veiling in his society. It was understood between us that I would continue to work as a physician in Qatar. It had been my understanding that the veil for Muslim women was not compulsory but voluntary. I presumed, naively, that I would not be expected to wear a veil. I was unaware of the politics of the veil.

That summer day, when we arrived, though I had not been much surprised at the particular kind of veil my mother-in-law was wearing, I was nevertheless astonished at her quiet welcome for her son. She did not make any sound on greeting him. My husband had gone to her and kissed her head. She had grabbed his hand, attempting to kiss it, but Hajar had deftly extricated his hand, kissing her head again. I could not see her expression because of the face cover, but her eyes had been moist. It was a quiet but loving greeting. Decades later, that scene would sometimes flash, like lightning, through my mind, when my son came home for holidays during his college years in the U.S.A. I would wait impatiently in the TV room so that I would hear the door open in the hallway. As soon as I heard it, I would run, arms outstretched and calling his name, ready to hug and kiss him. I had to stand on tiptoe while he bent to receive my showers of affection. Love has different ways of expression and wears many masks.

"Ummi," my husband had said to me, by way of introduction. *Ummi* is the Arabic word for "my mother." Ummi, as I also came to call her, gently touched my shoulder, murmuring softly in Arabic. I kissed her, pressing my cheek lightly on each side of her veil. She stretched her hand to my face, laughing softly; as she gently rubbed off the light purplish impression her face veil had left on my cheek.

After the introductions and greetings, Ummi turned her attention to the children, hugged and kissed them, and speaking in Arabic, gestured for us to follow her. She led us to a room furnished with Persian carpets and floor cushions. It was a large rectangular room, wallpapered with a stylized gold leaf design on light green background. It had two windows draped with thick curtains to block out the light. A window type air conditioner whirred in a corner. There was a large mattress on the floor with beddings and a baby crib in a corner, which had pleased me greatly.

"How thoughtful of your mother to have a crib ready" I said to my husband and, turning to my mother-in-law, thanked her. Her eyes, the only part of her countenance that I could see, smiled back. Emotions, unlike thoughts, transcend language and culture. "My mother says all bed sheets, blankets, and towels are new," my husband informed me. "We'll eat lunch after an hour when my father comes back from court." His mother left us so we could freshen up and settle in. Later, I learned from my husband that his mother and other Gulf women of her generation wore the face cover all the time, except when eating, praying, and sleeping. That information had greatly puzzled me and, as if reading my thought, my husband had added, "They feel 'naked' without the veil."

In the early days of my life in Qatar, when I was with my in-laws, my husband's mother, his aunt, and his sister would touch my dress, feeling its texture and commenting on the dress while gesturing at the sleeve length and hemline. I was modestly dressed—long sleeves and ankle-length hemlines. It was a mild and tender examination, done with a lot of smiles and in a playful manner. Then, they would point to their veils and ask how I liked them. My husband or his younger brother or a niece or nephew who spoke a little English usually translated. I had been amused, marveling at their child-like curiosity. Among the veiled ladies of the desert, I must have been as much a curiosity as a creature from another planet.

I had been blissfully unaware of the family's attitude towards my not wearing a veil. Naively, I had never thought or imagined I was expected to veil myself. At that time, it was quite unthinkable but I did not know much about my new society. Before our marriage, my husband did not talk much about his culture and society, even though I had asked a few times. He, however, had greatly entertained me with his humor and enthralled me by translating the poems of his favorite Arab poets. I had thought him the most fascinating person I had ever met. On religion, he was liberal and tolerant, and his witty remarks had amused me immensely, adding to his appeal. He recounted several amusing stories from his childhood but never once touched on veiling.

I remember, vividly, my first outing away from my husband's home. Hajar had wanted to show me around the souk (marketplace). Just before our souk adventure, I had sensed tension in the air. When my husband told his family that he was taking me out to see the souk, my in-laws had been shocked at my husband's audacity on two counts: I was unveiled and he was taking me out. That, he told me later, had been the problem. At that time an unveiled Qatari wife was unheard of, as indeed it still is. Men and women did not mingle freely in public. Women now have more freedom and can go to public places with their husband, but still they are veiled.

Curious, I had asked my husband how he responded. Hajar said, "I told them 'Rachel can't just sit here looking at the bathrooms.'" I had stared at him, incredulous. His reply had been so unexpected that I couldn't help but laugh. There had been five bathrooms in that courtyard house, four in the private family quarters and one Western style near the majilis and his father's library. The family bathrooms, however, had been interesting: the toilets were at ground level and the water closets were placed high on the wall above and equipped with a hanging cord for flushing. There was a low faucet near the toilet and sitting next to it, in a corner, was a metal vessel with a handle and long vertical spout that curved at the end. The metal vessel had tickled my curiosity. On asking what it was for, my husband had replied laughing, "For washing."

My in-laws opposition notwithstanding, I had gone to the souk gaily with Hajar; eager to see new sights and sounds. But that first trip to the souk, a public place, was a revelation that overwhelmed me: the souk was full of men; there were no women. It was like walking into a bad dream. Bewildered, I recall asking, "Where are the women?" The bizarre feeling was intensified when, while we were walking in the souk, my husband's subconscious seemed to take over and order him to walk fast, while leaving me trailing behind to occasionally stumble on little bumps and cracks on the streets, alleys, and pavement. I was fretful at being stared at oddly and I called out to him in alarm. "Wait . . . wait for me . . . please." In the U.S.A. we always walked side by side, with me frequently looping my arm around his. I had been very distressed and missed his arm profoundly.

At that time, I was only dimly aware of the social and cultural obligations required of a Qatari wife. I had thought that being modestly dressed was enough. Unknown to me, the issue of me wearing a veil had been raised with my husband, almost as soon as I arrived. My husband told me later that he had told his family, "Rachel is not an Arab. She did not grow up in an Arab Muslim society, so there is no need to try and make her act as an Arab." He had forbidden them to talk to me about veiling myself. His father, who considered me a Muslim, had said, "You are tying my hands behind my back. How can I preach in the mosque about veiling then?" Many years later, when my husband told me his father's predicament regarding the veil issue, I felt deeply how my father-in-law must have felt.

Life, however, is full of humorous moments, particularly if you're a foreigner trying to understand the philosophy of a different culture. One afternoon, I went with Hajar to visit his parents. He stopped the car near the men entrance and went in ahead of me. An old Mauritanian "religious sheikh" was sitting alone under the shade in front of the majilis, facing the gate. Hajar told me that such religious men from remote Muslim countries sometimes swept into Doha like gusts of wind, staying in his father's house for a few days to weeks. They slept in the small majilis, which was used as a guest room when the need arose. Some came to study a specialized Islamic subject; some came to collect charity donations; and some came to attend his father's majilis.

That old Mauritanian "sheikh" sitting in front of my father-in-law's majilis that afternoon had come from a remote village in Mauritania. He had a long gray beard and sat quietly reading the Qur'an after his prayer. My husband greeted him as he entered. He welcomed my husband and while he was returning my husband's greeting, he suddenly saw me—an unveiled foreign woman—entering through the men gate of a well-known Islamic scholar, Sheikh Ahmed Bin Hajar (my father in law). He could not believe such a sight, and turning his face away from my direction so that he would not commit the sin of seeing my face exclaimed, "I seek God's help from the devil." Then he added an Arab saying literally translated: "For every fall out, there is a lifter or a pick up." My husband told me to go quickly inside the house. I did not know what was happening and why the old man was so agitated, looking at the wall. When my husband explained to me the old man's reaction and the insulting remark, I was not offended but rather amused.

I was intensely interested in the face veil that my husband's mother, aunt, and sister wore. They were very pleased to show me their veils whenever I asked questions about the material and whether they were made especially for them. Sometimes my husband's aunt would remove her veil so I could examine it. They told me it was called *burqah* or *al-batulah*. It covered the face to the level of the chin and jaw with twin generous cutouts for the eyes. When spread out, the shape resembled a butterfly. I inspected it and was surprised to find that the contraption had a rigid middle pleat, which followed the ridge of the nose. The women explained that a small piece of wood was inserted through the pleat to retain its good texture, design, and rigidity. The rigid middle pleat also prevented the cloth from collapsing on the nostril, and so did not interfere with breathing! I thought it was quite a feat of engineering ingenuity. On closer inspection, the black cloth had a yellow gold sheen. I learned that the material was called kerja neel—pure cotton dyed with indigo—and that the fabric was imported from India. It was cut to fit the woman it was made for. The inside was lined with a gauze material to protect the face from color stains.

The *batulah* excited my curiosity. Obviously, the little contraption was designed and constructed with originality and cleverness as well as practicality. I supposed that its peculiar design probably evolved over time, according to the needs and requirements of the women who wore them. I wondered about the *batulah's* origins.

When looking into the origins of customs, it is sometimes useful to trace the derivation of the word that describes the object or practice, so I asked Hajar the etymology of *batula*.

"The word *batulah*," he said, "is not an Arabic word. It is not found in Arabic dictionaries." He said that the word *batulah* is widely believed to be of Persian origin. "The word batula is phonetically close to patella," he continued musing aloud. He had wondered whether the word patella was derived from the word *batula* or the other way around, *batula* from patella. It was an interesting thought. Patella is the medical term for kneecap. Both are used as cover, *batula* for the face, and patella for the knee. Merriam Webster's dictionary, however, stated that patella comes from Latin, from a diminutive of patina, which means a shallow dish, an apt description for kneecap.

I learned further, on reading the research work of local Gulf historians, that *batulah* is a word found in Sanskrit and Hindi to describe textiles made in Northwest and Southern India. The word *batulah,* "a facemask worn by women" is believed to be

Persian, from a coastal Iranian town called Siraf, a center of maritime trade during the tenth century. Historical descriptions of traditional costumes in Siraf include the *batulah* as a facemask worn by Balushi women. The inhabitants of Siraf were mainly immigrants from Baluchistan. When Siraf's importance declined in the eleventh century, the Balushis moved to ports on the Gulf's eastern coast to find work, migrating to Muscat and Dubai in the eighteenth century. Because of daily interaction between Balushis through work and intermarriage, local historical researchers surmised that the *batula* was first adopted as a new fashion before being picked up by Arab women in coastal areas and passed on by Arab traders to other parts of the Gulf. Although the basic form of the *batula* has been retained, there is subtle variation in style and shape in each Gulf country. In the Arab world, the batula was used only in the Arabian Gulf. Women in other Arab countries never used the batula.

Today, the batulah is worn only by my mother-in-law's generation. Young Gulf women have cast it off, considering it unattractive, but they continue to veil themselves. There is another type of face veil that many women still wear. It is called al-niqab, a piece of black cloth that covers the forehead, nose, cheeks, chin, and neck with twin slits for the eyes. Trendy young women, however, wear only *al-sheila*; a black head cover made of a light material, usually crepe or chiffon, worn with the face exposed or covered and the *al-abayya*, an overwrap worn over clothes. *Al-sheila* is worn in such a way that it could be either raised to expose the face or part of it made to fall over the face, like a curtain, for privacy when going out in public. A fashion industry has grown around the veil, catering to the fashion demands and whims of the younger generation. The severity and austerity are softened with elegant trimmings and embroidery, catering to youth fancies. There is a veil ensemble for every taste and budget, just like fresh-water pearls.

Throughout my years in Qatar, I have not noticed a rejection of the veil by young women in Qatar. Young Qatari women have college degrees, but veiling seems to run strong in this group. I have not been acquainted with anyone who thought of the veil as a symbol of oppression, as it is popularly perceived in the West. My general impression was that the veil was here to stay. The veil, however, has become a rallying point among champions of women's rights, and in the wake of the women's liberation movement, some Muslim women especially those from non-Gulf countries, no longer veil themselves. Recently, however, veiling among women in Muslim countries has been on the upswing, a phenomenon that has perplexed many feminists and new-age champions of human rights.

When my daughters came of age, they veiled themselves voluntarily. I occasionally overhear them discussing and exchanging ornamental veil details with their friends over the phone or when they got together. They sometimes designed their own sheilas and abayas and their little original embellishments added a touch of elegance to an otherwise subdued ensemble. The graceful trimmings gave them a lot of pleasure and the add-ons were also great conversation pieces. They are aware of the controversy over the veil in other societies but that world is not their world. The way they wear their sheila gives them the choice to expose or veil their face according to social need and requirement. In their world, the veil gives them anonymity and freedom from intrusive observation, desirable qualities in a society that puts a premium on privacy. Seeing them happy and comfortable behind the veil, I reflected how greatly misunderstood the custom of veiling is today.

It is interesting that, in our time, the custom of veiling is associated only with Islam. I learned, from reading about the history of veiling, that the practice was already an established social custom in Arabia before the coming of Islam. I read also that there are many references to different forms of veiling in pre-Islamic Arab poetry. Distinguished tribes considered it a manifestation of prestige, nobility, and honor. Women who wore the veil were perceived as completely honorable and therefore, chaste. During tribal wars, noble women would unveil to avoid being taken hostage for bounty.

But one does not have to read the history of veiling to realize that it was practiced in western societies as well. Anyone who has ever visited a museum in Europe would see portraits of ladies wearing veils either floating down from the peak of a hat, draped around the shoulders or under the chin, or sometimes even covering the entire face. The material used, however, was transparent so that the features of the face were visible but subdued. Veiling was so prevalent among the upper classes that in the houses of the wealthy and aristocratic families, there are probably portraits of lady ancestors wearing a veil, glaring down at their unveiled female descendants!

In museums too, I have seen statue representations of Roman, Greek, and Byzantine women wearing a hooded cloak over their dresses. It would appear then, that the tradition of veiling goes back to antiquity, before Judaism, Christianity, and Islam. Historians trace the custom to Mesopotamia (present day Iraq), where inscriptions dating back to 3000 BC, mention noble women veiling themselves when appearing in public. Reportedly, inscriptions exist mentioning that slave women, courtesans, and prostitutes were forbidden to wear the veil. The veil was a mark of respectability and honor. With time, veiling, a custom that was originally a social and cultural tradition, became a religious heritage. The ruling that women veil themselves is found in all the three world religions but Islam retained the custom of veiling, which became part of the dress code for Muslim women.

Nowadays however, a storm of controversy swirls around the age-old custom of veiling. In many Muslim countries, among those for and against the *hijab* (head cover), the type and extent of veiling are subjects of controversy. Qatari women feel that covering the face is a matter of "personal interpretation" of the Qur'anic verses that suggest its use. Within a family, some of the younger women may be fully veiled whereas others may leave their faces exposed.

There is wisdom in history. Looking into the history of veiling has given me better understanding and insight on the practice of veiling. I have come to the conclusion that veiling is a custom whose roots are deep and complex, transecting social, cultural, and religious as well as personal convictions. At stake are issues of identity and heritage. Through Islam, veiling has stood the test of time. But in the Arabian Gulf, veiling is more than a religious issue. Veiled women in the Gulf command high respect, for the cultural message attached to wearing the veil is still very much alive in the region. The veil code is embedded in the collective subconscious of the society. Veil language, like any language, has nuances understood by members of the society. In public places no Gulf man will initiate conversation with a fully veiled woman who is not a family member.

Since veiling is entrenched in the society, it is not surprising that veil-lore abound. My favorite story is about the poet and the black veil. My husband, who has in-depth knowledge of Arabic literature and poetry, narrated the story to me when I asked why black was the preferred color for veils in the Arabian Gulf. He added, "The story also illustrates the powerful influence of poetry on the Arabs."

The story involved a well-known Arab poet, Rabia ibn Amer, known as Miskeen Aldarami (d. 708 AD). When he grew old he gave up poetry and devoted his time to prayer and worship. He lived in the prophet's city of Medina, praying and fasting. During that time, an Iraqi merchant and friend of the poet came to Medina selling a large load of veils. He sold all except the black veils. Black veils were not popular in Medina then. The merchant was desperate to sell all his veils and go back to his country, so he went to the poet, his old friend, requesting his help. The poet felt sorry for his friend and decided to help him. He took off his religious cloth and wore normal cloth, composed a short poem, and gave it to a singer to sing it. The singer was delighted to sing a new poem written by the famous Miskeen. After the poet accomplished that task, he went back to his mosque and his prayers. In the poem the poet claimed that he was going to start praying when he saw a woman in a black veil standing by the door of the mosque. He asked her to redeem his prayers and fasting and not to kill him [with her love]. News of the poem and its words spread fast in town. Women rushed to buy the black veils. The merchant sold all the black veils in one day. Black veils then became widely used in Medina and the surrounding regions, a preference that has survived to the present.

According to my husband, that poem made Miskeen famous over the centuries and an Iraqi traditional singer sang the same poem in the 1960s. The story charmed me and I requested Hajar to translate the poem for me. He said it is very difficult to translate poetry but the most famous line was: "Say to the beautiful woman in the black veil, 'What have you done to the man who dedicated himself to prayer?'"

CHAPTER 6

The Majilis: Lesson in Culture

Two hours before sunset, usually from four to six, Sheikh Ahmed, my father-in-law, sat in the big majilis receiving visitors—male guests. There was no TV or radio in his majilis but he was not against such small marvels and did not forbid their use. My husband told me that when he was eleven years old, his father had permitted him to have a radio. His father had also allowed him to have a TV in the house even though the conservative religious associates of his father did not approve of television. They considered television an instrument of *shetan* (devil) because they thought watching TV might make people forget prayer time, enable them to see pictures of women, and spoil the society. Hence, when radio and television first came to the area, the conservative religious leaders had stood against it.

Religious people, whether Muslim, Christian, or Jew, have always regarded technical and scientific innovations with suspicion. The story of medicine in particular is full of glorious new discoveries and since medicine encompasses all spheres of human activity, such new ideas and discoveries frequently generate controversy. For example in mid-nineteenth century Britain, news that a physician had successfully used chloroform to eliminate the pain of childbirth in women caused hullabaloo in the medical community as well as religious circles. Straitlaced physicians claimed that pain in labor was a biological necessity. Churchmen cried from the pulpit, "Heresy!—For had not God told Eve: 'In sorrow thou shalt bring forth children?'"

According to Hajar, his father and the people who frequented his father's majilis preferred conversation to watching TV. The visitors exchanged news; sometimes even news heard on the radio or TV. Besides local and international news, a variety of other topics were discussed such as history, literature, religion, society, and the human condition in general. His father had visitors from all walks of life: scholars, religious people, poets, writers, doctors, teachers, businessmen, and other ordinary people. He frequently had visitors from other Arab or Muslim countries as well. Because he was an Islamic judge and scholar, many people frequently asked him questions about Islamic ruling on every aspect of daily life such as praying, fasting or family relations since religion is a way of life for many Muslims.

My husband's descriptions of what took place in the majilis excited my imagination. The majilis seemed such a fascinating place for exchanging ideas, news, and thoughts. It sounded so highbrow. I wondered aloud, however, if the gathering might engage in trivialities such as gossip. The majilis is a gathering of people after all and with human nature being what it is, harmless chitchat would be inevitable. He was offended and, drawing his whole body upright, informed me frostily: "Gossip is a disgraceful word in our society. It is insulting to link it to my father's majilis."

The Arabic word majilis means "a place for sitting" and it traditionally connotes a reception room for male visitors. Although rare, a woman can have her own open majilis but only for women. One exception was the Princess Wallada who lived in eleventh century Cordoba, the capital of Moorish Spain. Her majilis was open to men and women. She was the daughter of an Arab prince and a native Spanish woman. I never knew about her until a few years ago, when my husband and I toured Cordoba, Spain. After visiting La Mezquita (The Great Mosque of Cordoba), we had strolled leisurely with our guide along the streets of Cordoba, encountering statues of well-known historical figures who were born at and are residents of Cordoba, such as Ibn Rushd, known in the West as Averroes (1128–1198), an Arab physician, Muslim jurist, and philosopher. Passing by the ruins of a Roman aqueduct and medieval walls, we came across an arresting statue of two hands reaching towards one another. We learned from our guide that the statue was dedicated to Los Enamorados (The Lovers), a tribute to the greatest Andalusian poet, Ibn Zaydun (1003–1071) and the Princess Wallada, also a poetess, whom he loved. Inscribed on a plaque attached to the marble pedestal were excerpts of love poems they exchanged (in Spanish, translated from Arabic).

The Princess Wallada was famous for her majilis where the finest poets and musicians of Andalusia, in Southern Spain gathered. (Today, Andalusia, known as Al Andalus to the Arabs, is a symbol of an earlier Golden Age of Arab civilization and it is an important cultural icon in both Western and Muslim culture). In Princess Wallada's majilis, her literati crowd would sit around her on cushions and rugs, composing impromptu poems and verses and improvising ballads to the sound of lute and guitar. She attained notoriety for her sexually liberated lifestyle, taking on many lovers, but her great love was Ibn Zaydun. Their love affair was public and stormy, with each one apparently lacking the fidelity gene. She also refused to veil herself. The supreme judge of the city accused her of being a harlot. In response, Wallada composed a poem, embroidered the lines on her gown, and defiantly wore the dress in the streets for everyone to read: I deserve nothing less than glory / I hold my head high and go my way / I will give my cheek to my lover / and my kisses to anyone I choose.

The lovers lived at a time when Cordoba, as the capital of Moorish Spain, was renowned as the greatest center of learning in medicine, mathematics, sciences and the arts. Descriptions of court life during those times suggest a hedonistic flavor. It was a multicultural and sophisticated city with Muslims, Jews, and Christians living peacefully. Undoubtedly, there are many women like Wallada through time and across cultures but very few are remembered. And when those few are mentioned in history, it is mainly because of their association with illustrious or great men; hence, their promiscuity and flaunting of convention become legendary and romanticized. Although Wallada was a poetess, she became famous only because of Ibn Zaydun's love poems to her.

My husband is a poet too and although I secretly wished he would compose love poems to me, I never aspired to have my own majilis. The ritual of hosting a majilis requires patience, discipline and a high degree of sociability and loquaciousness. For company and recreation, nothing could surpass the delights and pleasures of books, but the majilis seemed just the right place to talk about what you've read. Reading a book does not require an invitation so, too, in the majilis. It is like an open house. The host sits in his majilis at a particular time and people drop in casually to greet the host, staying around for a little chat, and to meet other people.

My father-in-law had two majilis: a small majilis where close friends and selected guests were received, and a big majilis, which was open to the public. The small majilis was furnished with floor cushions and also doubled as a guest room for out of town visitors. The big majilis was furnished with sofas and armchairs. Both majilis were carpeted wall to wall and in the center of each majilis was a large Persian carpet. The Persian carpets were beautiful with large central medallions and geometric and arabesque designs on a red background. The walls were painted off-white, their monotony broken by a four-inch dado paint running horizontally and designed in arabesque on a light, pale green background. There were no pictures or paintings.

The chairs and sofas lined the wall, reminding me of official functions. The room looked so severe, so ceremonial, so intimidating. It had puzzled me that the seating arrangement was rigid. My husband informed me that a majilis sitting protocol is formal, with the host sitting in the section facing the door and flanked by the most important guests or most senior visitors since age is accorded much respect in the society.

But I had not fully understood the nuances associated with a majilis. When my father-in-law moved from his courtyard house to his new house, he gave me the honor of choosing the upholstery for the chairs of his new majilis. His majilis had marble flooring with a central skylight; and it was big, in keeping with his status as an Islamic judge. The room required several sets that had to be ordered. With much excitement and enthusiasm, I had gone with my husband to the furniture shop to choose the fabric. At that time, furniture and upholstery shops offered a very limited range of materials and styles to choose from, but I had still found it difficult to make up my mind. Finally, thinking to soften the severity of his majilis and keeping the skylight in mind, I chose a blue flowery print on white, to give the room a light and airy look, so I had thought. I had assured my husband the design on the fabric would "cheer and lighten up" the room, and so the chairs and fabric were ordered. After they had been installed and my father-in-law saw them, he was very unhappy. He thought the fabric "feminine." He had wanted a solid and restrained color. I was deeply mortified but he sportingly used it for a couple of months. Later, dignified-looking chairs arrived upholstered in plush deep red velvet with stylized faint brown-colored medallions. It was a cultural lesson I shall never forget.

Wherever there is a gathering of people, there is food and drink. The majilis is a gathering of people, so naturally I was curious about what was served. Hajar said that in his father's majilis, guests might be served: orange juice, Vimto drink (a purple soft drink containing the juice of grapes, raspberries, and black currants), tea and hot hibiscus drink. When I first came to Doha, I was woefully unaware of the charms of hibiscus as a drink, but it has long been used as herbal tea in many parts of the world such as India, Mexico, and the Middle East; in Egypt it is known as karkadee or red tea. The liquid is a deep red and when served ice cold with mint, it is delicious and refreshing.

Coffee, however, is the preeminent drink served in the majilis. Serving coffee is an integral part of Arab hospitality. In my father-in-law's house, as in the old days, the coffee beans were roasted and then ground with a pestle in a brass mortar. Water was boiled in a beaked brass coffee pot and clove or cardamom was added while the water was still boiling. Ground coffee was then poured into the pot and the coffee again brought to a boil. An electric coffee grinder has replaced the mortar and to make life even easier, coffee beans can be bought already ground. The coffee is amber, light and diluted, not thick and concentrated.

Serving coffee is a ritual carried out with great care, just like a Japanese tea ceremony. As with any ritual, there are accoutrements associated with its practice. I particularly admired the dainty and lovely tiny cups without handles used to serve the coffee. The cup is called a *finjan* and is about half the size of a ping-pong ball. The cups are made of glass or porcelain and are decorated in flowery or geometric designs, occasionally rimmed with silver or gold color. Coffee is poured from a *dallah*, "a brass coffeepot with beaked spout". The shape and form of the dallah is so distinctive that it is recognizable as Arab from New York to Peking. It is the embodiment of Arab hospitality.

In my father-in-law's majilis, a male attendant served the coffee. According to my husband, in every majilis in the Arabian Gulf, serving the first cup of coffee is steeped in protocol. For example, in his father's majilis, the attendant serves the honored guest first. Custom dictated that the honored guest refuses the first cup and then requests the host to take the first cup. An "argument" then ensues over who should be honored with the first cup. The "debate" may continue until one of them accepts the cup. I have occasionally witnessed this part of the ritual when my husband and I socialized with family friends. It had exasperated me in the beginning but now I look on it with amusement. When one of the major protagonists finally gave in and accepted the honor of the first cup, serving coffee continued clockwise.

Traditionally, for Bedouins in the desert, the host or son or younger relative served the coffee. With a stack of the little cups in his right hand and the coffee pot in his left, he pours a small amount of coffee for himself and tastes the coffee to ensure his guests that the coffee is suitable and the right flavor. Then, he pours coffee for the primary guest and then serves each guest. After each guest is served, he pours a cup for himself. Affluent households train their domestic staff (males) to serve coffee in the appropriate manner, and the coffee is poured from a thermos (to keep it hot) that is sometimes shaped like a dallah. Dates or *halwa* (local sweets) used to be served before coffee but not anymore in the modern majilis. The taste of Arabic coffee takes some getting used to because it is light and has spices, but it is delicately scented imparting fruity notes and pungent undertones. I find it particularly good after eating dates.

The amount of coffee served in the little cup is small, one third of the cup, so a guest could drink as many cups as he wished or every time one is offered, but etiquette dictates that he stops after the third serving. When a guest has finished or does not wish to drink coffee anymore, he quietly and gently shakes the empty little cup to signify that he has had enough. He never verbally says, "Enough, thank you" because that would interrupt the flow of conversation and distract the person speaking. This reminds me of an amusing incident I experienced when I was new in the region. Once, my husband and I were invited to the house of one of his friends. I was being served coffee endlessly. At a loss what to do, I sipped the coffee very slowly to avoid being served again, but still, my cup was refilled at regular intervals. My husband, pausing in his conversations had glanced at me and realizing my predicament, announced amusedly, "Rachel, if you do not want anymore coffee, just shake the cup like this," he said, gently rocking his little cup like a cradle between his fingers. Since then I have perfected the technique and I rock the little cup as adroitly as any Arab.

Occasionally, my husband attended his father's majilis and on those occasions, I eagerly awaited his return but not because I had missed him. I looked forward to listening to his entertaining and interesting anecdotes about his father's majilis. One time, he came back smiling broadly.

"My father had a visitor from Yemen," he said, "and the majilis talked about coffee."

"Well, what's new in the world of coffee?" I asked.

"Did you know that the English word "coffee" is derived from Arabic?"

"No. Really?"

"Yes, really," he replied, mimicking my disbelieving voice. "The Arabic word is *qahwa*, which originally meant wine. In pre-Islamic Arabia, wine was a social drink and qahwa was one of the names for wine. The English word 'wine' is also an Arabic word, pronounced *wain*, which means 'dark grape.' Wine was prohibited by Islam and when coffee became popular as a social drink supplanting wine, the Arabs used the word qahwa to refer to coffee hence coffee became known as the 'wine of Arabia.'"

"That's fascinating!" I exclaimed. "I suppose you'll tell me now that the Arabs knew all along coffee contained caffeine," I said teasingly.

"Well, the Arabic root of qahwa is *qaha*, a word which means 'to suppress the appetite'" he said, pausing to allow me to digest the information. I was thoughtful. Coffee decreases appetite because it contains caffeine. Many people believe that drinking coffee or other caffeinated drinks helps them lose weight. This is not true. Although caffeine is an appetite suppressant, this effect lasts very briefly and so, does not lead to weight loss or keep weight off. It is the diuresis—increased excretion of water in the urine—induced by caffeine that creates the false perception of weight loss. It does not enhance fat metabolism. The initial decrease in appetite with caffeine is offset by its effect on the stress hormone, cortisol. Caffeine increases cortisol levels in the body, and that hormone stimulates appetite.

"Did you know," my husband continued, "that long before coffee was known as a drink, the early Arab physicians used coffee as medicine?" When I shook my head, he went on to say that Al-Razi in the ninth century and Ibn Sina in the eleventh century wrote of the stimulant effects of coffee. They had been referring to the coffee bean, known as *bunn* in Arabic. Al-Razi, known in the West as Rhazes (864–930 AD), is considered the greatest physician of Islam and the Medieval Ages. He was the first physician to differentiate smallpox from measles and his descriptions are unsurpassed to this day. Ibn Sina, known in the West as Avicenna (981–1037 AD), was the most famous physician and philosopher of his time. His major contribution to medical science was his famous book *The Qanun (Canon)*, which became the textbook for medical education in European schools from the twelfth to the seventeenth century. Ibn Sina's portrait adorns the great hall of the Faculty of Medicine in the University of Paris.

It was intensely interesting to know that the stimulant effect of coffee was known by the early Arab physicians but this is hardly surprising since those early physicians were astute and very observant. Anthropologists say that caffeine occurs naturally in over one hundred different plant species and that humans have been ingesting caffeine since the time they were using stone tools in 700,000 BC. Every human being on the planet probably ingests some kind of drink that contains caffeine, with coffee and tea being the most common. Caffeine is a psychoactive substance and can be addictive. I presume that the world is probably evenly divided into coffee drinkers and tea drinkers. Many people cannot function without their morning cup of coffee. I welcome the morning with a cup of hot tea, and so do many people. Samuel Johnson, an English writer who reportedly drank forty cups of tea a day wrote, "Tea amuses the evening, solaces the midnight, and welcomes the morning." Coffee devotees would say the same. Chocolate, that perfect food, contains caffeine too. Who can resist its delights? I thought nobody could until I met my husband. He can't stand chocolate because his mother used to purge him weekly with a castor derivative covered with chocolate when he was a child. But he drinks tea and coffee, both stimulants, which may explain his extraordinary sociability.

"When coffee supplanted wine as a social drink, coffee-drinking quickly caught on and spread throughout the Arab world," my husband continued.

"So, coffee-drinking originated in Arabia?" I asked.

"Oh, yes. It reached Europe via Venice and Vienna through the Ottoman Empire."

The Ottomans were Turkish nomadic tribes who converted to Islam during the 8th and 9th centuries. In the fourteenth century, they became powerful, eventually governed large areas of the Arab Islamic lands and expanded to Europe. Their empire lasted until the twentieth century.

"Were there coffee houses in Arabia just like in Europe? I asked.

"Of course. In fact European coffee houses are very similar in function to Arabian coffee houses, especially those found in Egypt."

"Is there a link between the European coffee house, European bar, and Arabic majilis?" I wondered aloud. Under the influence of coffee, people held lively discussions on politics, religion, life, and anything under the sun.

"Most likely," he replied. "Coffee houses were suspected breeding grounds of revolutionary ideas." Laughing softly, he informed me that in sixteenth century Arabia, controversy had swirled around coffee: Does drinking coffee, like wine, lead to immoral behavior? Is coffee beneficial or detrimental to health? When no ill effects were observed, except a tendency towards conviviality, coffee was gradually accepted.

That was certainly fascinating. The same health debate about coffee had preoccupied Western doctors a century later. In seventeenth-century Marseilles, for instance, the leading medical man of the day pronounced that any man who drank excessive amounts of coffee "would be unable to perform his marital obligations." Overnight all the cafés in Marseilles were abandoned. Today, the debate about the effects of coffee on health continues. There are many studies citing the harmful effects of too much caffeine as well as the benefits of its antioxidant effects.

"The coffee plant is originally from which country? Yemen?" I asked.

"The Yemenis, like my father's guest, would like to think so but others say the home of the coffee plant is Ethiopia. The formal cultivation of coffee started in Yemen and Yemeni coffee is still considered the best in the world."

"So, how long has it been since the Arabs adopted coffee as drink?"

"Uh, perhaps more than five hundred years but no one is quite certain when coffee was first brewed as drink."

I read later on that there were colorful anecdotes and legends regarding the discovery of coffee as a beverage. One legend recounts that a Yemeni mystic traveling in Ethiopia, noticed, high on the slopes of a mountain, goats prancing, dancing, and displaying about with frisky vitality. Watching them, he observed that they were eating berries from a plant. He tried the berries and found them bitter, so he boiled them, drank the liquid, and thus, the first cup of coffee was born. The mystic had felt good, wide-awake, and his mind was wonderfully clear. He brought the seedlings back to Yemen where he introduced the new drink to his disciples. They found it kept them awake during their meditations, producing a condition of dreamy mindfulness and euphoric well being.

Coffee is a psychoactive substance and it certainly didn't take too long for the little coffee bean to get the world dancing, twitching, and jumping to the sound of its crackles on the fire. But in Arabia, the land where the coffee brew originated, life went on as it had for centuries, with people gathering in the majilis to socialize and sip a light, delicately scented golden beverage—Arabic coffee— in dainty little cups, while listening or talking animatedly and alternately looking serene, grave, or philosophical.

"I can imagine how fascinating it must have been, listening to people discussing coffee," I said. By the way, how do people know the majilis session is over? When it's time to leave?"

"Oh that. Well, the majilis gathering comes to an end with the burning of incense. An attendant brings the host a *mubkhar* (clay incense burner), with glowing charcoals inside. Then, the host puts a piece of *oudh* (sandalwood) on the hot coals. Smoke slowly swirls out and up and fills the room with fragrance. The attendant goes around holding the smoking incense burner in front of each guest. The guest leans forward and wafts the smoke towards him or perfumes his headgear by loosely enveloping the mubkhar with the flowing portion of his headgear."

I thought his description was exotic but the idea of signaling the end of a gathering with fragrance was enchanting. *Oudh*, however, is extremely expensive with prices ranging from $2,500 to $28,000 a kilo depending on quality. It is burned only for special guests and on special occasions.

I reflected that the pleasant and calming smell of oudh—rich and woody with rosy undertones—was a fitting end to the majilis ritual where coffee and conviviality reign supreme.

CHAPTER 7
Abui

My husband called his father Abui, and so did our children and my father-in-law's other grandchildren. I, too, called him Abui, which means "my father." People called my father-in-law bin Hajar (son of Hajar) or Sheikh Ahmed bin Hajar. Abui's title—sheikh—came from his being an Islamic scholar and judge. Because of their unique position in the world of Islam, Islamic judges are given the title of sheikh. The Arabic word sheikh has three meanings: an old man (original meaning), a religious leader or Islamic scholar, and Arab chief or prince, a somewhat crowded category in the Gulf States.

When I first met my father-in-law, he had just come back from court where he worked as judge. He was wearing a spotless white *thawb*—an ankle-length garment with long sleeves, and a tan-colored *bisht*—a loose, sheer, and transparent cloak spun from wool and trimmed with gold. His white and immaculate *ghatra* (head cover) cascaded loosely past his shoulders to his chest. As he walked, his *bisht* billowed behind him like the sail of a dhow. His feet were clad in a pair of tan leather thong sandals. They were the most comfortable-looking sandals that I had ever seen. The sight of my father-in-law in his finery was my first real-life vision of a man in full Arab regalia. He had looked very dignified and distinguished. I learned later that VIPs and religious sheikhs usually wear the *bisht*. On special occasions, like weddings, men wear it as formal dress.

I had been uncertain how to greet my father-in-law on that first meeting, so I had merely smiled hesitantly. He welcomed me with a warm smile and exchanged greetings in Arabic with my husband. He hugged and kissed the children. He was shorter than my husband and a little overweight. His eyes were dark and deep-set and the tip of his nose was bulbous and fleshy. I had liked his eyes—intelligent, expressive, and observant, but what had struck me was that in the middle of his forehead he had a lump, the size of a coin. My husband said it was a prayer callus, caused by touching the forehead on the prayer mat five times a day. He was the only person I ever met with a forehead callus. He walked to the mosque five times a day, to pray. I thought that if walking was the unintended side effect of going to the mosque five times a day to pray, then the ritual was good not only for the soul but for the heart too.

In the beginning I was puzzled why Abui, a judge, preached in the mosque. Gradually, I learned that Islamic judges don't have to preach in the mosque but by virtue of their high education and knowledge, the community preferred that judges give speeches in the mosques on Fridays. A man of knowledge is accorded great respect in Islam.

I was very interested to know where Abui went to school and how one became an Islamic judge. In those early days, we visited my in-laws almost every day, in late afternoon, after the siesta hour. During such visits, I would usually meet other relatives who were also visiting. I enjoyed those visits. It was a nice change from the quotidian of everyday life. At that time, Abui's house was only five minutes drive from where we lived. There was not much traffic in Doha then. Sometimes my husband would visit Abui in his room, and I would tag along.

There is a time and place to say or do things. My opportunity to ask my burning questions about Abui's past schooling came one lazy evening, after sunset prayer when the family was sitting around conversing and Abui sat reading. I asked my husband to ask Abui if he had always wanted to be a judge and where he had studied to become a judge.

"Rachel wants to know how you became a judge," my husband informed his father. There had been a pause. Abui had peered at me, quizzically, I thought, over his reading glasses. He seemed thoughtful as he removed his glasses and closed his book. Then, in a reflective voice he began, "When I was a child, my mother told me my destiny as Islamic judge was revealed to her in a dream."

I had not expected him to use the word destiny. Implicit in the word was a predetermined course of events, something inevitable or preordained. I had wondered momentarily what his thoughts were on pre-destiny and free will but I did not want to interrupt him. I listened intently to my husband's translation of Abui's narration. I felt, rather than saw, shadows in the room lengthen as Abui continued the tale of the dream and his early school life. Abui's mother had dreamt that she was holding a bowl filled with milk. In the dream she gave the bowl to Abui, and he drank the milk. Her dream had been so vivid that she was convinced it signified something.

"My mother was a great believer that dreams had meanings," Abui continued. "So, she consulted an old religious sheikh who interpreted the dream for her." The old man had told his mother, "Milk is white in color; the color white symbolizes knowledge. That he was drinking milk means he was drinking knowledge. He is going to be a very knowledgeable person; he will be an Islamic scholar."

My husband had told me of another of his grandmother's dreams. She dreamt that an angel came to her and told her she would live another twenty-five years. She was convinced that she would die twenty-five years after that dream, so she made Abui promise he would tell her if the twenty-five years had passed. Every time she got sick, she would ask Abui how many years had passed since she had the dream. On the 25th year she came down with a fever. She had asked Abui if 25 years had passed since the dream and Abui, who never lied to his mother, had answered yes. She prepared herself, saying her goodbyes to everyone. She had called for my husband and his sister to come, hugged and kissed them, and sent them off to play; half an hour after that my husband heard women wailing. His grandmother was dead. It was an extraordinary story and his family still wondered about it generations later.

When Abui's father died, Abui was only two years old; but his mother did everything possible to make the meaning of her dream come true. Abui was five years old when his mother had the dream, and when he was fifteen or sixteen years, his mother sent him to a famous Islamic school in Al-Ahsa, Saudi Arabia. A Bedouin had escorted him from Doha to Al-Ahsa for a fee of five rupees. The journey from Qatar had taken three days of travel on a camel. Al-Ahsa at that time was renowned for its creeks and underground springs, gardens, palm trees, and agriculture. But life had been hard for Abui and the other students. As a student, he did not have much money and he and the other students lived on whatever their religious teachers provided for them. In winter it was very cold, so at night, they would take the mats from the mosque for warmth.

The school curriculum was rigorous and the method of teaching was several centuries old. Students studied daily, from morning till night, twelve months of the year. There was

neither vacation nor holiday. Each teacher specialized in a
particular branch and taught that specialty. The students studied
the Qur'an and its interpretation of several volumes written by
scholars throughout thirteen centuries. They studied Islamic
jurisprudence, called *fiqh* in Arabic. The word fiqh means
"knowledge, understanding and comprehension" and refers to
the legal rulings of Muslim scholars based on their knowledge of
the shari'a. Shari'a refers to the laws and way of life prescribed by
the prophet Mohammed and dealt with ideology, faith, behavior,
manners, and practical aspects of daily life. Furthermore, Abui
also had to study Arabic language grammar. The duration of
study for the course was open. There was no specified length
of time. The student finished his studies when he had finished
studying all the scholarly volumes of Qur'anic interpretation
and all aspects of Islamic jurisprudence.

I had admired the extraordinary determination of Abui's
mother to make a conviction revealed in a dream come true.
The inspiration had come in a dream, but it was human will
and hard work that made the destiny contained in the dream
a reality. Abui and his mother made his destiny. At the same
time, I was humbled to learn of the hardships he had endured
and the long years of study required for qualifying as an Islamic
judge. I had had no idea. I had thought the study of medicine was
tough but judging from the experience of Abui, it had seemed
to me that the process of becoming an Islamic judge through the
old system of schooling was more laborious. The educational
system since his time has been modernized, and there are now
universities in the Gulf countries offering structured curricula in
Islamic jurisprudence, just like the way a law degree is obtained
in Western universities.

My husband teased that not everyone in the family had
Abui's temperament. "My family has colorful personalities too,

like my uncle—and me," he said, laughing. "You've met my uncle," he said.

When I was new in Qatar, my husband and I had visited his uncle and his wife, and his uncle had proudly shown me the kitchen shelving he had made for his wife. I had been impressed, thinking how sweet he was to do that for his wife. It was clear that after so many years, he was still in love with his wife. When we left them, my husband told me that before the discovery of oil, Arabs in the Arabian Peninsula lived a semi-nomadic life; and in his youth, his uncle had kept horses, swords, and guns. Family legend had it that he boldly visited tents at night until he fell in love with a woman whom he wanted to marry. Their mother (his uncle's and Abui's mother—my husband's paternal grandmother), who is described as a "strong woman," had opposed the marriage. His uncle, in spite of his mother's opposition, married the woman he loved, which was quite admirable considering the social conditions of his time. In contrast to his brother, Abui's marriage was arranged according to custom.

Abui was introspective and had a scholarly disposition. He had books in his room on tables, chairs, and on the floor. In his spare time, he occupied himself with reading and writing books.

When Abui had finished recounting his story, I absentmindedly picked up a book on the floor near where I had been sitting and leafed through it. To my surprise, it was in English. "That's one of the books Abui wrote, translated to English," my husband informed me. The book had been about Muhammad ibn Abd al-Wahab and his Wahhabi movement in Saudi Arabia in the eighteenth century. I had no idea why it was translated into English, but I took it home to read because I was interested to read a work written by Abui. I was pleasantly surprised that it was written simply, in a logical way, reminiscent of the exposition style of classical Greek writers like Plato, Aristotle, and Socrates. I had been very impressed. The author's name—Abui's name—was written, Ahmed bin Hajar bin Mohammed Al'bu-tami Albinali. "Why is your father's name so long?" I had asked my husband. My husband had laughed, translating to his father.

My husband then explained that Arabs trace lineage on the father's side, so names were written in the following order: first name, followed by the father's name, then grandfather, then family name and last, the tribe's name. Thus, my father-in-law's name told people that he was Ahmed, son of Hajar son of Muhammed of the family al'bu-tami of the people of Ali. The Arabic word *bin* means "son of" and the prefix *al* before the tribal name means "people of." The grandfathers could be as many as could be traced backward chronologically. He said it was not unusual for some people to orally trace their genealogy seven to ten generations back. He added, "Young people nowadays shorten their names and just write their first name followed by the tribal name." On official forms and documents, like a passport, order of descent is preserved. I learned that the name of the tribe a person belongs is still a source of pride. The Arab system omits the mother's name since descent is patrilineal. Upon marriage, a woman kept her original name.

When my husband went to study in the U.S.A., he was unfamiliar with the Western system of writing names: First or given name, middle name which is the mother's surname and last name which is the father's surname. In this respect, the American and Philippine system of surname usage was similar, unlike the patronymic Arab way. My husband's first name is Hajar, after his grandfather. Sons are named after their grandfathers. Locally, my husband wrote his name, Hajar bin Ahmed bin Hajar Albinali, omitting the al'bu-tami. During his student days, in an attempt to simplify and shorten his long name, he dropped both his family and tribal name, and simply wrote Hajar Ahmed Hajar. That the first and "last" names were the same was a source of puzzlement to his Western friends—and to me, when I first met him. It was unusual and a novelty to meet someone whose first and last names were the same. But he never explained, merely saying it was a "long story." It was, indeed, a long story, and even if he had explained, I wouldn't have completely understood the omission of the mother's surname. I was familiar only with my culture's way of using family names. I suppose I had been insensitive for failing to understand that each culture had its own rule with regard to family name use.

In his letters and ordinary notes, Abui signed his name as Ahmed Bin Hajar but as an author he always wrote his full family and tribal name. He was well known in the society as "Bin Hajar," i.e., son of Hajar. My husband thought that the name "Hajar" was adequate identification since no other individual or family had a similar name in the Gulf. He recounted that in 1961, he received an airmailed letter from a friend in Kuwait. On the envelope, his friend had written only, "To: Hajar, Doha, Qatar." The letter had reached him. A couple of decades ago, the Qatar government adopted and implemented a strict identification code for ID card, passport, and official documents. The identification required the following name sequence: First name, father's name, grandfather, family or tribal name. Everyone complied with that regulation.

My husband further elucidated that the tribal name appended at the end of a person's name is like a coat-of-arms and the Arab carried his tribe's name like a crest. "In Arabia, in the old days" he said, "membership to a tribe ensured survival." He said it was impossible to survive in the desert alone, and so families banded together into clans and tribes to collectively establish

and guard necessary resources such as water and grazing areas.
A person became a member of a tribe by birth. The tribe instilled
solidarity and fierce loyalty in its members. He said, "Arabs seek
honor, self-esteem, prestige, and sometimes anonymity in the
tribe. People cherish their tribal name."

"We belong to the Albinali tribe," my husband continued.
"We trace our lineage to the Banu Sulaim." He said the Banu
Sulaim (also spelled Saleem) was one of the pre-Islamic Arab
tribes that used to roam the Arabian Desert. Those Arab tribes
branched out into various tribes and traced descent to Adnan,
one of the twelve sons of Ishmael, the son of Abraham.

According to my husband, the Banu Sulaim originated
geographically north of Al-Medina city in the west of Saudi
Arabia. They migrated in the thirteenth century to several places
in the Arabian Peninsula and North Africa.

I learned from my husband that the Albinali tribe has an
archive in Bahrain and members continue to collect information
on the whereabouts of members and update their records. The
Albinali tribe was formed as a result of alliances with other tribes.
The tribe is mentioned in books written about tribes in the region.
They are not a big tribe in Qatar but they are in Bahrain. The
tribe's historian visits my husband every two years to get more
information on members of the Hajar family. Abui's family had
migrated to Ras-al-Khaimah after he finished his Islamic studies,
and then in 1958, his family moved to Qatar. The Hajar family is
a direct descendant of the Al-bu'tami branch, which is one of two
branches that are purely descended from the Banu Sulaim.

Throughout my years of living in Qatar, I observed that even
in the era of oil prosperity, the society is still strongly tribal and
preoccupied with pedigree—Arab ancestry through the father's
bloodline. More than any other people, Arabs, especially Gulf
Arabs, are obsessed with ancestry and the topic almost always

comes up as a favorite subject when they socialize. They seem to have the genetic ability to follow the innumerable branches and offshoots of their tribe. To an outsider, the bloodline maze can be dizzying but to Gulf Arabs, lineage is very important. I think that knowing who your ancestors were fosters and strengthens a sense of identity and heritage. I suppose that ancestry is to a person what anchor is to a ship.

Whenever I think of Abui, I see him sitting in his easy chair, reading—his pastime. He had books in his room, outside his room . . . and in his library, he had about 20,000 books. My husband told me that when he was born, Abui wrote the date of his birth on the page of a book he was reading. At that time, births took place at home and were not recorded officially. That particular book was later put back on the shelf and forgotten. So, for many years, my husband did not know the exact date of his birth in the modern calendar, but his father knew the date according to the Hijri calendar. On his passport, he had made up the day and month and the year of his birth had been an approximation, 1942. One day, he came home from visiting his father in a state of excitement. The exact date of his birthday had been determined using a conversion table. He finally knew the exact date of his birth! And he was younger—by one year! He was born on February 8, 1943. We had rejoiced. At least, when his real birthday came around, the family could greet him "Happy Birthday" without him muttering, "Well, today is not really my birthday . . ."

And with the breakthrough about his true birth date, I was able to pinpoint his zodiac sign with precision—Aquarius. The discovery sparked off a reading spree on my part on everything concerning The Water Bearer in an effort to gain better insight into the core of his personality and psychology. He is, however, one of those few people who defy their astrological sign. My

Aquarius would frequently tell me, "I could read you like a book" which I found rather unsettling because just like any woman, I wanted to retain an aura of mystery. He usually said it with confidence; in the way husbands often behave with their wives—prophetic. Each husband believes every person is an enigma with the exception of his wife. Husbands can be so blissfully myopic, making them such endearing creatures.

My husband sometimes narrated to me stories of Abui as a judge, and, listening, I wished I could have attended his court. There are challenging moments and ethical dilemmas in the career of a judge. My husband told me that in the early 1960s, there was a murder in Qatar. The murdered man was a VIP. The police arrested a man and brought him to court, claiming that the man had confessed to the murder. In court, the man denied committing the crime. After listening to the story of the police, Abui said that he could see no evidence that the accused was the killer. Because the murdered man was a VIP, there was pressure on Abui to condemn the accused to death but he had consistently refused. The ruler at that time summoned Abui and other "judges" who practiced officially and unofficially to his palace. The president of the court, Sheikh bin Mahmoud, had been in Saudi Arabia during that time.

The meeting in the palace began with the ruler saying, "Now that Sh. Mahmoud is not here, you are all incapable of making a decision. It's taking you so long. Why can't you just accept the police's story that the arrested man is the killer? Why can't you judge it?" According to my husband, Abui had been very irritated with the ruler's statements. Abui had stood up and taken his bisht, saying, "Tomorrow, in heaven, the rope will be put around my neck, not on you. I cannot condemn a man to death without real evidence. I will not." And he left the meeting. A year or two later, the real killer was found and the man wrongly accused was released from jail. Everybody felt that Abui was right in not having that poor man executed based on police papers. In Islamic law, the burden of proof is on the accuser.

Another of my favorite stories about Abui involved the story of one of his friends, Khamis, who built Abui's courtyard house. Khamis used to visit Abui's majilis and also would occasionally drop by Abui's court to visit as a friend and sit next to Abui, while sipping tea. One day, a worker employed by Khamis went to the police and filed a financial complaint against Khamis, who was then summoned to court. When Khamis arrived, he sat next to Abui as usual and had tea with him. When the complainant arrived, he sat in one of the chairs in front of Abui, one rung below, where participants in court cases usually sat. Abui told Khamis to go down and sit next to the complainant, Khamis' employee. Khamis was very unhappy with Abui but he did as he was told.

After listening to the case, Abui ruled in favor of Khamis' employee (the complainant), and so, the employee won the case. Khamis became very upset with Abui, asking him, "You gave the right to the worker? You had no consideration for me?" And Abui had replied, "If there are biases it should have been to a friend like you but you should appreciate that the law has no bias. The man had the right and if you do not pay him his money, I will throw you in jail." Khamis was very upset with Abui. He paid his employee what the court stipulated but for a year or two he did not visit Abui. Later on, however, he went back to visiting Abui and things went back to normal between them.

Khamis had blockage of his coronary arteries and he was one of our patients. He was hospitalized several times because of heart failure. During one of his hospitalizations, Abui visited him, but Abui by that time had also had a stroke and was in a wheelchair. Khamis cried when he saw Abui in a wheelchair.

Their meeting was very emotional. It was the last time they saw each other.

One early morning in May 1992, the phone rang. It was Ummi telling my husband that Abui was very weak, unable to get up, and had difficulty talking. "Abui has had a stroke," my husband said as he dressed quickly to go and see his father. He called me later to tell me that Abui had weakness in his left arm and left leg and had slurred speech. The incident had happened while Abui was in the bathroom. A CT scan had confirmed cerebral stroke. He decided not to hospitalize Abui because there was not much that doctors could do then, and he felt that his father would be more comfortable at home. That was Abui's first stroke. Abui was eighty years old at the time. He had long-standing high blood pressure that was well controlled on medications and gouty arthritis but he had been fairly well physically.

I had known Abui for almost fifteen years when he fell ill. Seeing him helpless was very sad. Our children were unhappy and frustrated with us. They asked, "Why are you not doing anything? You're supposed to know how to treat him. You're doctors, aren't you?" We understood their frustration, but they were too young to understand that doctors can't always make everyone well. Although medicine has progressed by leaps and bounds, there are still diseases whose treatment is beyond modern medicine's therapeutic miracles. Sometimes, the patient's own body processes—nature—does the healing.

In Abui's condition, there was interruption of blood supply to certain parts of the brain causing damage to brain tissues that control motor and speech functions. It is usually due to thrombosis (clot), embolism (a traveling clot) or hemorrhage. We know that risk factors for stroke include advanced age, hypertension, cigarette smoking, atrial fibrillation and diabetes. At the time that Abui had his stroke, treatment was supportive care and rehabilitation in the form of physical therapy and occupational therapy. But there has been progress in treatment since then, and the condition is now called a "brain attack" because it is analogous to a "heart attack." In both conditions, the interruption of blood supply causes death of tissues and quick restoration of blood flow is vital to prevent damage to either the heart or the brain. The use of thrombolytic (clot-busting) drugs for both conditions is now well established. There are, however, certain conditions that must be met for their safe and effective use.

Illness touches everyone but it is particularly poignant to witness people we love become incapacitated by illness. As physicians, my husband and I see sick patients on a daily basis. Doctors are trained to maintain professionalism, that is, to be knowledgeable, wise, and compassionate while maintaining a certain distance from patient and family. This is often a difficult balancing act, like walking on a tightrope. Doctors end up focusing mainly on the disease, ordering a battery of diagnostic tests and dispensing so-called evidence-based medicine. In our zeal to treat the disease, we sometimes overlook that the recipient of our highly technical poking, prodding, and peering is a confused, anxious, and terrified human being hanging on to dear life somewhere in the disease. How many times have I heard colleagues articulate a patient's symptoms and, yet do not know what the patient was doing at the moment of falling ill. When I know that someone was walking, running, eating, talking, sitting reading, watching TV or praying when the person fell ill, I can relate better because the sick person was doing something that everyone normally does. The same event could happen to me, my loved ones, and to anyone, hence the empathy is stronger. Stories of illness, when taken in the context of daily life, are full of pathos.

There is a thin and fragile line between "normal" and

"sickness." The moment of falling ill represents that line and marks a turning point, like crossing the river to the "other side." And once crossed, life is never the same. Such was the case with Abui. He was in the bathroom, doing his ablutions when illness struck, like an eagle swooping down on its prey. He was his normal walking, talking, and thinking self one minute and the next second or minute, crumpled on the floor, confused, unable to walk and talk. His story is also the story of countless patients, starkly illustrating the frailty of the human condition. Ummi—my mother-in-law—found him, helpless on the floor, and she called for help to carry him to the bed, and then phoned my husband—their son.

On the day that Abui fell ill, he was taken to the hospital for neurology evaluation and brain CT scan, and after discussion with the neurologist, my husband took him back home. In the evening, I took our children to visit Abui. My husband was sitting on the floor in Abui's room, reading to his father, who was seated in his reclining chair. That night, talking about his father, my husband said, his voice breaking, "This is the beginning of the end."

And it was the "beginning of the end" for although Abui improved over several weeks, he had a more severe stroke two years later, in 1994. He was taken to the hospital in an ambulance. It broke my heart to see him in the hospital flat on his back, semiconscious and unable to speak, with Cheyne-Stokes breathing (alternate periods of no breathing and hyper breathing). He was paralyzed and aphasic, that is, unable to speak. I watched as nurses attached oxygen tubing to his nostrils, inserted an intravenous line, and attached him to the monitor. How many thousand times have I witnessed such a scene . . . My husband talked to the doctors . . . it was hoped Abui's condition was a transient ischemic attack—stroke-like symptoms that resolve within twenty-four hours.

Standing by the window, looking out, I felt tears flowing down my cheeks. The sky was blue; the sun was shining; the streets were busy with cars and people going about daily life. Life was as usual but not for Abui. In such moments, we are at our most vulnerable. I felt helpless, as helpless as Abui, the patient.

I stayed with Abui a couple of hours that morning, collecting myself. Nurses and doctors came and went. As a physician I've seen numerous patients in Abui's condition, but it was my first time to witness near-death of someone close to me. My own parents were in relatively good health during that time. Knowing the limits of medicine, despair and resignation were inevitable but hope fluttered and glimmered somewhere . . . Throughout, my husband and I focused our conversation on the weakly positive medical prognosis—perhaps he'll improve . . . we did not dare go beyond. In such situations, patients' families hang on to a doctor's every word, like a decree from God. But doctors follow a blueprint and say, the condition is grave but there is a chance the patient will pull through . . . a miraculous line that ignites and fans the embers of hope. What would life be without hope?

Hope flickered in my heart as I watched Abui's abnormal breathing. I thought of him as he was before his stroke—a respected judge and well-known Islamic scholar, kind, loving, witty, and with a refreshing sense of humor. From the first day I met him, he welcomed me, a foreigner, as a daughter. It must have disturbed him that I did not wear a veil, but he never brought up the topic with me although he might have raised the issue with my husband. He was always kind to me and looked on me as part of the family from the first day I arrived in Qatar. He was an observant man and regarded my habits with amusement. I used to sling a bag over my shoulder everywhere I went and he wondered why. He was curious what it contained, and so I showed him its contents: ladies wallet, compact powder, small comb/brush, lipstick, pen and writing pad. He was very amused. One day, he went on a trip to India and brought back two bags, one made of tiger skin and the other of snakeskin. I was touched that he thought of me. When he learned that oriental carpets fascinated me, he also gave me a large and very good quality Persian carpet

Abui's wit and humor is well known to those who frequented his majilis. A newspaper columnist even wrote of the wit and humor in Abui's majilis in one of the local Arabic papers. The author recounted some memorable incidents demonstrating Abui's wit. One afternoon, Mahindin, the man who served tea and coffee in his majilis, was late. Mahindin was Indian and he was also the family cook. His name, Mahindin, meant, "reviving religion." When he arrived, Abui said humorously, "You are the killer of religion." On another occasion, a religious sheikh told the guests assembled that he had the key to paradise. To this Abui had replied, "And I have the key to hell. If you want, I'll give it to you." There was also the story of an old religious sheikh who went against the consensus that it was Eid, the end of Ramadan. Abui convinced the old man to retract his position. The old man's name was Sea, which meant "knowledge." To break the ice, Abui told the man lightheartedly, "You know you are Sea (knowledge). No doubt you are a huge sea but only in a small cup."

One story about Abui's wit that entertained me a lot was when my husband came home one day shaking his head and exclaiming, "My old man still has all his wits about him." Abui had hypertension and a skin problem, hyperpigmentation. A doctor had prescribed bleach cream and the cream successfully faded the dark spots. After we arrived in Qatar, my husband, fresh from his medical training in the U.S.A., was full of new modes of treatment. He gradually started changing Abui's antihypertensive medications and worked hard to convince his father to stop using the bleach cream. A week after discontinuing the bleach cream, dark patches reappeared on Abui's face and arms. While visiting Abui one day, my husband found that his father had gone back to his old anti-hypertensive drugs. "You never listen to me," my husband had reproached his father. Quick as lightning, Abui had replied, "I did listen to you and now I look ugly."

Abui was quick to spot the funny side of life. When I was new in Qatar and he noticed me following my husband everywhere around the house, he called me Hajar's *guls*, the Arabic word for a companion little boat tugged along by a big ship. And one day, while we were lunching with him, he asked me if I had ever eaten shark meat, one of the dishes for lunch that day. When I shook my head, he wanted me to try it, but I had declined, explaining that sharks eat humans and who knows what that particular shark had eaten before being caught. The explanation had provoked laughter. My husband explained that it was baby shark meat and that sharks found in the Arabian Gulf waters were not man-eaters. Still, I would not touch it. Abui told my husband that I had no brain, much to the merriment of my husband, who later informed me that shark meat was believed to be a potent aphrodisiac and that there were jokes about wives giving it to their husbands.

I quickly got used to Abui's humor, and the "no brain" phrase to describe what he considered my idiosyncrasies became standard fare. I had "no brain" because, among other things, I bought Persian carpets at prices he considered exorbitant. I had been boasting to my husband my prowess at bargaining every time I made a purchase. My husband in turn would narrate to Abui how much I paid for a piece of Persian rug. Abui would shake his head and cluck his tongue, commenting that the wily rug merchants were ripping me off.

One weekend morning, when my husband was out of town, Abui dropped by in my house to see the children. He had been visiting a friend who lived near our house. He swept in, his bisht catching the breeze as he walked and scooped up the children, showering them with affection and giving them candies and chocolates. After the customary greetings, he asked me, "Why is the front gate wide open? Why is the front door not locked? Anyone could walk into your house." I explained through my son Tami that I was told Doha was safe. "Risha," he replied, "You have no brain." He called me Risha, because it was the closest to my name phonetically in Arabic. My husband had told me Risha also means "feather." My son, Tami, translating, had informed me with alarm, "Abui says you have no brain, Mommy" and when I laughed, he had seemed relieved.

Many memories of Abui paraded through my mind as I sat in his quiet hospital room, the silence broken by the regular and rhythmic beeping of the cardiac monitor. The sight of Abui connected by wires to machines threw his illness into sharp relief, with depth and dimension. With a heavy heart, I realized that the change in his life would be overwhelming even if he pulled through and I mourned what he could no longer be. Once, I read a short story by the Argentine writer, Jose Luis Borges. The writer, already an old man, is sitting by a river when along comes his younger self, out for a walk. Recognizing each other, they talk. The younger man is shocked that the other (his older self) is almost blind. The older man comforts him (his younger self) telling him the condition is nothing to be feared.

Abui was a poet too, and wrote a long poem, *Al Laala' al Saniah, "The Shining Pearls."* The poem dealt with a variety of subjects in human relationships. On friendship, he wrote: "Every one must have a friend / to help with miseries and defend."

Abui did get over that stroke but he was never the same—he was wheelchair bound. He tried to go about his activities in as normal a way as he possibly could. My husband told me that he frequently heard him sighing about the "decrease in the quality of life." Just like many people, Abui searched for a "cure." People visiting his majilis had advised, "Go to Germany. The doctors there will make you well." He expressed a desire to go to Germany, to consult doctors about his weak legs, and so that summer, my husband took him to Germany, for stroke physiotherapy. When Abui came back, there was sadness about him. "My legs are still weak," he said wistfully and the way he said it was heartbreaking. Three years later, in the summer of 1997, he had another stroke that made him a complete invalid: quadriplegic and unable to speak and swallow. A gastrostomy tube was inserted for nourishment. The family brought him home and hired nurses to care for him. In the early morning of July 16, 2002, the Angel of Death came to take him away, rescuing him from misery and suffering.

Even though both my husband and I expected Abui's death, when the moment of death arrived, my husband broke down in tears, crying like a child. He expressed his sorrow and sadness in a poem he published the day after Abui's death. He said, "When my father died, I could not see the sunlight, the sun must have died." He lamented, "How could I bear the loss? No one on earth could ever replace him for me."

CHAPTER 8
Ummi

The Arabic word *ummi* means "my mother." I called my mother-in-law Ummi. It was the most natural thing but I had asked my husband first if I may call her that and he had said, "Yes, my nieces and nephews also call her Ummi." Ummi and I had one thing in common—we were both mothers: bearers of life, keepers of wisdom, and givers of love but we lived in different spheres. The world of Ummi was hidden from the outside world. Whereas life in the majilis was governed by protocol, traditions and customs, life in Ummi's world was more casual and relaxed. Her world beat with soft feminine voices and the laughter of children. Her life mirrored that of other women of her generation in the Gulf. Women and children came and went in that part of the house where Ummi roamed but adult males were forbidden entry, except the husband, father, son or brother. When entering her house, Ummi used a gate designated for women and located at the back of the house. To ensure the privacy of women, houses had a separate gate for men and women.

The women—veiled, gentle, and beautiful souls—oiled the wheel of life. They took care of the day-to-day affairs of the house, cooked, banished fear and anger, and provided warmth and security to loved ones. Giving love selflessly, their men loved them back, just as tenderly and protected them. Secluded from men, they lived quiet and sheltered lives. They do not complain, though they may sigh softly in the night.

Family life revolves around the kitchen in most households, across worlds of differing cultures and time. So, it was in my husband's home. The kitchen in my husband's family home was a separate building but adjacent to the main house. My first visit in that kitchen was strangely surrealistic. The utilitarian kitchen objects were not unlike that of any household but certain objects were remarkably striking for their size. Stacked in one corner were pots and serving trays so huge I could have easily curled up in one. I learned later such pots and trays were used for cooking and serving a whole lamb or goat, which was prepared for guests and used during special occasions, like Eid—a Muslim religious festival.

In our present house, there are also giant pots and trays but I don't have a comfortable relationship with them. When I first saw water boiling intensely and fiercely in the big pots, I couldn't help thinking, what if I trip and fall into the pot? I found them overpowering and unwieldy, seeming to have a life of their own. The enormous pots I never see now but sometimes I would catch glimpses of a massive tray containing a whole lamb on top of steaming rice being carried by two men attendants on occasions when my husband invited certain guests for lunch or dinner.

In the beginning, I was mystified how the whole lamb was cooked. I learned from Ummi that the whole lamb was bought early in the morning, cleaned, and then boiled and simmered for several hours in a big pot over a portable gas stove. Such cooking was usually done in open air and in her house; the portable gas stove was placed outside near the kitchen. When the meat was tender, the lamb was transferred to a huge tray and browned in the oven, a large oven. While the lamb browned in the oven, rice was added to the pot containing the water used for boiling the lamb and cooked with spices. When cooked, the pot of rice was emptied onto another enormous tray with the whole lamb placed on top, and served. The meat and rice were delicious but very unhealthy because the animal fat was not removed and the water used for cooking the rice was full of fat. Being prone to fancy, I imagined seeing cholesterol in the fat globules floating on the surface of the water.

I shall never forget the weekend my husband invited guests for lunch and decided that a whole lamb was appropriate. One of the cooks from his father's house came to prepare the lamb in our house. That morning, I had gone to the kitchen to make tea. The delicious aroma of meat roasting permeated the whole house and made me hungry. The lamb was browning in the oven. There were several pots on the table and curious, I opened one of the pots. *What do we have here*, I had thought gaily as I casually lifted the lid and got the shock of my life. The pot contained an animal skull!

"What's this?" I had asked the cook, stuttering.

"Lamb skull," he replied in Arabic. He was Indian but he could speak and understand Arabic. He also understood a little English.

"What's it doing here?" I asked stupidly, dazed. The cook again mumbled something in Arabic. I sat down in a chair, trying to compose myself. I asked the cook to take it out and get rid of it but he refused. Shaken, I called my husband who informed me that when serving the lamb, it was the custom to include the skull of the animal in the tray to show guests that a whole animal was butchered for them. He had wondered aloud why the skull was not with the rest of its body in the oven. It was too much. I hung up, shedding tears of frustration. Even though I am a doctor, I never expected a skull anywhere in my house, much less hiding and making itself at home in a pot in the kitchen! The image of a skull in a pot haunts me still, sometimes. Looking back on that incident, I marvel how sterile our modern world has become. The unpleasant side of daily life is hidden from us. With exposure to such disagreeable sights, more than half of the world's population would probably turn vegetarian.

The custom of serving a whole lamb to honor a guest persists, and the big pots and trays are integral objects of any self-respecting house in Qatar and across the Arabian Peninsula. Even though many houses employed a male cook, the lady of the house presided over the cooking. She still does, even though she may have an army of domestic staff. My father-in-law frequently invited guests for lunch, and sometimes more than one lamb had to be cooked. My mother-in-law supervised every aspect, from the cooking to the preparation of the tray for serving the lamb.

Ummi began her day at 4:30 in the morning, when she would wake up for dawn prayer. Then, she would feed her goats, chickens, and ducks. Many houses keep such farm animals in their backyard, even now. My mother, likewise, used to keep a chicken coop in the backyard of our home in the province, but I don't remember much about those chickens except that they lay eggs!

Many households in Qatar still keep goats for their milk and meat. The male goat is sacrificed for its meat but the female goat is kept for breeding. Ummi was fond of her goats and took very good care of them. I recall one incident when one of her pregnant goats went into labor. The mother goat had extreme difficulty during delivery; the kid's head came out but not its limbs. Ummi tried to help it, and not succeeding, she called for a veterinarian who delivered the kid. The kid, however, was dead, and Ummi grieved for a week.

Sometimes, Ummi would proudly show me the fresh produce from her backyard "farm"– eggs. The golden colored eggs, gathered in a painted aluminum bowl, looked splendid. She used to send us golden eggs from her "farm." My children always loved to eat anything coming from Ummi, especially her cooking.

I remember well my first breakfast prepared by Ummi. It was the morning after our arrival in Qatar. The family usually ate in Ummi's living room but that morning she came to our room carrying a large round tray. She spread a large round, thin, and soft plastic material on the floor on which she set the tray. I learned later that such floor lining was called *sufra*. It was the custom to eat on the floor. Nowadays, people eat on tables but for large gatherings people still find it more convenient to put large trays of rice and lamb on the floor. After washing their hands, people gather around each tray and eat with their hands.

I had been embarrassed that Ummi brought our breakfast tray herself but my husband explained that it was all right because it was the first morning after our arrival. On the tray that Ummi brought that morning were a thermos, dainty teacups, a bowl of sugar, rounds of hot Arabic bread, and cheese labeled KRAFT RAMEK CHEESE, a soft cheese individually wrapped in triangles and packed in a small rounded carton. Sitting on the floor, I watched with fascination as Ummi filled the little teacups with tea and milk from the thermos, heaped a teaspoon of sugar in each cup, and stirred the liquid with tiny gold colored teaspoons. The small glass teacups were the prettiest and daintiest I had ever seen. The upper part was ornamented with a gold band in a stylized geometric design. The little gold colored teaspoons were as slender and thin as toothpicks. Being served tea in such an elegant tea service from a thermos and sitting around a metal tray on the floor gave me the sensation of being in a dream, just like I had felt at the sight of the colossal pots and trays. The mélange of contrasts was somewhat overpowering as though illusory, fabricated by my imagination.

The tea with milk was delicious and the warmth of the hot drink was comforting. It had an exotic taste and fragrance that my husband said was cardamom. Our daughter Alia, who was already up and about and exploring her surroundings while her brother Tami was still asleep, came and sat with us sharing our breakfast. She must have felt like Alice in Lewis Carroll's *Alice in Wonderland*. Like me, she was charmed with drinking milk tea in the delicate little cups and drank several cups. Ummi laughed with delight watching Alia drink from the dainty cups.

The smell of the hot bread had made me hungry. It had such a delicious aroma. Nothing smells quite like hot bread. The bread was larger and flatter than the regular Middle Eastern or pita bread usually found in supermarkets. We let Alia tear them into halves and quarters. Alia and I enjoyed eating the hot bread with cheese. The Ramek cheese had a slightly salty and sweet taste that went very well with the flatbread. I marveled at the delicious taste and freshness of the bread. My husband informed me that Ummi had made the bread that morning. Surprised, I asked how she made the bread. Ummi only smiled and told my husband that in a couple of days, she would bake another batch and show me how it was made.

Ummi called the round flatbread *khubz*, which is Arabic for bread. The delicious smell of Ummi's bread stayed with me for days. I can smell it even now, and savor the taste. I watched how she made khubz one Friday morning. I was drying my hair after my morning shower when I heard my husband calling me.

"Rachel, Rachel, Come, Ummi is making bread."

"Coming," I called back, looking around our room for my sandals, which I kept inside although sandals were usually kept outside by the door.

"Hurry," he called again.

Gosh, what's the hurry? I thought as I hurried out. I found Hajar, Alia, and Ummi in a shed near the kitchen. Ummi was sitting on a low stool facing what looked like a hole in the ground. Alia was skipping around excitedly, calling, "Mommy, Ummi's making bread. Look!"

"That's the oven for baking bread," my husband said, pointing to the hole. Wondering, I gingerly approached the hole. The mouth was about fourteen inches in diameter. Peering inside I saw glowing red-hot coals at the bottom. The sides also glowed red.

"It's a clay pot buried in the ground," my husband explained. Ummi must have seen my confused expression for she started laughing. It was all so strange! Why bury an oven in the ground? I learned later through a little detective research work on my part that the oven was similar to a tandoori oven, which was a large cylindrical clay oven in which food was cooked over a hot charcoal fire. The sides curved inwards towards a centralized exhaust hole. To maintain high cooking temperatures of 480°C (900°F), tandoori ovens remained lit for long periods of time. Burying the clay oven in the ground allowed for the desired temperature to be reached faster and maintained throughout baking since the ground acted as insulation. Long and slender cylindrical tubing connected to the exhaust hole vented the buried clay oven. The exit end of the exhaust tube was placed a few feet from the oven.

Next to where Ummi was sitting, there was a large aluminum bowl covered with a moist cloth, and near it were a large wooden board and a rolling pin. Her right hand was sheathed in a very thick, large, and round glove made of layers and layers of cloth. She placed large flattened round dough on her glove and slapped it on the side of the buried oven. Tac! The dough snapped as it hit the hot oven wall. I watched with keen interest as small air pockets bulged, and then popped, as the pale dough turned beige and light brown.

When the bread was cooked, Ummi stretched her arm inside the hot oven and skillfully and deftly retrieved the bread and gave it to me. It was hot and I waved it about in the air to cool it down, sniffing its scrumptious smell. Calling Alia, I gave her one end of the bread to pull and the bread tore in half. We ate the bread with gusto, watching Ummi smack dough onto the oven wall with her gloved hand. Then she swiftly reached inside the hot oven with her bare hand, expertly and quickly peeled the bread off, pulled it away, and stacked it on a large tray covered with kitchen cloth. The side of the bread that clung to the oven wall had little burned black spots that my husband said were due to burned dough from previous baking. I didn't mind the burned spots. I thought they added to the flavor.

Years later, during one of his modernization frenzies, my husband bought a brand new stainless steel gas oven for "baking khubz" and was after Ummi to stop using the buried clay oven. His mother had resisted his efforts. My husband argued that the new oven he bought was cleaner than the buried clay oven, but I sided with Ummi contending that bread baked in the clay oven was far tastier. "Besides" I had added, "the intense heat kills bacteria anyway." My husband had sought to disprove my "tastier" statement by bringing home bread from Ummi, calling me to "come and eat this bread," watching me eat it, and then asking, "Huh, good? Was it baked in the clay oven or my new oven?" I always knew which one and he would walk away muttering, "crazy." He always maintained, however, that "nobody could tell the difference" and that it was just my imagination. But gradually, Ummi stopped using the buried clay oven. Baking bread in the comfort of an air-conditioned kitchen was just too irresistible.

Khubz is also known as Irani bread in some of the Arabian Gulf states because in the Gulf, people from Iran used to make and sell it. The flat slightly leavened bread is soft and thin, characteristic of breads in the Middle East from Syria to Turkey,

Jordan, Lebanon, Egypt, and the Arabian Peninsula. The size and shape are variable; it may be oblong or round, like pizza. The sizes and shapes are sometimes extraordinary and unusual, bordering on the bizarre like a Salvador Dali painting. In some restaurants in Yemen for instance, the bread could be rectangular and as huge as a table. A charming Middle East folklore tells the story of a British ambassador who was invited to dine in a mountainous district in Lebanon. That region baked its bread in paper-thin discs shaped like long-playing records but twice the diameter. Because the bread was so large, it was folded several times and left beside the plates. Not knowing this, the ambassador mistook his bread for a napkin and placed it on his lap, at which point everyone at the table immediately did the same rather than embarrass him.

The Middle Eastern flatbreads are the oldest breads known and they have changed little over thousands of years. The ingredients are wheat flour, water, salt, and yeast. Bread making is ancient and perhaps, its antiquity makes bread making so satisfying an experience—and its taste so delicious. Better bread comes from practice. The sight of Ummi sitting on a low stool in the shade, baking bread in a clay oven buried in the ground was like seeing a link to that ancient past. I cherish that memory of Ummi.

Ummi made other kinds of bread too. Sometimes, for breakfast, she made *mahalla* (thin bread). Another was *chebab* bread, cooked in a pan. The dough is flattened in the pan, then inverted and cooked over fire. The word *chebab* is derived from *kebab*, the original meaning of which was "to put upside down." She had her own ancient version of pancake, a liquid mixture of wheat flour, milk, and sugar. She would lightly oil a pan before spreading a thin layer of batter over it, and when almost cooked, brushed the top with eggs. It was very good with cheese or honey or sugar.

Another interesting activity of Ummi was making *laban*, "a

fermented milk beverage." Laban is like buttermilk but not quite the same. It is a popular drink in the region and has a sour and tangy taste.

My husband told me that one of his earliest memories was of Ummi making laban. Because life begins with mother, our earliest memories center on our mothers. My husband had written and published a memoir of his Gulf childhood in poetry form, consisting of over 1000 lines. He titled his poem *Lamia* because every line ended with the Arabic letter *Lam* (equivalent to the letter L in English). The poem, admired for the beauty of the words and imagery, is regarded as a classic in the region and a cultural poem since it described, and thus preserved a way of life that is gone forever.

My husband's *Lamia* contained a section devoted to Ummi vividly describing her day and the chores she did around the house, one of which was making laban. Briefly, my husband described to me his reminiscences of Ummi making laban. She poured yoghurt in a bag made of whole goatskin, which was then suspended on a wooden tripod. The goatskin was then rocked to and fro for about half an hour, and poured in a big pot. "The rhythmic rocking sound made by the yoghurt inside the goatskin was like the sound of beating drum," my husband recounted. When the yoghurt separated, butter floated to the top and the portion left at the bottom was laban, which was used as a beverage.

Ummi would remove the butter, which was used to butter bread or converted to oil by boiling. Sometimes she added herbs for flavor. The oil was considered the best as it was thought to be healthy. Because of its excellent taste it was frequently used for guests. Now, however, it is considered unhealthy due to its high cholesterol content. But the misconception that it was healthy food gave rise to a local Gulf saying, "like step-mother oiling" because of a joke that the stepmother poured more animal oil over the rice for her children than her stepchildren. I suppose that the stepmother stereotype cuts across cultures but jokes often contain a kernel of truth. Economists in the U.S.A. have claimed that studies have shown that children raised in families with stepmothers were likely to have less health care, less education, and less money spent on their food than children raised by their biological mothers.

As well as extracting butter and laban from yoghurt, Ummi also made curd from *laban* by cooking it over low heat. The water was poured off and the curd eaten with dates as a snack. It was also dried in the sun and could be stored for months. Dried, it was handy to take along when traveling; it was reconstituted by adding water to make it soft. Some people still make *laban* and distribute it to other houses. Dates dipped in the curd were considered a delicacy. On several occasions I saw my husband and Abui sitting together eating dates with curd. They coached me to try it and I had been surprised that it was very good.

Ummi was always busy and seemed to be everywhere in her sphere—that part of the house that was her kingdom. Though living a quiet and sheltered life, her mornings were like all stay-at-home mothers around the world: cooking, cleaning, laundry, sewing and doing other chores around the house—and feeding her goats and chickens. Her three children, two sons and a daughter have grown up, married and had their own children. Some of her grandchildren in turn have children of their own, and so she was a mother who was grand, a great grand the old fashioned way.

In the morning, before lunch, her house would fill with the delicious aroma of cooking. In the afternoon, after siesta and before sunset prayer, while the majlis used to fill with my father-in-law's male visitors, Ummi's world rang with the loud and cheerful voices of children, calling her and telling her news of their day or complaining that their mother or father had scolded them. Ummi always listened to each one, smiling, laughing, or talking soothingly, and they would follow her around before playing among themselves. Some were the children of her children and some the children of close relatives. A few minutes after the children, the lady visitors would arrive in a cloud of fragrance. They greeted each other with a kiss, usually cheek to cheek, twice on each cheek. It was easy for me to adopt this form of greeting because I was brought up to greet close relatives and friends in similar fashion.

The ladies in my husband's family usually gathered on Friday afternoons in my mother-in-law's living room, the only room with a television. It was also the room where the family ate. It was a medium-sized rectangular room lined with floor cushions upholstered in white cotton polyester with machine-embroidered blue flowery design. In the center of the room was a large Persian carpet with lovely geometric designs. The women would recline comfortably on the cushions, their veils discarded carelessly beside them. In that women's section of the house, they were free and at ease. The family quarter was Ummi's domain. There, she reigned supreme. In another section of the house, male visitors calling on my father-in-law streamed in and out of the majilis but they were never seen nor heard inside the house where the women were. That men's world was far away.

While the women chattered and gossiped, Ummi or one of her granddaughters would offer guests tea, coffee, fruits, and sweets. There were always children running in and out, weaving their way through the room to whisper or snuggle up to their mothers. Ummi would call the children, reaching down inside her pocket for candies and chocolates or opening a tin can of cookies. Her pocket never seemed to run out of candies and chocolates and seemed as magical as Mary Poppin's bag.

I did not always join those Friday afternoon gatherings but when I did, I was always conscious of the contrasting life experiences of the gathered women. The party consisted of three generations of women: Ummi, her daughter, and granddaughters. The young women—the granddaughters—were university graduates and students attending university; some of them had careers and worked full time. In contrast, Ummi's life and that of her daughter, Amna, had been totally different. Unlike the younger women, Ummi and Amna kept their face veils on, removing them only when praying or when going to bed. Victims of time and circumstance, both were illiterate and they were married at an early age. When they were young, Qur'anic instruction was the only education allowed and available for women. For both, marriage was arranged as was, and still is, the custom. Yet, watching Ummi and Amna chat contentedly, smiling and laughing with their children, it was as though the anxieties and fears of that episode in their life had never been. Wise and courageous, they are icons of endurance and resilience. Sometimes, in life, we are tossed about by forces over which we have no control and in such instances, all we can do is move along with the current.

The social conditions in which Ummi and Amna grew up have changed radically due largely to education. Many young women in Qatar now have college degrees and many are joining the workforce. Travel and modern media have fostered a tolerant outlook in the society but traditional male-female roles, the husband as breadwinner and the wife as caregiver in the home, are still deeply entrenched in the society. Arranged marriages, though not forced upon couples, remain the norm. Women now enjoy more freedom and are socializing more, but segregation of the sexes is strictly observed.

When it comes to the roles and expectations of women, the society leans towards conservatism. The young and educated women in Qatar have chosen to continue veiling themselves. They have not followed in the footsteps of those who have chosen more exposure. These educated daughters are making an informed choice. They are sensible. They are courageously trying to reconcile dreams and expectations with realities without compromising the ancient values, Arab heritage, and Islamic principles that remain the cornerstone of their culture. I think that it takes equanimity, wisdom, and insight adapting to the demands and pressures of modern life without sacrificing the uniqueness of one's identity and heritage. Striving to preserve the integrity of one's culture is something admirable.

In the society, Ummi and her generation are the guardians of tradition and are loved and revered. It is to Ummi that my husband turns to for advice in matters of custom and questions of social etiquette. Ummi's experiences and circumstance may have been very different but her heart, like all mothers around the world and across the millennia, sheds tears of joy, sadness, disappointment, pain, loneliness, and sacrifice. Her heart, like all mothers, is full of love, hopes and dreams.

And one of those hopes is the wish for a good wife for a son. My husband once told me that his mother had told him when he was a child, "Your wife will be lucky" for he never complained about his food and ate whatever food Ummi gave him. In that respect at least, I suppose she was right. The way to my husband's heart never was through his stomach; indeed, a real blessing for he has a penchant for no-salt-no-pepper-no-spices-no-garlic cuisine, posing a challenge to the most creative cook.

Once, for dinner, in the early days of our marriage, I had roasted chicken and cooked rice. When he carved the chicken, he found that I had forgotten to cut the strings tying the legs. I was mortified but he had the grace not to comment on it. I had added green peas to the rice to give a dash of color and I thought, flavor too.

"What's this?" he had asked, looking at the peas oddly, turning and flicking them over with his fork.

"Green peas" I replied with some disquiet.

"What are they doing in the rice?"

"Why, uh, well, just." I replied, at a loss for what to say. I couldn't say, "for aesthetics" because the peas seemed to have lost their pleasing appearance.

"You don't put peas with rice, silly," he said with a little laugh.

"Why not? There's no law that says I couldn't," I replied defensively, regretting not giving in to an impulse to sprinkle some raisins over the rice for additional contrast and texture— and to enhance his brainpower as well. I recalled that he had once told me that his parents had given him seven raisins soaked in water for breakfast daily when he was five years old on the advice of a religious folk "doctor." He had lagged behind his sister who was two years older than he in memorizing Suras (Qur'anic verses). It was thought a daily dose of seven raisins would make him smarter. Among Muslims, seven is a holy number since God created the world in seven days. The seven-raisin prescription must have worked for he eventually became a bright cardiologist.

He had the refinement not to make more fun of my cooking and the following day had given me a gift—a cookbook, titled, *Cooking for Two*.

I never could cook like his mother and I am sure that I was never Ummi's idea of a daughter-in-law, certainly not even in her worst nightmares. Nevertheless, she has welcomed and embraced me into the family like a daughter. Her heart is like that of my dear departed mother—and like mine.

CHAPTER 9
War on Evil Weed

One day over lunch, my husband told me jubilantly, "Today is a historic day. The cabinet finally approved my antismoking proposals." As minister of health in Qatar at the time, he was also a cabinet member. It was largely through his efforts that the government passed the new tobacco control law of Qatar.

I shared my husband's exultation. As cardiologists, Hajar and I see many patients with heart problems related to smoking. The harmful effects of smoking on smokers and non-smokers have been scientifically proven and smoking should be banned—totally. There are those, however, who say that banning smoking is an infringement on individual freedom. Everyone wants freedom, like the freedom to slowly commit suicide I suppose, or do whatever you want regardless of its effect on other people. Many desirable and noble qualities, however, are open to interpretation. Human nature being what it is, laws restricting or banning the availability of a health hazard to the general public and especially children are commendable and serve the common good.

"Did you know that in Islam, the punishment for drunkenness is flogging with eighty sticks?" Hajar asked. "Once, I jokingly proposed to the cabinet flogging a smoker with 80 sticks as therapeutic means," he continued. He added that the Qatar law on tobacco was not as harsh as the law made by Sultan Murad IV who ruled the Ottoman Empire between 1623 and 1640. A fire had erupted in the capital, razing 20,000 wooden buildings while the capital was celebrating the birth of Murad's son. Murad had blamed the fire on smokers and issued a decree prohibiting smoking and punishing violators by death. Many decrees issued by dictators, sultans, and kings are sometimes shocking but Sultan Murad's decree merely bypassed the "slow suicide" lane chosen by smokers.

Over the years, Hajar made several proposals to the government to combat smoking in Qatar, first as a cardiologist, then as Undersecretary of Health and later, as Minister of Health, a post, which he held until 2005. He tirelessly worked to get the government to implement his antismoking proposals. Some proposals were accepted, some rejected. He never gave up trying. "Press on" was his clarion call and on November 6, 2002, the government of Qatar implemented the new tobacco control law. For his antismoking efforts he was awarded the WHO Certificate and Medal Award both in 1992 and 2003.

Hajar's stance on smoking demonstrates that persistence is the key to success. My husband is a dream chaser and to go after your dreams, you need perseverance, resolve, and determination, which he had aplenty. It reminds me of his struggle to gain admission to a medical school in the U.S.A. I had found the story of his admission extraordinary. It is well known that state universities in the U.S.A. rarely admit foreign medical students. A student has to be an American citizen to get into their medical school system. After finishing pre-medical school from the University of Colorado in Boulder, Hajar had applied to the University of Colorado School Of Medicine in Denver. He was called for an interview, which was, and still is, a routine part of applying to medical school. One of his interviewers was a woman who was the Dean of Admission. After the interview, she had sat and chatted with him. She told him that his application, grades, and performance were good but that the University of Colorado was a state university, and State universities were obligated to give priority to its citizens who pay taxes to the state. It was very unlikely that the university would accept a foreigner into its medical school.

With a brave and mighty heart, Hajar told the dean his concept of medicine as being a humanitarian profession and his desire to help people and alleviate suffering from illness and disease. He added that his country was dependent on foreign doctors and that he thought the spirit of medicine was helping others. "Medicine is an altruistic profession," he told the dean. "Well-developed countries like the U.S.A. should help undeveloped nations without medical schools by accepting a few of these foreign medical students to study in their universities." He had ended his speech nobly:

"I think this is an honorable thing to do." The dean had replied, "If it were my desire I would admit you but I have only one vote. However, you could influence the Admission Committee by getting private citizens, especially your professors in college, to call the committee to support your application."

The following day he had gone to talk to seven of his professors as well as several American families who were his friends. By 6 p.m., the Dean called him in his dorm, telling him, "Your supporters were calling us the whole day. You have already enough support. Please stop asking people to call us." A week later, he received a phone call from the Dean. "Congratulations," she had said. "The committee unanimously approved your application."

He had celebrated that news in his own way by inviting the professors and the American friends who had supported him to dinner, to break the good news. The Arab students and the wives of those who were married had prepared the dinner, serving Arabic food. At the time, he was also president of the Arab Student Club in Colorado.

I had been very impressed when he told me that medical school admission story. It was a remarkable feat. In a lighter vein, he also told me that in class, in the large lecture hall, his physics professor used to look for him when writing difficult physics problems on the board. The professor would ask good-humoredly, "Where's that Arab? Get up. Come down solve these problems. Your Arab ancestors were the leaders in math and physics." Hajar said it was easy for him to solve the physics problems, not because he was smarter than the rest of the students but mainly because the physics course he took in Doha high school was of the same level as the freshman physics course in the university.

"That professor had a cigarette in his mouth all the time," Hajar had added with a laugh.

My husband's war against smoking started soon after he started working as a cardiologist in Qatar in 1978. He waged his antismoking campaign while struggling to establish a cardiology service and I witnessed his valiant efforts.

Central to the practice of medicine is the doctor-patient interaction. The relationship encompasses not merely delivery and receipt of care but also the interaction of two human beings dealing intimately with one another about issues of health, illness, and sometimes death. The arena of medicine is a rich field in the study of human nature. Particularly interesting and fascinating is the interplay of human behavior and health risks. Although new advances in molecular biology and genetics have opened up wonderful new possibilities for the prevention of disease as well as treatment, we know very little about the behavioral determinants in health such as substance use and abuse. Why do people engage in high-risk behavior? Why do young people experiment with tobacco? Why do some people become addicted and others don't? The medical scientific community is just now beginning to realize that understanding human behavior is essential to improving health.

In the meantime, while research tries to unravel the mysteries of human behavior, clinicians are exposed daily to the mystique of the ill patient and consequently deal with nuances of the doctor-patient dynamic.

In those early days, my husband brought home stories that I found incredible. One of the most astonishing was his first medical round in Doha. Young, full of enthusiasm, and eager to practice new-age cardiology, he had gone to make rounds at seven in the morning. He went to the room allocated for cardiac patients but there were no patients in the room. There were two empty beds. An old and dusty Siemens cardiac monitor sat on a small table in one corner of the room. The nurse told him that she did not know what the machine was for but she had seen doctors attaching the machine's wires to patients for a few minutes, and then removing them. There had also been an ancient defibrillator in the room, covered with dust and out of order although it was never used. A defibrillator is a machine used to deliver a therapeutic dose of electrical energy to the heart during life threatening cardiac arrhythmias (ventricular fibrillation and ventricular tachycardia), allowing normal heart beat to be restored. The company agent sold those machines to the hospital but nobody knew how to use them properly.

A file of one patient had been on the table. Opening the file, he found only a very short note with a folded electrocardiogram strip. There had been no proper history or physical examination in the file. The electrocardiogram showed acute myocardial infarction (heart attack). The nurse told him that she had seen the patient in the corridor earlier that morning, so Hajar had wandered through the hospital corridors, looking for the patient who had been admitted with a heart attack the night before. One of the Indian cleaning aides had helped him look for the patient. The aide had found the patient. He had pointed to an Indian man sitting on a bench, chatting with other patients—and smoking a cigarette!

Hajar found early on that about 60 percent of patients admitted to the hospital in Qatar were smokers and that 45 percent of local physicians smoked. When he conducted a smoking survey in the hospital in 1979, smoking was considered normal social behavior. "Smokers smoked everywhere," he said, "in shops, offices, living rooms, hospital wards, cars." He observed that many physicians and surgeons smoked while talking to patients. He was convinced that smoking was a major cause of coronary artery disease (blockage of the arteries) and a leading cause of death in Qatar. He was determined to drastically reduce the prevalence of smoking in Qatar, and started a public education campaign against smoking. While he struggled to establish a proper cardiology service, he wrote articles in the local press about the harmful effects of smoking; he gave lectures in the hospital, the university, schools and clubs and gave several interviews with the newspapers, radio, and TV discussing the damaging effects of smoking on health.

The first Arabic antismoking TV interview was filmed in Rumaillah Hospital. When the TV crew came to the hospital, Hajar arranged for one of our patients who had emphysema and heart failure to appear with him on television. The patient, a sixty-five year-old male, was a heavy smoker and needed continuous oxygen supplement to ease his breathing, a graphic illustration of one of the fates of a smoker. He had to have an oxygen cylinder with him all the time but he was happy to be on TV. If nothing else, at least he was famous for ten minutes. It was also ironic that smoking was the reason for his ten minutes of glory.

Hajar took the TV crew and the patient to our stress laboratory where he asked the patient to walk on the treadmill while he supported him. The patient tried but could not walk on the treadmill. Hajar then asked him about his medical problems. The patient, wheezing, coughing, and complaining of shortness of breath, answered his questions. He said he knew his problems were due to smoking and had been advised by his doctors to quit smoking but he never listened.

"What advise would you give people based on your experience?" Hajar asked him.

"Don't do the mistake I did. Don't smoke," the patient answered, adding, "I have a young wife and I cannot go to the side of my wife." According to Hajar, the patient said the last phrase in local Arabic Gulf slang, which meant "I cannot have sex with my wife."

The TV crew who were Egyptians did not understand the local slang, so what the patient said was aired on television as it was. That part of the interview sent shock waves through the community and HH the Amir at that time had called Hajar asking why he had allowed the patient's sexual declaration to be televised. My husband, however, was unrepentant. He thought what the patient said was an effective incentive to quit smoking and powerful deterrent to smoking. The Amir, nevertheless, had been amused at the incident.

There was one interesting Qatar television show where he was interviewed together with some religious leaders, one of whom was Sheikh Al-Qaradawi, a well-known Islamic scholar from Egypt who is a resident in Doha. During that interview, the topic discussed was drugs. Ever the opportunist to advance his antismoking position, Hajar said that nicotine, which is contained in cigarettes, was a drug also. My husband, being the son of an Islamic judge, is familiar with Islamic literature. Drinking alcohol is one of the worst sins in Islam. He told me that Islamic religious sheikhs frequently cited a classic story to illustrate why alcohol is considered the worst evil. In the story, a bad king made a wise man choose between death and one out of three sins. He brought before the wise man a bottle of wine, a girl, and a slave. To avoid death, the wise man must either drink the wine or rape the girl or kill the slave. The wise man thought the wine was the least of the three evils. He drank the wine, became drunk and lost his mind; then he killed the slave and raped the girl under the influence of alcohol. The moral of the story was that alcohol as a sin leads to other sins.

With his background in Islamic literature and the fact that a famous religious leader was sitting next to him in front of the cameras, Hajar was bold enough to use the opportunity to make a statement considered shocking to Muslims. He said, "Alcohol is bad for health and smoking is also bad. But if a person were to ask my opinion if he were made to choose between death or a choice between smoking one pack of cigarettes or drinking one glass of wine, I will tell him wine is the lesser of the two evils."

Hajar's statement had created intense controversy in the country. Someone told his father, an Islamic leader and scholar, that his son was advising people to drink wine on TV! He told his father, "Sh. Al Qaradawi would have contradicted me if I said something wrong. He did not."

Smokers have a hard time quitting smoking because smoking is an addiction. Only about 10 percent of smokers who try, succeed in giving up smoking. This is because nicotine, the addictive ingredient found in tobacco, causes changes in the brain that make people want to use it more—and more. When an addictive drug is present in the body, the addicted person experiences good feelings and when absent, bad feelings (called "withdrawal") result. Consequently breaking any addiction is very difficult. Nicotine addiction has historically been one of the hardest addictions to break.

I remember one patient in the coronary care unit who was brought unconscious by the police to Rumaillah hospital one morning. He was about forty to forty-five years old and his electrocardiogram showed acute inferior infarction (heart attack). While we were examining him, he went into ventricular fibrillation (fast, irregular, ineffective beating of the heart). Hajar quickly grabbed the defibrillator, told everyone to clear away from the bed, and shocked the patient. The patient's heartbeat went back to normal with normal blood pressure and pulse. The patient required mechanical ventilation and drug infusions to prevent more episodes of ventricular fibrillation. Despite the drug infusions, the patient had recurrent ventricular fibrillation five times that morning. And each time, we defibrillated him successfully. No one knew his identity but a relative of another patient informed Hajar that perhaps the man worked in the Amiri Diwan (official workplace of the Amir) because he had seen a man there who resembled our patient. My husband called the Amir's office and requested someone to come to the coronary care unit (CCU) to identify the patient. After establishing his identity, the patient's family was informed. His first name was Mohammed.

Mohammed improved remarkably and was weaned off the ventilator on the third day. He had no neurological sequelae. He was smiling. He filled us in on missing medical information on the history of his illness. He told us that he was a heavy smoker and had no previous history of any illness. He had been walking on the street when he lost consciousness.

The following day, Mohammed's wife was with him when we made rounds. She told us that a few weeks before Mohammed's heart attack, they saw Hajar on TV talking about the dangers of smoking. Mohammed had shouted, "Go to h . . . " then he had turned off the TV and continued smoking his cigarette. The story of that incident embarrassed Mohammed. He said he would never smoke again. Then pointing to his wife, he told Hajar, "If she gives me another son, I will call him Hajar, after you."

A year later, Hajar told me that he saw Mohammed in the Amiri Diwan and he had told Hajar that he was in "perfect health." One of his officemates informed Hajar that Mohammed was smoking again but Mohammed denied it, saying, "Do not believe them. They are trouble makers." One of the people whispered to Hajar to look in Mohammed's pocket. Hajar pulled out a pack of cigarettes from Mohammed's pocket. Denying owning the pack of cigarettes, he had told Hajar, "It belongs to a friend." He then admitted that he smoked only occasionally. Hajar had reminded him that he almost died of a heart attack the previous year and how dangerous smoking was to his heart. Mohammed had thanked Hajar for his concern and again promised to stop smoking.

My husband had wanted to bring home the point forcefully to Mohammed about how dangerous smoking was to his health. Hence, he told Mohammed in the Amiri Diwan, "Since you are not quitting, you will die at an early age. Come to my office so I could take your picture and write your story. After your death I will show the story to people and tell them, 'this is a man who died because of smoking.'"

Mohammed had replied, "I will come to you, but you must say in the story that I was a good man."

Mohammed had taken that conversation seriously and gone to Hajar's office to have his picture taken by Hajar and write the story, which Hajar did. A few years later Mohammed had another heart attack complicated by severe heart failure and died at the age of fifty-five.

Hajar published Mohammed's story in our medical journal, *Heart Views*, under the title "The Smoker."

After finishing medical residency and fellowship training in the U.S.A., Hajar returned to Doha with me and our two small children, to practice his subspecialty—cardiology. At the time of his return, Rumaillah Hospital was the only general hospital in the country, and there was no trained cardiologist in Qatar. The medical department staff in the hospital was composed of two general internists, a chest physician and a handful of house officers. There was only one intensive care unit in the country— a surgical intensive care unit—at Rumaillah Hospital. Most Qatari citizens and non-Qatari government employees with cardiac problems or other medical problems were sent abroad for treatment, mainly to London, at the expense of the government. Hajar realized immediately that he had to start the difficult task of establishing a cardiology department and a proper coronary care unit from scratch.

Soon after setting up a coronary care unit and a cardiology outpatient service, he set up a medical record system. At that time, patients kept their own medical files, x-rays, ECGs, and laboratory results. He also established an appointment system. Ordinary patients used to wait outside the clinics for hours and hours to be seen by a doctor, many in the heat. The doctors who worked in the hospital were from different countries, mainly Egypt, India, Sudan, and a handful from the West. They had been very skeptical about the appointment system, predicting that an appointment system would fail because "the people just won't keep their appointment and they will come anytime they wished." But Hajar's appointment system for cardiology was hugely successful.

My husband was appointed Undersecretary of Health in 1981, three years after he returned home from his studies and training in the U.S.A. and Minister of Health in 1999. In 1982, the state of Qatar inaugurated the opening of a new hospital— Hamad General Hospital—and Hajar was appointed Managing Director And Vice Chairman Of The Board.

As Managing Director of Hamad General Hospital, Hajar implemented an appointment system for the hospital, which incensed the VIPs. Hajar was summoned to appear before the Advisory Council to explain such an outrageous regulation. The Advisory Council is composed of individuals appointed by the Amir. They function like a parliament but their decisions are not binding. Hajar narrated with amusement that during the "confrontation," one of the members of the Advisory Council had asked, "If I walked in tomorrow to the hospital clinic without an appointment, will I be sent back without being seen?" And my husband had replied, "Yes. The fact that you are a member of this council does not mean you are better than any other citizen with an appointment waiting to be seen." That answer had angered the council and some had shouted that the appointment was a bad system.

During Hajar's stewardship of Hamad General Hospital, the hospital was equipped with the latest medical technology and well-trained senior physicians were recruited to staff the hospital. Under his management, Hamad Hospital expanded and grew. It evolved into Hamad Medical Corporation (HMC), having under its wing Hamad General Hospital, Women's Hospital, Rumaillah Hospital (for geriatrics) and later on Al Amal Hospital (dedicated to cancer patients).

As Undersecretary of Health and during his term as Minister of Health, with the support of the Amir of Qatar, Hajar greatly improved the infrastructure for health and implemented health strategies to enhance the country's health care system such as the adoption of a nationwide vaccination program and the building of satellite health centers. The labor force in Qatar is composed mainly of people coming from poor foreign countries. Hajar introduced medical screening of workers for major communicable diseases such as tuberculosis, leprosy, and HIV Aids before obtaining a resident visa. The success of that system attracted the rest of the Gulf countries to adopt similar screening programs.

From 1980 to 2005 there was a steady decline in crude death rates, infant and child mortality rates, and an impressive rise in life expectancy in Qatar. The WHO health statistics on Qatar show that in the 1970s, life expectancy in Qatar was 58.7 years and in 2005, life expectancy had gone up to 73.6 years. One of the indicators of the state of health care in a country is child mortality, particularly the under-five mortality rate, which is defined as the probability of dying between birth and the exact age of five years, expressed per 1000 live births. The under five child mortality was 107/1000 in the 1970s but by 2000, that figure had declined to 14/1000, a decrease of over 50 percent and one of the lowest in the region.

The outstanding decline in child mortality and increase in life expectancy were mainly due to remarkable upgrading and development of public health services in the country during those years as well as implementation of a nationwide vaccination program in the schools. Hajar succeeded in getting the government to adopt a law that no school will accept any child entering first grade class without a certificate that the child had received all the required immunizations.

Many health services that were previously non-existent became available and consequently, very few Qataris were sent abroad for treatment and only if such treatment was not available in Qatar. This became a touchy issue between the public and doctors. If patients were refused referral abroad for "treatment," the patients felt that they were being deprived of their inalienable right to go abroad for "treatment" at the expense of the government. In the scorching summer months, the desire to go abroad for "treatment" peaked and every doctor was swamped with requests from patients and their families to be sent abroad for "treatment." This particular "malady," known in the local medical community as abroaditis, existed long before Hajar came back to Qatar. The phenomenon gave birth to the humorous saying, "If you die in Doha, it is the fault of the doctors; if you die in London, it is God's will."

With the improvements in health care in Qatar and local availability of specialty services equipped with the latest in technology and staffed with qualified physicians, the public found that those idyllic summers and free vacations abroad had ended.

I am proud to say that my husband was responsible for catapulting medical care in Qatar into the twenty-first century. In addition to upgrading medical care services to keep up with modern progress in medicine, he raised the public's awareness of health risks such as diabetes and risky health habits such as smoking.

As a cardiologist, Hajar was convinced that smoking was a major cause of coronary artery disease. Several scientific studies have since proven that smoking is a major and important risk for coronary artery disease. The tobacco plant belongs to the plant genus Nicotiana, so named in honor of Jean Nicot, the French ambassador to Portugal, who in 1559 sent it as medicine to the court of Catherine de Medici. Many plants contain nicotine, a powerful neurotoxin that is particularly harmful to insects. However, tobacco contains a higher concentration of nicotine than most other plants. Nicotine acts like poison to human arteries by preventing or deactivating nitric oxide, a chemical that protects and keeps blood vessels relaxed and prevents clots from forming on the lining of arteries. Smoking promotes the rapid development of atherosclerosis i.e., hardening of the arteries due to plaque deposition, which in turn leads to heart attack, stroke, and gangrene. Lowering the amount of nicotine in cigarettes does not prevent the bad effects of smoking.

Hajar campaigned incessantly against smoking. Many physicians in Hamad Medical Corporation have admitted that the number of doctors who smoke in our hospital is one of the least in the world due to Hajar's efforts. The incidence of doctors who smoked in 1983, 1989, 1995 and 2002 steadily declined as follows: 46, 32.2, 13.6 and 7.46 percent respectively, but that had not been achieved by intellectual convincing alone. Any hospital employee caught smoking inside the hospital was fined QR200 (US$55). That regulation was implemented years before the tobacco control law of Qatar was approved. Hence, a doctor could not smoke during working hours, which was from 7 a.m. to 3 p.m. It was embarrassing for them to keep going out of the hospital for a cigarette. Quitting was the best solution for most of them. Many of them were glad they did.

My husband's interest in the harmful effects of smoking started long before he studied medicine. As a little boy, he used to hear his father preach against smoking in mosques. In 1971, when he was a second year medical student at the University of Colorado in Denver, his father started to write a book on drugs and smoking in Islam. His father had asked him to write a chapter on the ill effects of smoking. He had spent his two-week Christmas vacation that year in the library researching the health hazards of smoking. He had titled his chapter, "Smoking: a slow suicide." His father had put his name as co-author of the book, which thrilled him and boosted his student ego sky high. In an era when smoking was fashionable across all strata of society, a warrior against tobacco was born, remaining nascent for many years like a microorganism germinating in a Petri dish. Many years later, in one of his articles on smoking Hajar wrote, "In the seventeenth century, tobacco was considered the miracle drug for every disease, including asthma and tuberculosis. Now we know tobacco has a miraculous effect in shortening the lifespan."

For my husband, who considers tobacco the evil weed, the tobacco control law of Qatar was the culmination of years of Herculean struggle and debate and a dream come true. But he said, "We won only one battle but the fight against tobacco will continue as long as there is tobacco for smoking . . ."

CHAPTER 10
Driving in Doha

My first car in Doha was a four-door blue Volvo sedan: solid, reliable—and very boring. It was a hand-me-down from my husband. He said it was the safest car for me to drive. I believed him. Two weeks after he discarded the car and gave it to me, a driver—a woman—crashed into the passenger side of his new car, a blue Mercedes Benz, smashing the door. Fortunately, no one was hurt but my husband was disconsolate. He reviled women drivers for weeks after. The door, beyond repair, had to be replaced with a new one, ordered from the factory in Germany. Hoping for sympathy, he told his father that a female driver had smashed the door of his new Mercedes. His father had replied with a shrug, "Why do you drive an expensive car?" His father known for fairness and justice most probably did not share the prevalent bias among men that women drivers were inherently worse drivers than men. Recent statistics reveal that women had fewer fatal auto accidents than men, were less likely to drive drunk, were more likely to wear seat belts, and paid less car insurance than men.

Women drivers, however, were not the hazards on Doha roads; those were the aggressive XY chromosome drivers who drove fast, cut in front, flashed their headlights, changed lanes recklessly, and beat red lights, as though it was some kind of sport; albeit a bloody sport. Non-Qatari women were permitted to drive but a Qatari woman was issued a driver's license only under exceptional circumstances, i.e., her profession (medicine, teaching) required that she drove to work, there was no available family driver, and there was no objection from her guardian, i.e., father or brother or if married, her husband. Women in the other Gulf States drove their own cars, except in Saudi Arabia.

Before we came to Qatar, my husband had a Qatari passport issued for me so, when I applied for a driver's license, the regulation concerning female Qatari women drivers was applied to me. I was issued a Qatari driver's license by virtue of my being a physician, and certainly my husband did not object to my driving.

I speculated that the reason for the strict regulation on female drivers probably lay deep in the Gulf Arab male's patriarchal psyche since there was no legal or religious basis prohibiting women from driving. Perhaps, I thought, a woman in the driver's seat symbolized a woman in control and independent, an image that generated extreme anxiety and set alarm bells ringing loudly in the male ego. Underlying many of the social restrictions on women is men's fear of female sexuality. I deduced from conversational overtones that family honor was closely interwoven with the chastity of the women and governed male/female dynamics in the society. The stark reality that filtered through to me was that to a Gulf Arab, honor was everything, dearer than life itself.

There has been some relaxation on the restrictions imposed on women due partly to education and practicalities of modern life. Today, a Qatari woman can drive provided she is eighteen and her father or guardian allowed her. It is more practical and economical than hiring a driver and a maid to chaperone. In Qatari society, a woman must be chaperoned when she ventures out of the house. Most Qatari families employ a driver and a maid. Many young Qatari women now drive their own cars but many well-to-do families still prefer to employ a chauffeur for the ladies. Driving in Doha is far from being a pleasant experience, however, and hence, many young women do not like the hassle of driving. The adoption of many modern practices and innovations are actually driven by economics and practicality.

When I got my Qatari driver's license, I had felt free, like the wind, in control and independent, although freedom and independence have nothing to do with driving a car. Police, however, frequently stopped me asking to see my driver's license. The exhilaration I had felt on being given a Qatari driver's license was soon replaced with frustration and disillusionment. I shall never forget the first time I drove my daughter to school. The family chauffeur was late, so I had to drive her to school to get her to class on time. Schools started early, around 6:45 a.m., because many of the schools had no air-conditioning at that time. We arrived at the school to find the road in front of the school clogged with cars facing in all directions, the drivers honking their horns, leaning out rolled down windows, and gesticulating wildly. It was bizarre and I don't think I would ever forget such a sight. It was chaotic. I was dismayed. The drivers were all males, employed family drivers mostly from the Indian subcontinent whose apparent goal was dropping off children in school, the same purpose that I had that morning. Resolutely and with a brave heart, I inched my car and willed my way towards the gate, waving my arm outside the window to clear a path. The drivers gaped at me with curiosity and amazement but miraculously, to my relief, a path was cleared, enabling me to park just in front of the gate and get my daughter through the school portal.

I have no doubt that driving conditions vary from country to country and I believe that this is due mainly to the temperament of the inhabitants. Basic road rules are similar around the world with slight variations but differences in road courtesy probably vary like the oscillations of a pendulum. For example, whenever I visited Geneva, Switzerland I was always astonished at the courtesy of the drivers. Road manner among drivers was the best in the world. I was very surprised that while waiting to cross the road, on the street in front of our hotel, oncoming cars would stop so that I could cross over, even though the light was green for cars and red for pedestrians. This happened so many times that I suspected it must have been a road rule. I had never experienced such a phenomenon in other cities.

In Doha, keeping my sanity became a struggle while driving. I had to be careful and stay on the right side of the road because drivers going faster than me flashed their blinding headlights constantly until I changed lanes. Once, a Bedouin driving a pick-up truck forced me to change lanes even though I was on the right; he wanted to pass me on the right and having passed me, he drove slowly in front of me and then would not allow me to pass! The aggravation was more than enough to transform a normal, peace-loving individual into a murderous criminal. Luckily for me, I had no gun, because he probably had a loaded shotgun sitting in his lap.

Whatever romantic notions I had about patience in the desert was shattered in Doha. This was most evident at intersections with a traffic light. I perceived that Doha drivers considered a traffic light an imposition, perhaps on their freedom to come and go as they pleased. I fancied how free and in control they must have felt in the old days, in the middle of the vast desert, when the only means of transport were camel, horse, and donkey. A traffic light must have been deeply aggravating to these free spirits, so I thought on observing their behavior. At intersections controlled by a traffic light, drivers would watch the color change like a falcon, accelerating to the intersection on flash yellow and with horns blaring to clear any stragglers from their path. If my car did not move on yellow, cars behind me bombarded my ears with their horns. In time I learned to keep up with the "yellow onrush" to preserve my hearing and to avoid being left behind.

I found too, that pedestrians posed a danger to drivers. They would suddenly materialize in the middle of a main road, as though they were strolling in a park. On seeing them, I would hit the brakes and honk, uttering "Idiots!" under my breath. Driving in Doha was a harrowing experience. Moreover, I frequently lost my way if a diversion forced me to follow another route. It was seldom that streets had names. I remember my children asking, "Are we lost again Mommy?" as I drove round and round the roundabouts, struggling to get my bearings.

Early on, I was surprised to learn that the leading cause of death in Qatar was motor vehicle crashes and not cardiovascular diseases. Despite the adoption of strategies such as lower speed limits and speed bumps, radar cameras, seat belts, child restraints, and motorcycle helmets, motor-vehicle deaths still remain high, especially among the young. Qatar had the highest mortality in the world from road accidents. This alarming statistic may have been due to poor compliance and implementation of safe driving measures. Another reason was that many drivers were illiterate and unskilled; they were brought from poor Asian countries to work as family drivers. Drivers only had to know the signs and what they meant; they had never heard of road manners. At the other end of the social spectrum were the numerous Qatari teenagers who drove fast and recklessly. The morbidity and mortality in this subgroup was quite high.

Most fatal traffic accidents occurred outside the city where people drove fast because the road was almost empty. There may be other reasons too, why people speeded up outside the city. The desert, always there, at the periphery, had always filled me with awe. During the day, for the better part of the year, with the sun blazing down from a cloudless sky, the landscape was baked and desiccated; desert plants and gnarled trees struggling to survive dotted the landscape. I thought nothing could be living there except scorpions and spiders. Driving at night outside the city, the vast desert seemed to breathe, come alive, engulf, and swallow you. Along the solitary desert highway, it was not unusual to see remains of wrecked cars in the most bewildering positions and locations. I once saw a picture of two wrecked cars that had crashed into each other, on the roof of an abandoned single-story house. It was an eerie sight but how those two cars got to the roof was a mystery no one could explain, unless it was a Photoshop trick.

When a car accident occurred, both drivers had to wait for the police to arrive, to file a report. A police permit was necessary for a garage to repair any damage to the car. Repair shops will not touch any car involved in an accident without a police permit. Some people drove without a driver's license. One evening, Hajar came home distressed. While driving, a truck had slammed into the back of his four-wheel drive Toyota. Stopping, he had gotten out of his car to inspect the damage. The other driver, dressed in long flowing jalabiya (floor length shirt) usually worn by an Egyptian fellahin (farmer), had run to my husband and prostrated himself, kissing my husband's feet and pleading, "Please let me go. I don't have a driver's license. The police will put me in jail and deport me. I am a poor man and I have children." Many cars had stopped, and a crowd was gathering to watch the spectacle. Hajar had been very embarrassed when the driver kissed his feet and had told him, "Okay. Go." But the police were unhappy that he had let the driver go. It took a lot of effort on his part to convince the police to give him a permit to repair his car at his own expense.

There have been changes on Doha roads since then. There are now more traffic lights, four-lane roads, and overpasses but the one difference between driving in Doha, then and now, is the traffic. Traffic jams were almost non-existent in the 1980s and 1990s. They are now a common occurrence. Qatar's ambitious development projects have caused a massive influx of foreign labor, consequently increasing the population, putting more cars on the road, more construction, and more road diversions. These have all caused more traffic congestion. Whereas before, it took me only ten minutes to commute to work, commute time is now a nightmarish half an hour or more. Progress is a good thing but everything comes at a price and in Doha, that price is traffic jams, frustration—and high levels of stress.

CHAPTER 11

It's Time for Fish

My husband frequently entertains the family with his in depth knowledge of fish. For Gulf citizens, fish is a major part of their economy, recreation, and food history. Even though fish is also a principal component of the national diet in my country, my fish savoir-faire is pathetically non-existent, unlike my husband. Hajar even made up fish bedtime stories for our children, modifying and expanding the stories as they grew up. He told me that at age seven, he started fishing on the seashore with his playmates and even now, he enjoys going deep sea fishing for recreation.

One Friday morning, my husband took me with him to the fish market. My experience in buying fish is confined to the supermarket so naturally I was curious and excited. I found during that visit that the fish market in Doha was a fascinating place, a world unto itself. For one thing, there was the peculiar smell, the brackish odor of fish.

The fish market used to be near the seashore but it is now located in the Doha Central Market, away from the sea. The sea front, however, is the best place to buy fresh fish and even now, a few fishermen still sell their catch by the seaside. People like to buy fish there. In the early evening, fishermen sell their fresh catch by the seashore along the Corniche. The fish is so fresh you can see fishermen selling fish off the boats. Most of the catch, however, is auctioned at the fish market between 4 a.m. and 6 a.m. Fish retailers purchase fish at this auction and transport the product to their stalls in the fish market for sale to the public. For the local market, fish are sold chilled, whole, and fresh. Most of the fish is consumed locally but some are exported to Saudi Arabia or Bahrain.

I found the Doha Fish Market surprisingly very clean but it reeked of the sea and was a noisy place, with everyone talking in loud voices, their words bouncing off the walls so that the sound was like the magnified low frequency humming of thousands of pigeons. The fishmongers, wearing aprons, cut, chopped, and sliced fish or weighed them on a scale located in a corner or in the center of their stall. They shoveled ice, making tinkling sounds, and then swoosh-whooshed them over the fish. Most of the shoppers were men. The fish sellers, although wielding sharp knives, seemed unsoiled, uncontaminated with blood and fish guts. Conventional fish markets in the world of books teem with vulgar characters—unbridled smokers, peddlers, hawkers, thieves, criminals—and rats, but such characters were conspicuously absent. The place was startlingly wholesome.

Some newly caught fish were busy wiggling, jumping, quivering, or making thumping and clunking noises as they blindly collided against the wall of the metal containers. There were fish of different kinds and different sizes, some as tall as myself. I was surprised to see small sharks. Hajar told me before that there is an old myth in the Gulf that shark meat is an aphrodisiac. There were also crayfish, crabs, prawns, clams, and squid—huge, some surprisingly bigger than a man's head, like the stall owner's.

The walls of the fish market were tiled in white and the fish sellers frequently poured water on the floor and over the fish in their metal boxes. There was a cat behaving like the sovereign of the place, a fat cat, with a grey coat streaked with beige. The vendors occasionally threw it fish, and the cat, fish firmly wedged between its canines, would run up a wooden rampart above, survey its kingdom, sit, and there, devour its special treat.

Stopping at one of the stalls, my husband asked me what kind of fish I'd like to buy. I looked blankly at the variety of fish posing like beauty queens in the metal box but none looked familiar. In the supermarket, fish is sold pre-packed whole, cut like steak or filleted and the name of the fish clearly stamped on the package. Without their stamp, the fish had all looked the same to me even though the heads were of different sizes and shapes. I looked at the google eyes . . . the drooping half-open mouths . . . they looked dazed and confused out of the water but quite comical. Fish seem to have a talent for looking funny. In their natural habitat they scurry about or glide indifferently, royally, some preening, displaying their magnificent colors but put them in an aquarium and they become philosophers: self-contained, floating calmly, surveying the human world through the glass tank. When caught as food, they wiggle and jump frenziedly or loll dejectedly, as if to say, "It's a cruel world."

In a world where big fish eat small fish, sub-phylum Pisces is at a distinct disadvantage especially since brainy Homo sapiens discovered that fish possess omega-3 fatty acids—health-giving oils. The human body cannot produce omega-3 fatty acids and they must be taken in through the diet. Large population-based studies have suggested that a diet rich in omega-3 fats can reduce the risk of cardiovascular disease. Research has shown that these fats decrease risk of irregular heart rhythms, which can lead to sudden cardiac death. Omega-3 fats decrease levels of triglyceride—a type of fat found in the blood which has been linked to heart disease, and reduce the clumping together of small particles in the blood called platelets, which can cause potentially harmful clots. Furthermore, omega-3 fatty acids have been shown to decrease the growth rate of fatty plaques that clog the arteries and it also lowers blood pressure. Omega-3 fatty acids have been linked to a wide range of other health benefits including: good fetal development, prevention of memory loss and dementia, improvement in behavior and mood, and may cut the risk of cancers such as prostate and skin.

With these health benefits in mind, I did not feel sorry for the fish at all as I stared at them, trying to decide which of them I should buy as food for my family. It was my turn to be philosophical, while surveying the fish. No one feels sorry for a fish, perhaps because fish are cold—cold as a fish. These cold-blooded creatures tolerate freezing temperatures, and some vegetarians even eat them. Fish are caught, cooked, and eaten gleefully by both adults and children alike. My children who are not fish eaters used to relish eating fish they caught whenever they went fishing with their father. I remember how breathless with excitement they were on coming back from those fishing trips, calling out to me:

"Mommy, Mommy, we saw seven dolphins and we caught a lot of fish!"

"Tami fed the dolphins with fish!"

"The dolphins spit water out from their mouths!"

"Mommy, you should have come with us!"

"I caught five fish!"

"I caught a baby shark!"

"A fat fish jumped into the boat, brushing Salma's arm and landing on Haifa's feet!"

We would cook the catch for lunch and each child would tell me who caught which fish. Everyone caught the fat fish! The kind of fish was not known but they recognized them by the size, shape, and form.

On that Friday morning at the fish market, not having had the honor of a prior meeting, I failed to recognize any of the fish in the stall but I knew some easy and tasty fish recipes such as Fish Meuniere and Fried Fish Masala. Of the local fish, hammour (grouper) and safi (streaked spinefoot) were good for both.

"Let's buy some safi," I suggested.

"I was stung once by safi fin as I tried to free them from the fishing net," Hajar said. "It was very painful. Its fin has poison that causes severe pain. Immersing my fingers in warm water relieved the pain. Hot water is the antidote for sea fish poison. Heat neutralizes the poison."

"I would like four kilograms of safi, please," I said to the fish vendor. He selected a handful, showed them to Hajar and me for inspection and slid them on his scale.

"Did you know that safi is a vegetarian fish?" Hajar asked. "It does not eat other fish; neither does it eat baits like worm or squid." I was pleased that safi was vegetarian.

"Maybe we should buy hammour also. I like hammour." I said.

"That's hammour" Hajar said, pointing to a grayish, dumb-looking fish with a big head. "Tell me, is it male or female?"

"How should I know?" I countered, but then he told me it was a female fish! I thought he was joking but he was serious.

"Hammours have a unique sex life," he said. "When young, they are all females and when they grow larger, like say, ten kilograms, they transform into males." That was fascinating. I had no idea hammours had such exotic sex lives. The hammours had all looked so dull and dumb, which just goes to show that when it comes to sex, one never knows! Can you imagine what fun you'd be missing if you judged people by looks alone?

"The males are polygamous. They have a harem of several females," Hajar continued.

"That is very interesting and very charming!" I exclaimed. "I am pleased to hear that hammour is the counterpart of a dirty old man!"

"Give me that hammour, please," I said to the fish vendor, pointing to a squirming and stupid-looking hammour. He captured the hammour and showed it to Hajar for inspection before sliding the fish onto his scale. It was seven kilograms short of becoming a male.

"Fish must be fresh," Hajar said, glancing sideways at me.

Freshness is a sacrament in fish cuisine. My husband considers himself an expert on fish. On that Friday outing to the fish market, he demonstrated to me the great science of buying fish—the pearls. I surmised that growing up in a small fishing village, he must have acquired fish expertise through an extra sense, just like the way a man born blind acquires knowledge of his world. When we have fish for lunch or dinner, he has an uncanny knack of enlightening the family that "the fish does not taste fresh because it was bought frozen" or that it was on the "verge of spoiling" at the time of cooking, as though the fish had willed itself to undergo such change to spite and spoil our fun of eating it. The family was never quite sure if what initially tasted like an excellent dish was really only fish in the nascent stage of rigor mortis. He would quiz each of us, "Does the fish taste good or not?" After several hesitant, careful, and thoughtful tastings, most of us would concur with him "the fish is not so fresh." Then he would quiz our children. "If the fish is spoiled would it float in water or sink?" Some would say, "It will float" and some would state, "It will sink." To which he would smile and say, "It will float."

During that expedition to the fish market, while walking and looking around, greeting the friendly and smiling stall owners enticing me to buy their fish, Hajar, intent on my education, decreed, "The fish must be fresh." My only social interaction with fish was picking up frozen packets in the supermarket unlike Hajar who swam with fish in the sea as a child. Buying fish can

be tricky so I whispered, "How do you know that fish is fresh?"
With a little smile conceived in hidden wisdom, he revealed the
precious pearls. The secret was careful physical examination.
Examine the eyes—they should be bright, clear, shiny, and
protruding; dull, hazy, opaque, sunken eyes indicate that the fish
is spoiled. Look at the gills—they should be red or pink. Inspect
the skin—it should be moist and shiny. Feel the flesh—it should
be firm and elastic. "Press the flesh with your fingers, and if
there is pitting edema, the fish is spoiled." Pitting edema is a
medical term referring to the persistent indentation on the skin
when pressure is applied to a swollen area of the body and that
persists for some time after the release of the pressure. It is one
of the signs of heart failure in humans, not in fish. My husband
advised me, "Exercise your sense of smell—fresh fish emits a
fresh, slightly ocean-like, mild odor; if there is a distinct fishy,
sour smell, do not buy it." He said he could tell from a distance if
the fish was fresh or not. "Remember," he said; "check the eyes,
the gills, the skin and flesh. Use your nose." Since a fish market
already has a naturally unpleasant odor I had no idea how good
my nose would be in such a place, but I had been very impressed
with my husband's fish savoir-faire and teaching style. It was an
educational tour-de-force worthy of Plato's school in Athens.

The fish market still plays an important role in the life of its
native residents and has retained the essence and spirit of a small
fishing village. Although I never went to the fish market again,
I frequently bragged about that particular visit, highlighting
the market's cleanliness, the absence of shady characters, the
courteous and affable fish vendors, the variety of choices, the
freshness of the fish, and the bargain prices. There have been
many changes in Doha but the fish market has been spared. To
this day, the sights and sounds of the Doha Fish Market linger in
my memory. To me, it is the epitome of the old Doha.

CHAPTER 12

The Adhan

I heard the chant, "Allaaaahu Akhbar," flowing out from the minarets five times a day. The first time I heard the sound, I was intrigued. I wondered what it was. I thought someone was singing but my husband said, "Shhh, don't say that. It's the *adhan*, 'the call to prayer'."

He was shocked that I had described the adhan as "singing." He told me that some Muslims who were very religious did not listen to songs and, so, it was inappropriate to refer to the adhan as singing.

"Not listen to songs!" I exclaimed. "But why not? I would have thought religious people would encourage people to listen to music since it soothes the soul. I relax to music and so do countless people. Music is one of the little pleasures of daily life. I don't see any harm in listening to music and songs. I even read that music was used as a form of therapy for psychiatric conditions during the Arab empire."

"Well, some religious Muslims do not approve of it and there is some debate on the issue that you might find tedious. Anyway, if the sound of the adhan bothers you, you had better get used to it," my husband said.

"Oh, not at all," I replied. "It doesn't bother me. I like it. I think it beautiful." I had found it melodious, in a melancholy way.

Interestingly, the beneficial effects of music have been confirmed by research using PET scan, which showed that music activated parts of the brain that made us happy, enhancing feelings of physical and mental well being, just like exercise. PET stands for positron imaging tomography, an imaging test that uses a radioactive substance to show how organs and tissues in the body are functioning.

Human beings are aware of the powerful effect of music since, probably, time immemorial. For example Homer, the ancient Greek poet, in the Odyssey, one of his two epic poems, tells of the adventures of Ulysses on his voyage home after the Trojan War. Ulysses' ship had to pass by the island of the Sirens, sea nymphs who had the power of charming by their song all who heard them. Their song was the sweetest and the seamen who heard their song were so enthralled that they were irresistibly impelled to cast themselves into the sea to destruction. As Ulysses' ship approached the Sirens' island and following the advice of Circe, the enchantress, he instructed his men to seal their ears with wax; but Ulysses, a man of never-ending curiosity and characteristically seduced by danger and mystery, desired to hear the siren's song. He did not plug his ears but instead instructed his men to tie him to his ship's mast and gave strict orders not to release him even if he raved to be set free until they had passed the Siren's island. As their ship sailed past, the music grew fainter and then ceased. With joy Ulysses gave his companions the signal to unseal their ears and they relieved him from his bonds. So, Ulysses was the only mortal who experienced the ecstasy of the sirens' enchanted song and lived to tell the tale.

Music affects everyone. It is hard to imagine anyone immune to the charms and pleasures of music. I thought that the adhan, with its rhythmic cadences, was akin to music and that was why

I had found it appealing. At dusk, when light faded and shadows fell, I loved listening to the gradations in tone, textures, and contrasts of the adhan. In Qatar, as in the rest of the Arabian Gulf, that time of day is called *maghrib*, which means "sunset," and the prayer at sunset is called *salat al maghrib*. *Salat* in Arabic means "prayer." *Adhan al maghrib* is the sunset call to prayer.

Maghrib became my favorite time of day. The world seemed to pause and sigh sadly, as though it regretted the day's passing. The subdued mood was intensified by the plaintive call to prayer emanating from the mosques. The sound of the adhan will always be one of my enduring memories of the Arab world.

One time, I woke up at dawn to the sound of the adhan. I remember sleepily glancing at the luminous green hands of my alarm clock—3:30! *Who wakes up to pray at this hour*, I had asked myself incredulously. Sleep flew away and I lay in the darkness listening to the undulating tones tumbling from the minarets. The sound was like a restrained wail—striking, compelling, and haunting but soothing in a way that the ringing church bells of my childhood were not.

Like the adhan, ringing church bells signified the time for the worshippers to pray or go to church. In the days before watches and clocks, religious communities had to devise some sort of a signal to announce prayer times and sing the Divine praises. It seems that religious leaders had always devised a method to remind people of their obligation to pray. In ancient times, the Greeks used a wooden board or sheet of metal struck with a hammer. The Romans did not seem to have used a specific instrument for religious purposes but joyfully rung bells during triumphal processions to express gratitude to the gods for success in battle. The ancient Egyptians supposedly used bells in their worship of their god Osiris and it is claimed that the practice of ringing bells among Christians may have originated from the ancient Egyptians. Moses, who had been educated in the priestly class of Egypt, is said to have introduced bells into the ceremonial of the Jewish religion. In those early and unsettled times the church bell was useful not only for summoning the faithful to religious services but also for sounding the alarm when danger threatened.

Eventually, other uses for church bells evolved and bells rang out to announce a church service, to celebrate a special or happy event such as marriage, mark the time of day or announce the death of a parish member, in which case the bell would toll once for each year of a person's life. With expanding use, church bells developed a unique language of their own. Differences in the manner of ringing and the number of bells employed indicated many details of the particular service or event. In Christian Rome, on the evening of a fast day, bells ring for a quarter of an hour to remind people of their obligation to fast the following day.

Ringing church bells are no longer as important in Christian daily life as they once were, and some Christians would rather not have the sound of church bells in their area. When rung overzealously, the bells can be noisy but I have a nostalgic fondness for the sound of church bells. I remember them clanging and pealing exuberantly in the morning, at midday and in the evening for the Angelus prayer, the daily prayer of the Roman Catholic Church. I fondly remember the Sanctus bell. *Sanctus* is a Latin word, which means "Holy." It was a small, shiny, bronze colored handheld bell, which was placed conveniently on the left side of the altar. During Holy Mass, the acolyte dressed in his liturgical finery—a black robe under a white surplice—rang the Sanctus bell just prior to and during consecration. Consecration is that moment in the Holy Mass where the priest prays to the Holy Spirit to change the gifts of bread and wine into the Body, Blood, and Divine Soul of Jesus Christ. The transformation is called the Eucharistic Mystery, and it is the heart and center of the Mass. The mystical transformation is supposed to be a supernatural occurrence but for me, it was easier to reconcile its symbolism. Like the rest of the congregation, I would kneel and with head bowed pray to be worthy to receive the Body of Christ. The solemn ringing of the bell intensified the deeply spiritual nature of the Mass. The sound of the bell, though solemn, was sweet and joyful. I always felt profound during that moment and later, sitting and waiting for my turn at communion, I would experience deep peace. Sometimes, the priest perfumed the Mass with incense reinforcing feelings of serenity and harmony.

I grew up a Catholic and the "bells and smells" of the Catholic Church have stayed with me through the years. The passage of time has made me realize that the rituals of the Church are potent and stay with you forever, no matter what. When I came to live in Qatar, my memories of those rituals underlined for me the importance of heritage and made me more aware, open, and tolerant to the cultural and religious practices of other people. I felt that each culture must have practices that are interesting and enduring. Our customs and traditions become personal and intimate experiences for us, as well as integral parts of our sacred space. I thought that learning about other people's religious and cultural rituals would enrich me as an individual.

The adhan is uniquely Islamic. I was immediately drawn to it on first hearing it, feeling its magnetism. Once, I told my husband that sometimes the dawn adhan woke me and made me remember the ringing of church bells. I then compared and analyzed the effect each had on me. The comparison had prompted him to quote one of his favorite Arab poets, Al-Ma'arri (973–1057 AD): "There is noise in Al-Lathiqye between Muhammad and Christ; this one with his bell ringing, and the other crying from the minaret. Each one is supporting his religion. I wonder which one of them is right?" Al-Lathiqye was the city where Al-Ma'arri lived and is now a modern seaside resort on the Mediterranean coast of northern Syria. Al-Ma'arri is a famous poet in the Arab world and was born in Syria. He was stricken with smallpox at the age of four and became blind. Some religious authors have accused him of being a non-believer because his poetry reflected his skepticism of all religions, including Islam.

Unlike Al-Ma'arri however, I never considered the adhan and ringing church bells as noise. I liked both. Each had a timeless quality, but I felt that the controlled tone and tempo of the adhan gave it beauty. The more I listened to it, the more I noticed subtle variations in its recitation. The reading was embellished with pauses, repetitions, and variations in tone and tempo. I found out that the modulated form of the adhan was due to adherence to certain fixed rules during its recital.

In contrast to the church bell, which had other functions, the adhan is used solely for the purpose of summoning worshippers to pray. It is said that the function of the adhan was foreseen in a dream by one of the first Muslims who saw a person calling out for prayer from the roof of a mosque. The prophet Muhammad agreed to add this element to the *salat* (prayer) and chose Bilal, a black Ethiopian slave, as the first person to call out the adhan for he had a "beautiful and far-reaching voice." Bilal had converted to Islam on hearing that the new religion championed fairness, justice, and equality among people irrespective of color.

The adhan begins with an affirmation of the supremacy of God, repeated four times, and then comes the shahada or profession of faith, which consists of the declaration that there is only one God and negation of polytheism followed by confirmation that Muhammad is the Messenger of God. After that comes the call to prayer and to success in attaining paradise, and return to the Creator. Each successive line after the first is repeated for emphasis. The words of the adhan are as follows:

Allahu Akbar, Allahu Akbar.
God is the Greatest, God is the Greatest.
Allahu Akbar, Allahu Akbar.
God is the Greatest, God is the Greatest.
Ash-hadu anna la ilaha illa-allah.
I bear witness that there is no God but God.
Ash-hadu anna la ilaha illa-allah.
I bear witness that there is no God but God.
Ash-hadu anna Muhammadan-Rasulullah.
I bear witness that Muhammad is the Messenger of God.
Ash-hadu anna Muhammadan-Rasulullah.
I bear witness that Muhammad is the Messenger of God.
Hayya 'ala-s-Salah, hayya 'ala-s-Salah.
Come to the Prayer, come to the Prayer.
Hayya 'ala-l-falah, hayya 'ala-l falah.
Come to real success, come to real success.
Allahu Akbar, Allahu Akbar.
God is the Greatest, God is the Greatest.
La ilaha illa-llah.
There is no God but God.

I wondered a lot why the *adhan*, at least to my ears, sounded like "singing." Reading the words of the adhan and following the recitations, I noted repetitions of the lines. These prescribed set of line repetitions, combined with the muezzin's own variations in tone and tempo, gave the adhan its lyrical and melodious quality. I was told that the muezzin was free to modulate the sentences to what he felt was best. That was why each recitation varied in subtle ways. It is preferable that a person with a good voice delivers it, for a good voice deepened the inherent beauty and rhythm of the language. At first, the sound may be bothersome to some non-Muslims but those with an ear for rhythm cannot fail to appreciate its cadenced beauty. I have tried repeating it aloud to myself whenever I have heard the call; however I had never approximated the muezzin's skill, but then I never had a good voice! Muslims say it must be recited appropriately, pleasingly, in a way that attracted attention but never sung. To be a muezzin required long sessions of practice in diction and pronunciation. If art is the conscious use of skill and creative imagination, then I suppose recitation of the adhan is an art.

Since that early morning hour, when the adhan woke me up and beguiled me, I endeavored to listen when the lilting chant resounded throughout the day. However, due to the commotion of daily life, I heard mainly the adhan al maghrib, the sunset call to prayer, although I was aware of adhans at other times. There were so many new, strange, and unfamiliar sights and sounds when I was new to the region, but the sound of the adhan represented for me an oasis of serenity and harmony. Near the hour of sunset, it became my habit to sit in my library or on the terrace when the weather was nice, in anticipation of adhan al maghrib. I would hear the first of the adhans, a low sinuous sound from the mosque nearest our house followed by other low-pitched lilting voices from other more distant mosques. The graceful tones rippled through the city, echoing the flowing voices rising and falling and then, silence. In the sea of stillness that followed, I sensed and saw in my mind people praying in their mosques and in their homes.

One *maghrib*, I was in my library listening attentively to the modulated inflections of the adhan when Hajar walked in. I wondered out loud why the adhan sounded magical at sunset.

"It is curious that the adhan should fascinate and preoccupy you," he said. "Did you know that sunset in the Islamic clock is equivalent to midnight in our modern clock?"

"The Islamic day begins immediately after sunset," he continued. I stared at him, incredulous. *What was he talking about? Was he pulling my leg?* I thought. But no, he was not teasing me. He was serious! What he said was extremely interesting and fascinating but puzzling to me, and it took a lot of explanation by my husband and research on my part to clear up my confusion.

In our modern clock, day begins immediately after midnight, which is Egyptian in origin, whereas the Islamic day starts immediately after sunset, which is Babylonian. The Babylonian day began with sunset. Therefore, sunset—the twelfth hour—is equivalent to midnight in our modern clock.

Different civilizations have different ways of measuring time because the concept of time is complex, but we know that events take place and have duration in a dimension called "time," which we measure by the clock and the calendar. In addition, our concept of time has changed over the centuries. Today, we think of time only in the context of "What time is it?" or "There's not enough time to do everything" and our modern 12-hour clock is perfect for such pursuits. In ancient and medieval cultures, however, the division between night and day was important, because human activity and the business of living were carried out during daylight hours. Since the time from sunrise to sunset was longer in summer than in winter, the "hours" of summer were also longer than the "hours" of winter. Historically and geographically, the Arabs were closer to the Babylonians than to the Egyptians, and so it was not surprising that they adopted many Babylonian customs and ways such as timekeeping. In addition, since praying five times a day is central to the Islamic way of life, the Babylonian method of keeping time was suitable and practical for Muslim religious activities. Immediately after sunset, the fasting Muslim could break the fast and then perform maghrib prayer. Since sunset marks the end of a day and beginning of a new day, Muslims end and begin their day in prayer.

With time, I noted that the adhans did not start simultaneously so that adhans in different stages of recital would fill the air at the same time, like ripples. I wondered why this was so since daily adhan timings were fixed according to a preset time. I learned later that in each country, the adhan time is the same in each time zone and special clocks were installed in the mosques to make the call to prayer more precise. All the mosque clocks were synchronized to 12 o'clock at sunset but the muezzins who led the call were not, confounding efforts at precision and uniformity. Some started on time but others started one, two, three, four or more seconds later, thus producing the delightful ripple effect. I was considerably charmed to learn that human touch was responsible for such an enchanting phenomenon.

Listening to the adhan enabled me to pause, think, reflect, and be in touch with my innermost self when life was busy or disheartening. To make sense of life, it is integral to have a sense of the spiritual, the sacred. The adhan transported me to sacred time—to moments when the cares of our modern world dissolved and maybe put aside. For me, it was—and is—a small window to spirituality that I cherish.

CHAPTER 13
Romancing the Souk

The marketplace is called souk in the Arab world and when Arabs say "souk," they mean the old traditional bazaar, which is still very much a part of every Arab town and city. In the Arabian Gulf modern shopping malls and designer boutiques are now common and many are as sophisticated as those found in Paris, New York, and Milan. In fact some shops in the region are branches of famous brand names abroad, but I preferred wandering around the old souk.

When I asked my husband the origin of the word souk, he said it was derived from the ancient Arabic word *sak*, which meant, "drive." So, the marketplace was the "drive" place where camels were driven for exchange or barter. In those ancient times, goods were paid for mainly with camels or goats. Therefore, the buyer drove the money to the seller.

The basic structure, function and motif of souks are the same everywhere and probably have not changed much over the centuries. Architecturally, regional variations exist depending on the size, sophistication, and antiquity of the city. For example, one of the Arab world's greatest and historic bazaars is Khan al Khalili souk in Cairo and known simply as the Khan. It is the oldest souk in Cairo—about six hundred years old. It was established on the site of a Fatimid castle. Some information

143

about Khan al Khalili souk claimed that the Khan might have been indirectly responsible for the "discovery" of the United States of America! Such assertion may not be so implausible considering that the Mamluks (slave soldiers who seized power from the Muslim caliphs and who ruled Egypt from the 13th–16th centuries) controlled the spice trade monopoly, spurring the Europeans to search for alternative routes to the East, and led Columbus indirectly to discover the Americas. I thought it highly entertaining that an old Arab souk may have played a role in launching a serendipitous "discovery" that resulted in the establishment of a rich and powerful country such as the United States of America. Such playful musings about souks enticed my brain to shake and gyrate like a Macarena dancer, profoundly enhancing the natural charms of the souk.

On the few occasions that I visited Cairo, Khan al-Khalili souk was one of my favorite places. I was disoriented the first time I visited it. On passing through its medieval carved stone gate, I felt as though I had stepped into another world, a strange and astonishing place where little had changed since the Middle Ages. It was a bustling, vibrant place consisting of a confusing maze of narrow alleyways lined with tiny shops displaying all sorts of merchandise and peopled with a rich array of locals, tourists of many nationalities, shopkeepers, vendors, and craftsmen. There were men smoking shisha (water pipe) in almost every corner, which unfortunately seemed to be an integral part of that souk. The details of life seemed to crowd in, thrown in relief, threatening to overwhelm. It had a kind of medieval commercialism. Vendors and shopkeepers inveigled passersby to come into their shop to look around. Tourists, me among them, wandered around in a daze, marveling at the seemingly endless variety of merchandise: leather, brassware, gold, silver, jewelry, textiles, carpets, incense, perfume, coffee, tobacco, spices and other things. Souvenirs were everywhere, many mediocre in quality and mass-produced for tourists. But some items were of good quality and would have been difficult to find anywhere else in the world. The souk was full of a pungent potpourri of smells, sights, and sounds—a place throbbing with activity and spilling over into the tiny alleys, so topsy-turvy, like life itself.

After getting over my initial bewilderment, I fell in love with the place. It had a dream-like quality. I loved walking in that souk. You never know what "treasure" you might stumble on. On my first visit, I found—and bought—a beautiful large 215 carat (43 grams) unset amethyst stone of the loveliest shade and perfect to make into a pendant. I couldn't believe it. Amethyst is not so expensive but it was rare to find one that big and beautifully cut. I was surprised to learn that those shops imported precious and semi-precious stones from all over the world.

When I saw the gorgeous amethyst, the fabled *rukh* (griffin) floated from the depths of my imagination. Being prone to flights of fancy, I had wondered if perhaps the shopkeepers kept a rukh who flew them to a secret valley full of jewels, just like in Sindbad the Sailor, one of the captivating stories in the Arabian Nights. I became ambitious and started to look for an emerald stone. I have always thought emeralds beautiful—fresh and radiant with lush green hues like a spring morning. The ancients believed the emerald symbolized hope and rebirth and that the gem rewarded its owners with love, intelligence, and eloquence. In addition, it was believed to have a soothing effect on the soul, an effect attributed to the relaxing and calming properties of the color green. It was also believed to ward off evil spirits.

I am not superstitious but I desired to possess such a mystical stone and looked for it with excitement and hope fluttering in my chest, like bird wings flapping. Those tiny shops were lined wall to wall and floor to ceiling with tiny drawers that seemed to contain everything from tourist bric-a-brac and precious and semi-precious stones to rolls of sewing threads, needles and other unlikely items such as nails and bookmarks. The shopkeepers opened drawers noiselessly, whispering, and voila, whatever a customer requested materialized. It was mesmerizing, like watching a magician pull a rabbit from a hat, and the thought flashed through my mind that perhaps Aladdin's wonderful lamp was hidden somewhere in those drawers.

I saw many customers leave the shops clutching bundles wrapped in cotton wads and newspapers, and teasing my imagination with their furtive manner. I went to numerous tiny shops in search of the mystical green gem. I was certain that somewhere, in a drawer in one of the little shops, an exquisite, exceptionally rare and flawless emerald lay wrapped in velvet, waiting to be discovered. But I had only a limited time and my desire to possess a magical emerald stone spirited away from the valley of the mythical rukh remained merely a dream, beyond reach like a distant moon.

The allure and excitement of that first visit to Khan al Khalili souk has endured and for me, each visit to that shadowy and chaotic place full of whisperings, imagination—and life—was like stepping through the pages of the Arabian Nights. For inspiring whimsy in its visitors, Khan al Khalili souk is matchless.

Souks have mood and character, in various shades, but they are essentially pragmatic places, which is not surprising since barter was the fundamental impulse that inspired their existence. They have, however, many aspects that appeal to the imagination, especially in someone like me with a tendency to whimsy.

Souks are everywhere in the Arab world, in every city and village. Souks are small worlds within worlds, multilayered and multidimensional, with secret hidden spheres—a microcosm of Arab society. Their design echoes underlying traditional elements, spaces, and themes, but each souk preserves the unique local flavor of the region and reflects its history and culture as well as the customs and habits of its inhabitants. They all give an insight into the daily life of the country.

Souks in the Arabian Gulf are not as old and grand as Khan al Khalili souk in Cairo but they have a lighter charm, like watercolor painting. They are smaller with their own inimitable qualities. In Doha, the old souk is called Souk Wagif, which means, "standing market" and I often wondered out loud why. Hajar informed me that the souk began as a makeshift marketplace where people, especially Bedouins, brought goods on camels or donkeys and unloaded them for sale. Staples sold were milk, cheese, dried dates, meat, wool, handmade crafts, and other items. Since the market lasted only a few hours, the merchants sold their goods standing, hence the name Souk Wagif (standing market).

When Qataris talked of "the souk," they usually referred to Souk Wagif. There are, however, other souks scattered across Doha with names like Souk Hamad, Souk Al Ali, Souk Al Badi, and Souk al-Asiery, etc. Souk Wagif had recently undergone a massive makeover. It has been modernized and revamped to look "old" so that people sometimes referred to it as the "new Souk Wagif" or "new old souk." But I still fondly remember Souk Wagif before its modern facelift, and I won't ever forget my first visit with my husband. It had narrow and bumpy dirt alleys partially paved with cement that separated clusters of small shops—humble shops. I had been initially disappointed at the dilapidated state of the place but strolling through its heart, the shops charmed me with their casual air of disarray. They were crammed with goods that spilled over the front of the shops. The informal and relaxed confusion of merchandise displayed added considerably to the appeal of the place, so I had thought. The alleyways had no permanent roofing, but corrugated iron covered some of the spaces between shops cutting off most of the sunlight during the day. The setting was shabby but in a comforting sort of way, like a worn out old rug. What appealed to me most was the air of intimacy and lack of pretension of the old souk—and an odd feeling of changelessness, as though the tiny shops and little streets had been there for ages. Changelessness implies stillness or lack of activity but the souk was not a place of repose. It was filled with life: vendors, shoppers, tailors, weavers, carpenters and other craftsmen—all busy engaging in commerce.

I was amazed to see on the street shoe repairers squatting or sitting cross-legged in front of toolkits or toolboxes, mending anything from shoes to luggage. I regretted that my sandals didn't need patching. It would have been immensely fun to watch them renovate my sandals. They did their jobs quickly, cheaply, and efficiently. There were also tailor shops and tiny shops that specialized in repairing watches. The shops sold an infinite variety of merchandise: textiles, kitchen utensils, cutlery and crockery, pots and pans, large cauldron-sized pots for cooking a whole lamb and huge serving trays to serve the lamb. There were hardware shops, which stocked tools, nails, screws, and other household items. There were shops that sold toys, luggage, groceries and sweets, as well as those that sold perfume, spices, and herbal medicines.

On that first visit, one scene that had attracted my attention was a group of men sitting quietly on floor cushions and inhaling through a mouthpiece connected with a long hose to a bubble-shaped base. When I asked Hajar what those men were doing, he said, "Smoking shisha, water pipe." I had been very curious and had thought the sight exotic, but Hajar started walking faster, as though he had wings on his feet, like the god Mercury. Being an ardent anti-smoking advocate, he wanted to flee from that place as fast as he could. Trying to keep up with him, half running, the image of the hookah-smoking caterpillar from Alice's *Adventures in Wonderland* rose unbidden in my mind. The water pipe used for smoking is also called hookah. That caterpillar was the first shisha smoker I ever encountered and I remembered my fascination at the illustration. It was so unusual, so oriental, in a Middle Eastern sort of way. I recalled, somewhat incongruously, that the caterpillar was three inches tall and spoke in a languid, sleepy voice. The human shisha smokers I saw were definitely taller but looked heavy-eyed and indolent and if I stared at them, I fancied them taking their shisha hose out from their mouths and asking drowsily, "Who are you?" just as the caterpillar did to Alice.

In the old Souk Wagif, there used to be only one section for shisha but tobacco smoking using water pipes is increasing in popularity, especially among young Qataris. In the new Souk Wagif, there are many cafes considered fashionable where the young hang out to smoke shisha. It was popularly but erroneously believed that water pipe smoking was safer than cigarettes. Numerous researches have shown that it is worse than cigarettes. The local Ministry of Health Laboratory analysis had shown that each shisha head of tobacco contained 52-fold more nicotine than one cigarette. Carbon monoxide gas, the most poisonous substance to the heart and arteries does not dissolve in shisha water but goes directly to the lung. Water pipe smoke contains the same harmful substances as tobacco smoke that is detrimental to health and could cause cancer, pulmonary disease, coronary heart disease, and pregnancy related complications. Smoking shisha against a background of oriental cushions and carpets may sound romantic and exotic but I wish its use was banned in public, just like cigarettes, for it is a risky habit that is damaging and injurious to health.

Usually, I went to Souk Wagif not so much to shop but to soak up the atmosphere. In the winter, when the weather was pleasant, I liked strolling leisurely in the old souk. It was a refreshing change from the uniformity and monotony of air-conditioned supermarkets and shopping malls with marble floors, escalators, and uninteresting and repetitive window dressings.

Walking along the narrow and bumpy dirt alleys, peering through or entering the small shops crammed with merchandise was like romancing the past. Arabia was the crossroads of ancient caravan routes. The sight of little items, like souvenir wooden replicas of camels decorated with colorful saddles and reins, fired my imagination and I saw, in my mind, camel trains laden with goods—textiles, ceramics, precious metals, foodstuffs, spices, frankincense, perfumes, and raw materials. The fanciful thought of thousands of camels in every shade of brown, from cream to almost black, saddled with brightly colored cloths, bawling and grunting with heavy loads and rhythmically swaying side to side like rocking boats in the arid desert landscape was hypnotic. The camel caravans used to be a familiar sight in Arabia and such scenes are featured and preserved in art. The camel—that magnificent desert animal—made overland caravan trade routes between East and West possible.

The interconnecting little lanes and streets of the souk became, in my imagination, the great and lucrative spice trade routes linking Africa, Europe, and Asia. I usually got a whiff of this perfumed heritage when coming upon the spice shop in the souk with its attractive array of aromatic and rainbow-colored spices. Throughout history, spices were appreciated for their fragrances, their medicinal properties, and enhancement of flavor in food. All traditional Arab souks took pride in the excellent quality of their spices, and Souk Wagif was no exception.

Walking through Souk Wagif, taking in the sights and

sounds, I was always delighted to suddenly come upon the spice stall. The spices were displayed in large open metal boxes and their rich and dazzling colors offset their modest backdrop. They looked glorious, so unlike the dull rows of uniform spice bottles in supermarkets. In the souk, the colors of the spices were incredibly vivid, vibrant, and eye-catching, like a medley of bright-colored lipsticks in cosmetic counters. The spice shop had a rich assortment of whole and ground spices on display: pepper, cinnamon, nutmeg, ginger, curry, sesame, cumin, turmeric, cloves, saffron, paprika, coriander, chili, cardamom and other spices and condiments that were unknown to me. They emitted indefinable scents and their fragrances held the promise of pleasure and delight.

Spices evoke memories of gustatory enjoyment through the vivid world of odors. I had been delighted to recognize cardamom, turmeric, and cumin among the numerous spices. They had been unfamiliar to me before I met my husband and I remembered the first time he introduced them to me. We had invited some friends for dinner and he said he had a special recipe for a leg of lamb that was simple and effortless. I had been skeptical but he said, "Trust me. I'll show you." We had gone to the supermarket and of the spices he chose, I knew curry and cinnamon but the others were a mystery. Hajar identified the spices that I did not know: turmeric was yellow-colored and odorless and he used it only for "color"; cumin was yellowish-brown with a pungent smell and he used a small amount to add a "bit of flavor." Of the spices my husband had used, the powder that had interested me most was cardamom, which was light green with a pleasant smell, reminding me of menthol. Hajar had added cardamom to "add fragrance and flavor." He told me to sprinkle sliced onions, lemon without the rind, and raisins and nuts under and over the lamb, wrap it tightly with foil twice over and then pop it in the oven.

"Well, now what?" I had asked.

Hajar had replied, shrugging, "That's it. Leave it for three to four hours. Very simple." Indeed it was! While the lamb baked in the oven, a delicious aroma filled the house and I had no doubt that the lamb would taste wonderful. I have since used his recipe several times for family and guests and passed it on to friends who named the recipe "Rachel's Lamb."

I have since learned that cardamom is an essential ingredient in the straw-colored coffee of the Arabian Peninsula. It is also a standard spice in the traditional Arabian dish kabsah, a lamb-and-rice stew and a common ingredient in fruit desserts. Many English names of spices are Arabic in origin such as saffron (*za'faran*), ginger (*zangabil*), tumeric (*kurkum*), and cumin (*cummoon*). Historically, spices were referred to as the "perfume of Arabia" and Herodotus, the Greek historian, wrote of Arabia "the whole country is scented with them [spices], and exhales an odor marvelously sweet." We have no inkling now, however, of the greed they aroused and the warfare and barbarism they incited through the ages. The Assyrians fought and killed for the spice tribute of Arabia, and the Genoeses and Venetians engaged in a long struggle for the spice trade of Medieval Europe.

Spices may have dark associations historically but the spice stall in the souk beguiled passersby with their aroma and flamboyant colors. Passersby frequently bought small amounts. The spice seller was always helpful suggesting buying whole spices, pointing out that they were stronger and more aromatic since the volatile essential oils were lost much more rapidly after grinding. He often ground the spices on the spot. Although obliging, he would become as secretive as a spy agent when asked the ingredients of his mixtures. He would only smile and shake his head—the blends were top secret.

Not far from the spice shop was a shop called Ibn Abbas.

The shop was so inconspicuous that I was curious what was inside. Hajar said it was a little herbal shop and such shops were a unique feature of traditional Arab souks. He advised me not to go in since it was stuffy and musty inside and the smell might trigger my allergy. "As a physician, some of his goods might interest you but there's really not much to see inside," he said. I wondered aloud why the sign on the shop didn't proclaim "Herbal Shop" so more customers might stop by.

"Everyone in Doha knows it's an herbal shop," Hajar replied. "The shop is called after its owner's name, Ibn Abbas. He is the local herbalist and he inherited the profession from his ancestors."

Hajar told me that Ibn Abbas sold a variety of herbs, spices, incenses; flower extracts (perfumes) and mineral substances used as traditional medical therapy. He imported some of the materials such as gum, camphor, thyme, saffron, musk, castor, honey, coriander, cumin, cloves, sulfur, iron oxide and arsenic from Oman, India, and Iran. Frequently, people went to his shop for advice and treatment for various body complaints. He actually prescribed treatment for each complaint and gave detailed instructions on the preparation of the herbal mixtures and how to use them. He fulfilled the role of a traditional pharmacist or even a traditional physician.

"The role of the herbalist is not unique in Doha," Hajar said. "It was practiced all over the Arab and Islamic world for centuries." He informed me further that such herbal shops were known in history as *makhsan al-attar* (perfume shop) and the herbalist was called *al-attar*, which means the "perfume-seller." The word *al-attar* is derived from the Arabic word for perfume—*iter*.

The herbalist had an important role in the history of medicine. Patients must have benefitted from his "cures"—psychologically and physically—to keep the profession going for centuries. Modern medicine, however, has progressed by leaps and bounds and the herbalist cannot compete with modern medicine technologically. Neither does he have the resources and expertise to prove the value of his traditional remedies through experimentation and clinical studies. Some physicians worry that the herbalist might delay early detection and treatment of serious diseases. In turn, the herbalist claims that his remedies "cure" many patients after modern medicine failed to give them relief.

"People used to visit al attar to buy cosmetics and perfume even though perfume was a minor part of the goods sold in his shop," Hajar continued. "That role has been taken over by cosmetic surgery and modern cosmetic products. No one can accuse him now of trying to make an old woman younger and better looking." He quoted an Arabic verse and smiled, "It's an old saying beautifully phrased in Arabic poetry and maybe translated as follows: *What time spoils goes so far, that cannot be repaired by attar.*"

While walking in the old souk, the gold shops always caught my attention because of the glinting ornaments displayed: necklaces, bracelets, bangles, rings, earrings, and pendants. Doha has a gold souk that is separate from the old souk and consists of one whole block of small shops devoted to gold jewelry. Like the gold souks in the other capitals of the Arabian Gulf States, it is a dazzling and spectacular place.

There were only a few gold shops in the traditional section of the old souk. The gold shops sold only gold jewelry, in 22 and 24 carat gold, none less than 18 carat. Gold jewelry is sold by weight according to the current gold price of the day. Most of the items had traditional designs but some were modern. There were a wide variety of pendants, including pieces fashioned into individual letters of the English alphabet. You can have a necklace made according to your design specifications. Craftsmen can alter the composition of alloys in the gold to create pink, white, yellow or green hues in one piece. One popular gift with Western visitors is to have a necklace made displaying the name of the recipient in gold. Craftsmen can produce the necklace in either English or Arabic letters.

It was fun and marvelous just to look and quite absorbing to scrutinize the elaborate designs of traditional items such as the traditional gold bridal necklace, which is given to Qatari girls by their husbands to be. They looked somewhat similar to the family heirloom gold necklace that my mother-in-law gave me soon after I arrived in Qatar. My husband told me that the necklace had belonged to his paternal grandmother. It was the custom in his family to pass on the necklace to the oldest son's wife. Its size and old-fashioned design made it impractical to wear; but it had a small headpiece that I thought was charming and which I removed, occasionally wearing it as necklace. These days, the traditional gold bridal necklace is considered too old fashioned and brides now prefer modern and contemporary diamond jewelry.

Old Souk Wagif had a section that sold regional handicrafts and local traditional items: traditional dress and accessories, wooden chests, brass coffeepots with beaked spout, water pipes, stringed instruments, sword, incense burners and woodwork. On my first visit I found this section one of the most exotic. I found the Qatari dress section extremely interesting. For ladies, there were long Arab shift dresses heavily embroidered at the neck and cuffs, headscarves, *abayas* (black overwrap worn over clothes), delicate and sheer black head coverings made of crepe or chiffon called *al-sheila*, and different types of veils such as the *batula*, the black face mask worn by Gulf women of the older generation such as my mother-in-law. The batula attracted the attention of

newcomers to the Arabian Gulf because it covered the face to
the level of the chin and jaw with two slits for the eyes. I was
intrigued and fascinated to see on the shelves ladies' *sirwal*—
the long baggy trousers that ladies wear under their dresses; the
tight cuffs were decorated with gold or silver embroidery—very
pretty. For men, there were long white *thobes*, *ghattra* (the
long flowing headdress, white or checkered in red and white),
ghafiya, (the white crocheted or embroidered cap worn under the
headdress, the black *aghal* or rope ring which secures the Arab
head dress, and *bisht,* the ceremonial cloaks trimmed with gold.

For me, the Qatari costume and accessories section was
fascinating. I had always wondered where my husband, in-laws, and
Qatari friends and acquaintances bought the traditional garments
and accessories that they wore. It was quite a surprise to suddenly
come upon them on display and stacked on shelves in the old souk.
The garments were simple and there was not that much variation.
Sometimes, they commissioned a tailor or craftsman to execute their
sartorial desires, always traditional with a few personal touches here
and there. The most important parts were the overwrap and headgear.
It was a particular way of dressing, for both sexes, that affirmed their
origins and indicated an individual's identity and social status. I
thought that part of the souk was a small window into one aspect of
Qatari social life and values.

In the shops that sold local garment and accessories for men,
I saw strings of beads called *misbah* (prayer beads) hanging on
a nail or peg. Only a few samples of misbah were displayed.
Most of the misbahs were on trays inside glass display cases
or in boxes in drawers. There were misbahs made with beads
of ebony, mother of pearl, amber, cornelian, coral, ivory, and a
thousand other multicolored stones.

In the early part of my life in Doha, the sight of a man or
groups of men sitting and chatting while playing with their string

of beads had attracted my attention. I had thought the string of beads was a fad. The first misbah I saw belonged to my husband. The beads were round and smooth, opaque, the color of egg yolk, with faint white hues, and looped and gathered at one end with a tassel of the same color. That was one of his favorites. I remember that one of my husband's best friends gave him a gift of misbah made of hollow silver beads and each bead contained attar (oil perfume) of roses, but my husband never used it and I stored it in an undergarment drawer. Each time I opened the drawer, I would smell the heavenly scent of roses.

Hajar took his misbah with him wherever he went and he sometimes misplaced or lost them so that he would buy new ones even though he had a drawer full of misbahs. I supposed he felt "incomplete" without his misbah. Whether he was alone or with company, he sat fiddling with it, grasping each bead with thumb and index finger and then pushing and releasing the bead, knocking its counterpart below with a barely perceived click. Sometimes, he twirled the string around his fingers and flicked it over his hand. There was infinite variation in the clicking rhythm; intervening pauses, twirls and flicks that I imagined the sounds expressed a vast range of meanings, like a secret sound language. I wondered what sounds expressed boredom, annoyance, approval, agreement, amusement or rumination. I thought that if I understood the "language of the misbah" I would be able to read my husband like a book. I surmised that the misbah is the Arab male's social prop, much like Linus' security blanket in the cartoon series Peanuts.

When I first saw my husband's misbah, I had been struck at how similar it was to Roman Catholic rosary beads. The misbah's resemblance to the Catholic rosary had intrigued me. I have since learned that that there is historical evidence suggesting the rosary had its origins from the Arabic misbah. It has been claimed that the use of the misbah originated with the Sufi (a mystical Muslim sect), who used the beads as mnemonic device to mark recitations glorifying God. A popular recitation might include Glory be to God, Praise to God, and God is Great, each repeated 33 times. Each string of misbah has either 33 or 99 beads. The Catholic rosary has 50 beads to mark repetitions of the Hail Mary with five larger beads to count Our Fathers, and thus preserved the original religious function of the misbah. It was introduced into Western Europe during the thirteenth century, after more than two centuries of European-Middle Eastern contact during the Crusades.

Both Christian and Muslim Arabs use the misbah; however, time and cultural diffusion have erased the original religious distinctions and the misbah has become part of an Arab man's wardrobe, especially a Gulf Arab. I often thought the soft clicking sound of a misbah was a convenient way to fill in awkward gaps in conversation and an expedient means of expressing surprise, dismay, or amusement. Fiddling with something when you are nervous or stressed is a convenient way to hide your emotional state. I thought that twirling a misbah to conceal stress or nervousness was stylish as well as an elegant gesture while gathering your thoughts. I once asked Hajar about the origin and function of the misbah habit but he just replied with a shrug, "It's custom." His reply made me reflect on how most everything we do seemed to be steeped in "custom," traditions from long-forgotten civilizations but we never pause to think about them. When we look at a clock for example, we never think for one moment that we are using an old Babylonian method of reckoning time. I thought it interesting how the misbah developed from being a religious device to a social accessory. It illustrated nicely how customs and traditions can evolve with time to accommodate social and environmental changes.

The great game in the souk is bargaining, which I found fun and entertaining. It is a form of social interaction that requires grace, humor, and psychology. Bargaining is an art, and like art people respond to it differently. You either like or dislike it, just like a Picasso paining.

My husband does not enjoy bargaining but I do. One of the most amusing and entertaining bargaining experiences I've had happened in a little shop in Toledo, Spain. The salesmen spoke very little English and I had to summon my rudimentary Spanish to bargain. Browsing inside, I had been much interested in the plates, jars, and vases of a very unusual make displayed in cabinets with locked glass doors. The background of the items that had attracted me was black with flowery or geometric designs in a golden color, very pretty. There was even jewelry of the same make. A man had come, smiled, unlocked one of the glass cases, taken out a small round plate and handed it to me for closer inspection. I had been surprised that it was heavy.

"What is this?" I had asked. He explained that it was iron and that the decorative filigree laced through it was gold. I looked at the price tag and thought it a bit expensive for a tiny souvenir plate. I had thought the decoration was gold paint or bronze, but even so, the execution was superb.

"Why is it very expensive? This is not gold," I said pointing at the decoration. He explained patiently that it was gold thread inlaid through the iron. I was fascinated. I thought such craftsmanship did not exist anymore. Seeing that I was still skeptical, he told me to wait a moment. He disappeared and then came back. He showed me the thread. It was really gold thread.

"Can you give me a discount?"

"Yes, it is possible," he replied easily. I was delighted. He went and consulted another man, then came back. Yes, he would give me a discount.

"How much discount will you give me?" I asked.

"Five percent," he said.

"Señor, five percent discount is nothing," I said smiling and shaking my head.

"How much do you want, Señora?"

"Twenty percent," I said. He opened his eyes wide. It was all very amusing and I thought what a very nice man he was not to throw me out of the shop!

"Please, Señora, speak with him," he said gravely, gesturing to the man with whom he had consulted. So, we went over to the man behind the counter. I surmised he was the owner or manager, a dignified-looking man. My desire was explained to him. To my surprise he actually smiled pleasantly. He too seemed amused.

"Give me a good discount and I will buy these," I said, pointing to the plate and jar that the first man had brought.

"One moment, Señora." The man did some mathematics on a piece of paper. Finally, he wrote down on a piece of paper for me. 15 percent!

"Muchas gracias" I said, smiling. I was ecstatic. It was beyond my expectations. I had admired the composure of the owner or manager. Throughout the deal he was courteous and amiable and judging from the sparkle in his eyes, saw the humor of the situation. After all, how many non-Spanish speaking tourists went into his shop to bargain laboriously in Spanish?

I went over to Hajar elated to tell him the good news and that he would also be given 15 percent discount but he had been indifferent, which had slightly annoyed me. The money involved did not really matter that much. It was the goodwill behind the markdown that I appreciated. Unlike me, my husband did not enjoy bargaining. According to him shop owners never reduced prices without a profit. But of course! The seller is always interested in making a profit because that is his living but the buyer does not have to accept the sticker price. The price could be brought down considerably through the fine art of haggling. For me, the rich theatrics involved in the transaction was highly entertaining. The buyer always gets the raw end of the deal, but the fun was in not letting the seller eat the icing on his cake by getting him to reduce his price as much as possible. Buyer and seller agree on a price that is satisfactory to both parties. Bargaining is a game where both parties feel like winners. For me what counted were the good feelings and social interaction involved. Buying something at a fixed price was just so boring.

In the souk, the items I was most interested in and for which I indulged in bargaining were oriental carpets, specifically Persian carpets. The delicacy and intricacy of the design and color combinations of Persian carpets had always fascinated me. Many of my excursions to the souk involved looking for Persian rugs. There used to be a shop in Souk Wagif with the sign Iranian Carpets adorning its front façade. I had been thrilled to suddenly come upon the little carpet shop one day, while strolling along the alleys in the textile section. There was a beautiful area rug hanging in the display window. The background was red with a predominantly blue medallion accented with delicate flowery and arabesque designs in muted orange, reds, and yellows. The rest of the field was scattered with little flowers in varied hues of red and blue. It took my breath away.

Inside the shop, the walls were covered with hanging rugs and kilims and stacked in corners were folded carpets. A man was sitting behind a desk talking to two other men and when I went in, they looked up, murmuring "Salaam Alaykum." Souk traders were gregarious and they seemed always relaxed, while sitting, and interminably talking to people, perhaps friends, acquaintances, and visitors.

"Good afternoon," I said.

"May I help you, Madame?" The man behind the desk asked, standing up.

"Oh, I just want to browse around," I replied.

"You are welcome, Madame" he answered politely. He followed me as I looked around and I asked the place of origin of some carpets that attracted me. He told me the carpets were from Tabriz . . . Mashad . . . Khorassan . . . Isfahan . . . Shiraz . . . Kerman . . . and other exotic-sounding towns and villages that I had never heard of. The majority of the carpets had wool piling on cotton weft, some with silk threads through the delicate designs. There were pure wool carpets and a few were made of pure silk, from the city of Qum.

As I looked around, he would call my attention to certain rugs, telling me they were very "fine carpets." I asked the number of knots, and then flipping the rug over, I tried counting the number per square inch, just to impress him. I learned how to count knots from books about oriental rugs and had practiced the technique in other carpet shops I had visited. Weaving has a long and rich tradition in the Middle East. It inspired and was influenced by other arts. A poet living in eleventh century Central Asia even went so far as to compare composing a poem to weaving: "Each thread of its warp was drawn from within me / Each thread of its woof was painstakingly extracted from my soul . . ."

"Please sit down, Madame. I will show you some of our fine carpets," he said, gesturing to a chair in front of the desk.

"What kind of carpet would you like, Madame?"

"Nothing in particular. I was just attracted to the rug in your display window and I came in just to see," I smiled as I sat down, thrilled with the lovely carpets surrounding me and the prospect of being shown "fine rugs." Two men appeared from somewhere and the shop owner signaled for them to spread carpets on the floor for me to view. They spread carpet after carpet . . . As if by magic, tea in a pretty little cup and a small plate of cookies materialized and were offered to me.

"Thank you," I said as I accepted graciously even as I remembered my husband telling me not to drink souk tea because the cups were probably rinsed in water only, without soap. The tea had looked so inviting—very deep red, like liquid rubies. The cookies had aroma and flavor that I could not pinpoint. "These cookies are delicious. The flavor, what is it?" I couldn't resist asking.

"They're saffron cookies, Madame. I'm glad you like them," he smiled. I started to like the guy. He was very courteous, polite, and hospitable. He spoke good English.

The carpets he showed me were a visual feast in color and design. It is the breathtaking beauty of the colors that enchants the lover of Persian carpets. I recalled reading somewhere that the French painter Paul Gauguin said, "Oh you painters who ask for a technique of color—study carpets and there you will find all knowledge." The magnificent colors were achieved with vegetable or animal-based dyes. Natural dyes had remarkable beauty and subtlety of color, and they were durable.

"How did the weavers manage to get just this shade of red or blue?" I asked.

"Madder provides all shades of red," he replied. "Madder is readily found in Iran, my country, and blue color from indigo." He informed me further that different shades of yellow were obtained from turmeric and saffron; reddish-yellow from wild saffron and pure yellow from cultivated saffron. Beige was obtained from barley, and brown came from walnut husks. From these few dyes, skillfully thinned and knowledgeably mixed, all shades can be obtained. Unusual hues were obtained from pomegranate, alum, and heliotrope.

"That color, how was it achieved?" I asked pointing to a gorgeous turquoise blue silk rug spread out on the floor before me. It was so unusual that I thought chemical dye might have been used.

"That kind of blue is obtained by allowing the stem of the heliotrope to ferment in urine," he replied with a straight face, which had amazed and amused me. "Such dye is rarely used though," he added with a smile. Absurdly, I imagined rich collectors bidding for such rarity at Sotheby's in London, entertaining me greatly.

I was learning so many things just by sitting and chatting to the carpet dealer. The designs were beautiful and consisted of a central medallion with ornamental motifs of arabesque, palmettes, rosettes, and other vegetal designs. The most enchanting motif in Persian carpets is the garden as the earthly reflection of paradise. I was shown carpets with flowers, trees, bushes through which ran animals and birds of many kinds. Small songbirds, pheasants and peacocks perched on trees; lions, tigers, cheetahs, foxes and deer ran through the undergrowth. They were delightful and a pleasure to behold but I liked the medallion-arabesque and floral medallion designs best.

On that particular trip, I had been looking for a Nain carpet. Nain is a small town whose carpets are among the finest in Iran. The knots varied from 300 to 900 per square inch. I asked to see his Nains and samples were spread before me. One of them was a medium-sized rug with floral medallion motif on a navy field with a beige-ivory border, and jewel-tone accents; cotton warp and wool pile. It was very elegant and understated and I secretly desired it. I asked the price of other rugs first, before asking the price of the Nain, and he quoted a price.

"That's expensive!" I exclaimed, gasping a bit.

"It is a very fine quality carpet, Madame."

"How many knots per square inch?" I asked.

"530."

"It can't be that many," I said, flipping one end to examine the knots at the back. "It feels very loose. I think it's less than 300." It wasn't loose at all and my knot estimate was close to the figure he gave me.

"See, Madame, it is quite firm. It lies flat nicely on the floor." That was one quick way to tell a good rug.

"You know, it's not silk. It's wool. I don't know how you could tie that many knots per square inch as you told me."

"The weavers of Nain could, Madame." He answered patiently.

"Are they magicians?" I asked.

"No, Madame but they are very skilled," he answered laughing.

"How much discount would you give me?"

"10 percent Madame."

"Oh, pfff, that's nothing. Everyone here gives 10 percent discount. Besides, I didn't bring any cash or checks with me so I can't pay you," I said with a smile.

"That is no problem Madame. You can take the rug home and pay me later at your convenience. You could even take the rug home, see how you like it and if you didn't like it, I'll take it back." Rug dealers frequently did that but I didn't want to take the rug home without settling the price.

"How long could I keep the rug?"

"As long as you wish, Madame. Take your time."

"Thank you. That is very kind of you but it won't be necessary because I can't afford your price" I told him, smiling a little. "But you know something? I would pay only this much for this rug" I said, quoting a price 50 percent less than his quotation. He feigned offense then recovered his composure.

"You cannot get a rug this fine with that price Madame. But I have some good rugs in that price" he said, signaling to his assistants to unroll some rugs.

"You break my heart" I told him lightheartedly. "These rugs are not Persian. What is your last price for the Nain?" And so we negotiated the price to and fro with me upping my offer incrementally while pointing out imagined flaws in the carpet and him slowly lowering his original price.

"Oh, I've been sitting here so long, sipping your nice tea and munching on your delicious cookies but we seem to be getting nowhere. I had hoped to be one of your regular clients," I said, slowly getting up. "I'm quite disappointed." I added, smiling, "Nevertheless, I've had a wonderful time and thank you very much for your hospitality."

"I would like to please you Madame and I would like for you to own the Nain. This is my last price Madame" and he quoted a price that was only a hundred riyals above my offer.

"Thank you" I said happily. "Do you accept checks?" He consulted another man in the background.

"Not usually but we'll accept your check Madame." So, I sat down again and wrote out a check for the beautiful Nain.

The Nain looked lovely in the bedroom. I excitedly narrated to my husband my bargaining adventure and how I had gotten the price down by 30 percent. But still he said I had paid a high price for it, pricking my balloon and making me wonder if I was a lame duck the minute I entered the little carpet shop.

"You are a foreigner and do not speak Arabic. The shop owner probably doubled his price and then gave you 30 percent discount," my husband laughingly told me, pouring ice water on my self-perceived prowess at bargaining. No matter. I had had a wonderful and romantic time sitting in a small carpet shop in the souk being shown exceptionally fine rugs and learning about carpets while sipping sweet tea and munching on saffron cookies.

Nothing was ever what it seemed to be in the souk.

CHAPTER 14
Footsteps of Morning: Eid and Christmas

"When the happy Eid morning come / We compete with the feet of the morning, running / We go out with the bright light of our clothes / Our bright smiles brighter than the morning light / We gather to the musalla on the sand . . ." penned my husband exuberantly in a verse remembering the *Eids* of his childhood.

The Islamic calendar has two religious festivals called *Eid*. The Festival of Breaking Fast is called *Eid al-Fitr* and marks the end of Ramadan. *Eid al-Adha*, the Festival of Sacrifice commemorates the willingness of the Prophet Abraham to offer his son Ismael as sacrifice to God. In Judeo-Christian belief, this story involves Abraham's second son, Isaac. Eid al-Adha coincides with Haj, the annual pilgrimage to Mecca. The celebration of the two Eids is essentially the same except that Eid al-Adha involves the sacrifice of an animal, a ritual performed by Abraham when he killed a lamb in place of his son.

"What does the word Eid mean?" I asked my husband one Eid day.

"The Arabic word Eid literally means "return" or "recur." The Eid greeting, Eid Mubarak carries the same theme, 'I hope the Eid returns to you with happiness and good health every year.'" His reply made me remember the Christmas greeting, Merry Christmas.

I had never heard of Eid before coming to Qatar but I have found that taking part in Qatari festivals has been both an enlightening and a culturally and spiritually enriching experience. Festivals are windows into the heart of a culture. Eid is to Muslims what Christmas is to Christians. Although the two festivals differ in context, both are occasions for prayer as well as a time devoted to family and friends and the fulfillment of social obligations. There are, however, similarities and differences in their celebration, underlining the multidimensional nature of each festival.

Of the two Eids, I always felt that Eid al-Fitr was a more personal and intimate experience than Eid al-Adha because in Eid al-Fitr each Muslim celebrates his happiness at completing Ramadan, the Holy Month of Fasting. It is a time of thanksgiving to God for observing Ramadan and an occasion of hope for a new life and abundant blessings. Unlike Christmas, however, the official announcement of Eid was always preceded with uncertainty. Will it be or will it not be Eid tomorrow?

On the eve of the expected Eid al-Fitr holiday, just after the breaking of fast at sunset, people stayed glued to their radios or television sets awaiting the news with eagerness and excitement. Having embraced the spirit of Eid with zest, I would sit with my children in front of the TV waiting impatiently. Sighting of the new moon marking the start of Eid was officially announced by blowing sirens or firing cannonballs and the news broadcasts. The uncertainty exasperated my husband but I found it exciting. I thought it gave depth and dimension to the excitement and anticipation. The occasion usually reminded me of the night before Christmas, when as a child, I used to go to bed keyed up, anticipating Christmas morning and wondering what presents awaited me.

The beginning of Eid was always shrouded in uncertainty because the religious authorities depended on human sighting of the new moon, which can be a problem on cloudy days. The Islamic calendar, being lunar, has twelve lunar months in a year of about 354 days and each month is either twenty-nine or thirty days. It is shorter than the solar year by about eleven days so that Eid shifts eleven days earlier each successive solar year. Each month starts when the lunar crescent is first seen by a human observer's eye. New moons can be calculated precisely but in some Islamic countries such as Qatar, human sighting of the new moon in any Muslim country is required to officially announce the beginning of Eid. Actual visibility, however, depended on many factors such as the weather and hence, the uncertainty surrounding the beginning of Eid. People received news of Eid with jubilation. At home the telephone would ring incessantly from well-wishers, and all the lines at home would be busy as my family raced to wish relatives and friends Eid Mubarak. Today, with cell phones, such rivalry no longer exists. Every household became alive with activity and the atmosphere was electrifying as people feverishly prepared for the holiday. The streets jammed with traffic as people went out for last minute shopping, just like last minute Christmas shopping, and stores stayed open till after midnight.

The Eid festival was celebrated according to tradition. Grooming was a very important aspect of observing the feast. I learned from my husband that each item of clothing and footwear that was worn on this day must be new, which had surprised me. There was no such requirement for the celebration of Christmas but usually people, and especially children, wore new clothes and shoes. Gradually, I realized that for Muslims, Eid signified a new life, a new spiritual life, a time of renewal and hope. Wearing new clothing and footwear were outward physical expressions of a new internal self, like rebirth, and underlined the special nature of Eid.

Women usually dressed in caftans adorned with fine gold or silver embroidery and wore gold jewelry. I loved wearing the caftans; they were loose, cool, and comfortable. The ladies of my husband's family usually painted their hands and arms with henna the night before, which was called "henna night." I tried it once and although it was fun, the long time needed—at least two hours for the henna to "take"—was discouraging. The longer the paste was left on the skin, the more intense the color and the longer it would last. In the past henna painting was done at home by an older lady, family member or friend who was expert in painting beautiful and intricate designs. Nowadays, this is done in beauty salons or an expert comes to the house to do the service. The custom of henna painting to celebrate special occasions goes back to pre-Islamic times. Arabian women used henna paste to cool, soothe, and soften their skin as well as adorn their hands and feet.

In a poem redolent with nostalgia of his childhood Eids my husband described the Eid girl:

The Eid girl, dressed in bright color,
Throws her hair behind her collar.
Silver thread decorate her vest,
And shine with light over her chest.
Her necklace dances when she walks,
And shivers around her neck when she talks.
Her gold earrings look at her cheeks,
And dance with joy when she speaks.
Her gold bracelets ring

With music as they swing.
Henna on her hand is a duty,
But does not add to her beauty . . .

Grooming for men was less elaborate. It was socially and religiously required that a pleasant fragrance emanated from the individual. Incense was frequently used but my husband was satisfied with just modern perfume. The headgear was scented with a special incense burner, which was placed underneath the headgear before it was put on to allow the fragrant smoke to suffuse the outfit.

It was not the sweet smell of incense that inspired my husband to compose Eid verses but rather the remembered happy feelings aroused. Just as my husband had tender memories of past Eids so I had fond memories of Christmas. It is the feelings evoked by Eid or Christmas that makes our memories of those feasts so special. Sometimes I think that memories are like lights refracted through a prism; the colors and hues become more intense with remembrance. When my husband remembered past Eids, he talked of his childhood Eids and when I reminisced of Christmas, I talked of my childhood Christmases. I have warm memories of past Christmases and I realize that those experiences are pieces of my past and part of me. Our behavior, beliefs, hopes, and fears are all influenced by what we remember of our past.

The Christmas customs I was familiar with—Christmas tree, Nativity Scene, Santa—were borrowed traditions but the experience was magical nevertheless, and nostalgia as intense as ever. When I was small, my mother used to gently wake me up at dawn to attend Misa de Gallo, a dawn Mass. From that distant time, I still sometimes hear her soft whisper, "Rachel, Rachel, wake up my child. It's time to go to church." Blinking sleepily, yawning, and rubbing my eyes I would hear the distant sound of church bells. It was not fun waking up early for Mass but I looked forward to after the Mass. On coming out from church I would see vendors outside selling various native sweets and hot drinks. My favorites were bibingka, a glutinous rice cake; puto bumbong, a sticky rice delicacy steamed in bamboo tubes, spread with melted butter and sprinkled with brown sugar, and grated coconut. They were not gourmet foods but in the chill of early morning, in the open air, they were delicious and we would round off our breakfast with tsokolate, a hot cocoa drink.

The celebration of Christmas is a rich mosaic of traditions from many different cultures. The festivities in a particular country are flavored by that country's history and culture. In my country, the Philippines, Christmas season began formally on December 16 with attendance at the first of nine dawn masses called Misa de Gallo or Early Morning Mass. In most Catholic countries where the Spaniards left their footprint, Misa de Gallo was a midnight Mass held on Christmas Eve, but in my country this custom was held at dawn, lasted nine days, starting from December 16 and continued up to December 24. The literal translation of the Spanish phrase misa de gallo is "mass of the rooster." Perhaps the practice was so named because the mass was held between 4 a.m. and 5:00 a.m. just before light began to break in the morning, the time that the rooster crows. Catholics believe that by completing a nine-day devotion called novena, God would grant a special wish or favor. In Catholic scripture the number nine is believed indicative of suffering and grief and the nine days of Misa de Gallo supposedly commemorated the nine-day Census journey taken by Joseph and the pregnant Mary from Nazareth to Bethlehem looking for lodging before the birth of Christ.

One of my favorite Christmas rituals was Noche Buena, the traditional family Christmas Eve feast to celebrate the birth of Christ and which was eaten after the Midnight Mass (Misa de Noche Buena or Misa de Aguinaldo). The gathering was an opportunity for reunion with immediate and distant family members, but in my family just close members. (La) Noche Buena means "the Good Night" (or Holy Night) of Christ's birth but in the Philippines, the phrase evolved to refer to the meal at midnight on the 24th. Besides the pleasure of family reunions, it was always wonderful to attend Midnight Mass held at the stroke of midnight as Christmas Eve ticked into Christmas Day. The celebration of mass at midnight is based on the ancient belief that Jesus was born precisely on the stroke of twelve. The service began with holy and joyful music and readings of scripture and psalms. The midnight hour was heralded by the pealing of church bells and the choir singing "Gloria in Excelsis Deo" (Glory to God in the highest). I always found Midnight Mass beautiful, glorious, and spiritually uplifting.

After the midnight meal my family exchanged gifts but as children my sisters, brothers and I opened our presents on the morning of Christmas. One present that charmed and gave me pleasure was a doll—a flesh colored plastic doll with red hair and pretty blue eyes that closed when reclined and opened when stood up. The doll's eyelids closing and opening had greatly fascinated me. I spent many happy hours playing with that doll.

When I was small, Christmas day was an occasion for big family gatherings, with grandparents, aunts, uncles, cousins, nephews, nieces, and close friends. I remember going round, greeting the elderly members of the clan by taking their right hand and touching it to my forehead, as a form of respect and appeal for blessings. This was an old custom in the Philippines and an admirable tradition. With the passage of time, the festive Christmas celebrations in my family became simpler. Gatherings were not as large as younger family members became more mobile and moved to other towns and cities in search of better opportunities.

In those gatherings, there was always plenty of food. Festivals are great opportunities for sharing food, which serves to strengthen social bonds. Christmas was a time to renew family ties, and the preparation of traditional family Christmas dishes was basic to the celebration of Christmas. My favorite dish was my mother's chicken salad, the taste of which I never could reproduce no matter how faithfully I followed her recipe. I remember the queso de bola (Edam cheese), spherical in shape and looking very Christmassy in its glistening red paraffin cover; queso de bola literally means "ball of cheese." I remember its pale yellow color, its crumbly texture when sliced and its salty, sharp taste; it was very good with crackers. I remember also the fragrant smell and the rich deep red of *mansanas* (red apples); the smoky, pungent odor of jamon or cured ham. It was cooked in pineapple juice to reduce its salty taste but the end result was a sweet-salty taste. One of my favorites, which my family also prepared for Christmas, was arroz a la valenciana, a dish of glutinous yellow rice laced with saffron with chunks of chicken, vegetables, and topped with prawns and mussels. When I recall those family reunions, the images and flavors of those foods dart through the convolutions of my mind increasing my endorphins, the feel-good chemical.

Looking back on my past Christmases, I realize that prayer and family were central to the observance of Christmas and I could not help but notice the striking similarity with Eid celebrations. On the first day of Eid, Muslim men assembled for Eid prayer at sunrise in various designated open spaces called musallas. I usually saw pictures of those gatherings in newspapers showing thousands of men kneeling shoulder to shoulder in neat rows, humbly prostrating themselves in prayer, foreheads touching the ground. It was awesome and in my mind I would hear them murmur, "Allaahu Akbar" in unison, the sound resonating through the morning light.

After the Eid prayer, people greeted each other, "Eid Mubarak" (Blessed Eid), asked about family members and then hugged and kissed each other in a spirit of peace and love.

The first day of Eid was devoted to the family. Everyone breakfasted together on traditional fare, consisting of bulalit (sweet vermicelli topped with fried eggs), special sweet bread, and other kinds of sweets. Wishing their parents Eid Mubarak, children were given eidiyah, a gift of money from family, relatives, neighbors, and friends. Laden with eidiya and sweets, the children played happily. Except for the token of money given to children, gift giving was not part of the ritual and so it became my habit to write an Eid card to each of my children, in my uniquely clumsy Arabic script, that included their own Eid greeting and their eidiya. Doing so gave me a lot of thrill and pleasure and enabled me to relive the card and gift giving of Christmas. The first time I gave my children their Eid card written in my distinctive Arabic script, it created a sensation in the family. My newfound skill in writing Arabic letters languished when they outgrew eidiyas.

Groups of children went around the neighborhood singing Eid songs and were rewarded with more eidiyah, reminding me of Christian children singing Christmas carols. Throughout the day, guests were offered fresh fruits, sweets such as baklava (layered pastry and nuts sweetened with honey), gahwa (Gulf coffee heavily laced with cardamom), and tea scented with rosewater.

The clan met at the *beit al kabeer*, the big house, for lunch. beit al kabeer means the house of the oldest and/or wealthiest member of the family or the head of the clan. Lunch usually consisted of one or more lamb, depending on the number of guests expected. The lamb was boiled whole with spices in huge pots until very tender or baked to tenderness in large ovens and was served on top of steaming rice on massive trays. Sharing was an important element in Eid celebrations. Families usually prepared large quantities of food to distribute to neighbors. Beautifully wrapped baskets of sweets and pastries were exchanged among friends and relatives, and reciprocal invitations to lunch, dinner, or afternoon tea or coffee were common.

In my husband's family, the clan gathered and had lunch at his father's house where the men gathered in the majilis and the women and children in the family/TV room, in the women's quarters. After lunch, immediate male family members would join the ladies to catch up on family news and trade stories and jokes. My husband usually came to join us for gahwa and he would sit with a big enigmatic smile, cradling the dainty little coffee cup in his hand, while his mother fussed over him. I reclined lazily on floor cushions, watched the children come and go, listened to the quiet conversation around me, while intermittently dozing and drifting to another time and place—to Christmas with my family far away—and musing how right Tolstoy was when he said all happy families were alike.

But to Muslims, Eid is more than family bonds. The Islamic Eid has highly spiritual and moral qualities. The first Eid comes after a whole month of daily fast. The second Eid marks the completion of Haj or pilgrimage to Mecca in which the Muslim renounces worldly concerns. I was told that Eid was a day of victory, which had puzzled me at first and it was only when I joined the Ramadan fasts that I understood.

Fasting the Islamic way, from sunrise to sundown, was very hard and challenged and tested my will power. Taming my desires was a daily struggle, like doing battle with myself. Fasting was an ordeal and completing a full month was indeed a victory, a moral victory. To Muslims, each Eid is a thanksgiving day where they assemble for prayer to offer their gratitude to Allah for helping them fulfill their spiritual obligations prior to Eid. Muslims who complete the Ramadan fast expressed their gratitude to Allah by distributing alms among the poor and needy. Most of the sacrificed lamb meat is distributed to friends and the needy.

Christmas is also a spiritual feast since it celebrates the birth of Christ—the Savior—who was sent to redeem mankind from their sins. He symbolizes the hope of victory in the individual's struggle between good and evil and so, just like Eid, Christmas also means victory—the triumph of good over evil. This aspect of Christmas seems to have been forgotten in the way it is currently celebrated with its emphasis on material things and merry-making, but the template of the celebrations of Christmas that I remember is not so much different from the celebrations of Eid. The two feasts highlighted that Muslims and Christians shared the same beliefs and behaviors. The milieu for the celebration of Eid and Christmas may be different but both encode in their festival and prayer ritual the concepts peace, joy, love—and hope.

CHAPTER 15

Ramadan: A Special Month

There is one month in the Islamic calendar that I grew to cherish. That month is called Ramadan, the holy month of fasting. It is fondly referred to by many names: Blessed Month, Jewel of All Months, and Month of Victories. During the entire month of Ramadan, Muslims are religiously forbidden to eat, drink, and engage in marital intimacy from dawn until sunset. Ramadan is a month full of rituals. I found the practices and activities associated with it spiritually inspiring. I have come to value and treasure the month of Ramadan.

I knew nothing about the Islamic fast before coming to Qatar and my first Ramadan in Qatar was in the summer.

"Tomorrow, Ramadan starts," Hajar had gravely informed me one evening that summer.

"I know. Everyone was talking about it at work but no one was certain," I had replied.

"The exact dates of Ramadan changes every year because Islam uses the lunar calendar, which means that each month begins with the sighting of a new moon," he said.

"What does the word Ramadan mean?" I asked my husband.

"The word Ramadan is derived from the Arabic root, ramida or ar-ramad, which means "scorching heat" or "dryness." Hajar replied. "The month of Ramadan is not associated with any particular month in the Western calendar because Ramadan comes around eleven days earlier each year in respect to the Gregorian calendar."

I had been slightly disappointed that the name of the month—Ramadan—had nothing to do with the particular time of year that it occurred. I had romantically linked the month of Ramadan with the scorching heat of a desert summer. Ramadan moved, like Easter in the Christian calendar. If the month falls during the winter months, the duration of each day's fast will be shorter, or much longer if it occurs during the summer.

"The duration of each day's fast is shorter in winter but Ramadan comes in winter every thirty-three years," Hajar continued, smiling. Thirty-three years had seemed a very long time then.

"We will eat *iftar* with my parents," he had added, thoughtful.

"Iftar?" I echoed.

"The breaking of fast is called iftar in Arabic."

Since that first Ramadan in summer, I have spent all subsequent Ramadans in Qatar, the sequence of its arrival looping cyclically backwards, like a clock moving in counterclockwise direction because it came eleven days earlier each year in relation to the Gregorian calendar. The perceived effect, at least for me, was of time slowing down, as if one billion Muslims fasting reined in a world fast hurtling forwards.

During Ramadan, life seemed to roll in slow motion as the pace of life slowed down considerably. In Qatar and some Muslim countries, people usually went to work late because they stayed up late at night. During the day, after the official Ramadan working hours, the streets were almost deserted and hardly any activity or signs of life could be discerned. Day was turned to night and night into day. I used to hear my husband lament the loss of productivity but the change of pace thrilled me. I had been very surprised to observe how the people welcomed the month with enthusiasm and cheerfulness. I could not imagine how anyone could refrain from eating and drinking for nearly twelve hours or more during the day, and especially in hot weather.

Before coming to live in Qatar, I was as conscious of the realm of fasting as the next galaxy. I had read of the political fast, especially Ghandhi's, but I had thought that was only for the birds. At that time I did not understand the rationale for fasting except that it was a religious obligation.

"Why do people fast, do you know?" I asked Hajar one Ramadan day.

"Muslims believe that by fasting they will gain entry to Paradise," he replied with a shrug.

Even though I grew up Catholic I never associated fasting with Paradise. Yet, the practice of fasting is ancient and mainly related to religious rituals as I learned later. The Holy Scriptures in Islam, Christianity, and Judaism are full of the divine injunction to fast and fasting in one form or another is obligatory among Muslims, Christians, and Jews. Followers of these three monotheistic religions believe that to gain entry to Paradise, they must purify themselves from sin and fasting is one way to achieve that goal. Since my first encounter with the Muslim fast, however, I have wondered many times whether the concept originated in the creation story of Adam and Eve, the first man and woman. They disobeyed the divine injunction to fast by eating the fruit of the forbidden tree and consequently, God expelled them from Paradise, as punishment. Entrenched in the tenets of the three religions is the inference that man has been trying to go back to Paradise since. Every person is responsible for finding his way back to Paradise, and the three religions teach us that one way is through fasting. I always found the story of Adam and Eve riveting, even now, for it flows along universal motifs: transgression, punishment, atonement/purification, and the promise of reward.

In antiquity, however, fasting was primarily associated with rites of mourning. It was believed that fasting was a powerful medium to ward off demonic spirits. It was assumed that evil spirits could enter the body through ingestion of food and drink, like a food-borne disease. Fasting was an act of penitence and means of purification that rendered a person worthy to receive divine blessings. In addition, it was believed that the one who fasted was more receptive to divine revelation. Moses was fasting when God revealed the Ten Commandments to him on Mt. Sinai, and the Qur'an was revealed to the Prophet Muhammad during the Islamic holy month of fasting—Ramadan.

"Don't Christians fast?" My husband asked, rousing me from my reverie.

"Christians fast selectively with partial abstinence during Lent, the forty-day fast and penitence before Easter. My family did not eat meat on Fridays in Lent, but we had fish and that was considered fasting," I replied with a little laugh. "Christians may have crackers with soup and it still would be considered a proper fast with all attendant spiritual benefits—very easy on the body and spirit! That was the kind of fast that I am familiar with."

"A Muslim would not consider that fasting at all," exclaimed my husband

"The Christian fast varies in strictness depending on the particular sect. Catholics fasted by partially abstaining from food and drink," I said.

In the Middle Ages, Christian monks fasted during Lent by abstaining from food but not from drink. They brewed their own beer, drank it, and prayed—rather tipsily I would presume. It amused me to think that those merry monks probably conducted their prayer and penitence in a state of mild intoxication jazzing up monastic life. In ancient times, however, beer was a nutritious thick soupy liquid that was regarded as food rather than simply drink. In general, today, Catholics fast by abstaining from meat on Ash Wednesday (first day of Lent), Good Friday (Friday before Easter Sunday commemorating the crucifixion and death of Jesus Christ) and on Fridays in Lent.

In various guises, fasting is still observed by most religions. Fasting is abstinence from food, drink, and sex. Although there is interfaith and intra-faith variation as to the strictness and duration of the fast, I was fascinated to learn that the ancient beliefs on the function and purpose of fasting lived on in the fasting rituals of various religions.

People from different countries and with different religious backgrounds come to work in Qatar as skilled, semi-skilled, and manual laborers. Native Qataris are Muslims whereas the expatriate community is composed of Muslims, Christians (Roman Catholics, Orthodox, Coptic, Anglican, and other Protestant denominations), Buddhists, and Hindus. The diversity of race, religion, and lifestyle made life in Doha fascinating. It was quite stimulating to interact with people from different cultures and not unusual to meet someone from a remote or little-known country. I have always been curious and interested in the customs and habits of other people. When I came to live in Qatar, I found the opportunity to interact with people from different cultures exciting. The coming of Ramadan was an occasion to learn about fasting and the fasting practices of people from different religions and cultures.

We once had a cook from Nepal who was Buddhist, and so naturally, I was curious about how he fasted. He said he fasted by abstaining from meat on certain days. I learned later that among Buddhists, there were two types of fasting practiced: the partial fast and ascetic fast. Lay Buddhists observed only the partial fast by not eating meat on certain days, like on the new or full moon days. They believed that abstaining from luxury foods such as meat was already a form of fasting and brought merit to the one who fasted. Buddhist monks practiced the ascetic fast, which was undertaken only with supervision under the guidance of a skilled mentor. The standard ascetic fast period was eighteen days and only a small amount of water was drunk daily during that period. At the end of the fast, only small portions of thin porridge or gruel was taken every few hours for three days. Food had to be reintroduced gradually since it takes time for the digestive system to recover its physiologic function. Buddhist monks fast as a means to purify their bodies, clarify their thoughts, and thus, free the mind.

The Hindu community in Qatar is almost exclusively Indian. A large segment of the expatriate population in Qatar is from the Indian subcontinent. The majority is Muslim, some are Christians, and others are Hindus. The physician staff of the hospital is almost exclusively Muslim but one of the doctors, a lady, in the Non-invasive Cardiac Laboratory section of the Cardiology Department is Hindu. The Non-invasive Cardiac Laboratory provides electrocardiography (heart rhythm) and echocardiography (ultrasound imaging of the heart) services. As director of the Non-invasive Cardiac Laboratory, I was delighted to have a physician from another faith among my staff. Some of the technicians and nurses in my section are Christians, Muslims, Buddhists, and Hindus but the physician staff was predominantly Muslim. I was pleased to observe that the staff seemed to get on very well with each other. I like diversity and was charmed to learn from our Hindu doctor about the gods, goddesses, customs, and festivities of Hinduism. I knew nothing about Hinduism before I met her. She fasted habitually on certain days, like on the feast days of certain gods or goddesses. She firmly believed, as did other Hindus, that fasting rids the body of toxins so that it can function at its optimum level. It was interesting to learn that fasting in Hinduism was intricately linked with ancient health care practices such as Yoga and Ayurveda. Hindus believed that fasting kept a person healthy and disease free, so they fasted regularly throughout the year. The notion that fasting was a form of therapy is ancient and ancient people probably made the association on observing that people stopped eating when ill and then later recovered. As with Buddhism, fasting was used to enhance meditation, to build up self-control and discipline, and to strengthen the mind, body and soul. Hindu fasting may involve twenty-four hours complete abstinence from any food or drink, but was more often an elimination of certain foods and drink. Such method of fasting to promote weight loss has become fashionable and has been widely exploited in health resort spas around the world.

Although I did not meet Jews living in Qatar, my husband and I had Jewish friends when we were living in the U.S.A. In fact some of our best friends were Jews. I thought of them sometimes during Ramadan because I remember them mentioning that Jews observed fasting as a means of atonement for sins, on Yom Kippur—the Jewish Day of Atonement. One Palestinian colleague in our hospital, from Occupied Palestine, told me that the Jews in his neighborhood ate only thin dry bread on Yom Kippur fast.

The Islamic fast, on the other hand, was unusual in that it was fixed in time and stated in method. The abstinence demanded was total. When I first heard of total abstinence I thought the practice was unwise. Frequently, I encountered some patients in the hospital coming for diagnostic tests who refused intravenous infusion. If the test was elective, physicians usually postponed the test until after Ramadan. To my dismay, many patients also skipped their medications during the fasting hours, and we usually advised such patients to take their medicines after breaking fast, in the evening and at night. The sick and pregnant women were not obliged to fast during Ramadan as were children, the mentally handicapped, and anyone who would be putting their health at serious risk by fasting. There were also circumstances where people normally able to fast were unable to, such as when people were on a trip. In such situations the person must make up for the fast at a later date or give food to the poor or, in the days when slavery was common, by freeing a slave.

In Arabic, fasting is referred to as *sawm* (to leave things) and is the fourth pillar of Islam. It is practiced primarily for spiritual discipline and self-control as well as being a means of earning divine mercy and benediction to enter heaven.

One Ramadan, one of my daughters, Salma, came to my library to research a topic on "protective spirits" for her art class. She was fascinated to learn that the angels of Christianity, Islam, and Judaism had their origins in the protective spirits of ancient religions. I asked her what she thought of the belief that people went to heaven by fasting. Giggling, she replied, "Oh, Mommy, I don't know, I just don't know. Me, I might not even go to heaven. It might take a very long time for me to reach heaven. Hopefully, fasting will shorten the time."

When I narrated this conversation to my other children, they added, "Fasting without prayer is not accepted."

As with Eid, Ramadan was ushered in with the sighting of the new moon. A traditional saying states, "When Ramadan begins, the gates of Heaven are opened, the gates of Hell are locked, and the devils are chained." Cannon fire on the eve of the first day of the fast announced its arrival. People welcomed the news with gladness and religious fervor. I was always astonished to witness the passion with which the arrival of a month of self-denial was embraced. I, on the other hand, was filled with angst. Since I started participating in the fasting ritual, I found that fasting the Islamic way was very hard but I considered it a challenge.

On the run-up to Ramadan, I was usually afflicted with a floating, diaphanous anxiety, which was due, I thought, to the expectation of an impending struggle. Over the years, I have attempted to develop a strategy to deal with the expected hunger and thirst on the first day of fasting. On the eve of Ramadan, I generally embarked on a "body fortification" program, a process consisting of eating like there was no tomorrow, which prompted my children to comment humorously, "Mommy freaks out in Ramadan." My children had taken to fasting like ducks to water, unlike me whose only experience with fasting while growing up was the Catholic meat abstinence on Fridays.

During Ramadan, after *al-assr*, the afternoon prayers, a Qatari kitchen buzzed with activity as mothers and daughters prepared and experimented with new recipes for iftar—the breaking of fast. When my children were small, I was frequently in the kitchen trying new recipes because my family liked to try different kinds of food at iftar. As my daughters grew up, they also tried their hands at cooking new dishes. Ramadan was an opportunity for them to polish their cooking skills. In recent years, they would surf the net on their laptops searching for new recipes to try. As always I thought the dishes they made were the most delicious but they critiqued each other: "This is good" or "This is not so good."

Food was a preoccupation for me during Ramadan because I was not to the manner born. At work, I constantly daydreamed how lovely it would be to have a nice, hot cup of tea, scented with rosewater or jasmine, and the trace of their fragrance was never far away from my fancy. Two or three days before the anticipated beginning of the fasting month, I would work on the family menu for the entire month of Ramadan, pouring over cookbooks and, in recent years, surfing the internet, incorporating new dishes to try. Such overzealousness on my part was based on the assumption that when people fasted, they liked trying new foods at break-fast. At least, I did! Composing a menu can be fun but making one for an entire month can be a bother—and crazy! I did not have to but for me preparing the Ramadan menu in advance was an absolute must. I had to free myself from the daily vexation of being asked by the domestic staff, "Doctora, what shall we cook for tomorrow?" Daily life sometimes is burdened with such trivial but important pursuits. Hunger, thirst, and fatigue were the Ramadan triad that I had to contend with. For me, deciding what to cook the following day required vast expenditure of precious energy, which I needed to conserve to get through a day of fasting. My exceptional solution was to make a menu for the entire month of Ramadan. Call it the byproduct of an anxiety-ridden and mentally disordered person, but in our house the menu became an organizing principle that was posted in the kitchen, for every member of the family to see. Advance preparation should guarantee that life flowed smoothly, but humans constantly and perversely sabotage the best-laid plans. Unlike Hammurabi's code of laws, the menu I made had no such authority. Every member of the family was free to pencil in the dish of his choice and; consequently, the dishes in the menu were frequently crossed out, other choices scrawled in, or notes scribbled like, "don't like this" or "sick of this" or "terrible." The posted menu usually ended up like graffiti, and our cook, bewildered, ended up asking me, "So, what shall I cook tomorrow?"

As with any ritual, there were foods associated to the observance of Ramadan. In the Arabian Gulf, traditional Ramadan dishes were thareed, meat stew mixed with extra thin pieces of crispy bread, and harees, wheat and lamb cooked very tender and stirred into a puree. Thareed and harees were dishes known from pre-Islamic days. A very special traditional dessert poetically described as "cones of gold" was *Loqaimat*, fried dumplings dipped in honey. It was my favorite Ramadan dessert and I always thought our cook's loqaimat was the best in Doha. He made them crunchy on the outside and soft inside, nicely oval or round, colored a golden yellow and just the right amount of sweetness. My husband, ever the poet, composed whimsical Arabic verses in praise of loqaimat and which he translated as follows for me:

She was dipped in honey, before her wedding;
The golden honey, on her cheeks was spreading;
And she came shining,
Like a golden apple in a silver setting.
Her sweet dress, she was not shedding;
While her lips, to my lips, were heading.

Other traditional sweet dishes were Mahalabiya and Umm Ali, both with interesting histories. Mahalabiya is rice pudding scented with rose water. I was told that in the ninth century, during the Abbasiya period of the Arab empire, Muhallab, chief commander of the army, had a stomachache. His doctor prescribed a soft diet of rice powder cooked in milk and sugar. Since then it has been called Mahalabiya (after Muhallab) and has come down to the present time as dessert during Ramadan because of its soothing effect. Our cook made its variant— cornstarch, which was really light on the stomach and very good to eat when one was fasting.

Umm ali (mother of Ali) was a creamy bread pudding with nuts and raisins. It has a violent and bloody history. In Mamluk

Egypt (the Mamluks were the slaves who took power in Egypt in the thirteenth century and unique in the history of the Arab empire), there was a slave concubine Shajarat al Dur (the name means "pearl tree"), who bore the king a son. Apparently she was very smart and became very powerful, even ruling in the absence of the king. The king, however, was killed in battle during the Crusades, and she ruled against the wishes of her subjects. Wishing to preserve her power, she married the Wazir (Minister of State) to make him king so she could rule through him. But there was one snag—the Wazir was married, to Umm Ali (mother of Ali). Shajarat al Dur made the wazir leave Umm Ali. Years later, she discovered that he had been regularly going to his first wife, and so she ordered her slave to kill him in the bathtub. But the murdered man's son, Ali, arrested her and gave her to his mother (Umm Ali) to do with her whatever she wanted. Umm Ali, in turn, ordered her slaves to beat Shajarat al Dur to death. Umm Ali celebrated the queen's death by making a special sweet, which she distributed to the soldiers. That sweet was named after her, Umm Ali. When my husband first narrated the story behind the delectable dessert, I lost desire for it initially. Our cook, however, always made it superlatively so that its bloody history never again prevented me from the pleasure of eating it.

Adhan al-maghreb, the call to prayer at dusk, announced iftar, which was broken by eating dates in imitation of the Prophet Muhammad. Dates are food items of desire among Muslims during Ramadan because it is said that the Prophet Muhammad broke his fast with dates. I found that eating dates was the best way to break fast—it delivered instant calories. Dates are a high-energy food containing 50 percent sugar and one piece has twenty calories. The nourishing properties of dates have been known throughout the millennia. Nutritional analysis has shown that dates contain appreciable quantities of proteins, fats, vitamins, and mineral salts as well as high iron content. For these reasons, the date-fruit is ideal for breaking fast and much sought after during Ramadan. People stocked up on dates before Ramadan and the markets are usually flooded with dates. The Arabs have an intimate knowledge of the date palm and can identify different varieties. They discriminate between high quality and low quality dates. At home, the date connoisseur is my husband. He has about fifty-five date palms in our garden. During date harvest, in August, we usually dried most of the dates, vacuum packed and froze some fresh dates. A few days before Ramadan, we distributed dried dates to relatives, friends, colleagues, and the staff at work.

During fasting hours I generally suffered from low energy levels, like other people who were fasting. Going home from work in early afternoon, I was usually weak, tired, hungry, and thirsty but iftar (breakfast) would still be hours away. While lying in bed to rest, I would doze off. If I snoozed longer than usual, the *adhan al-maghrib* (sunset call to prayer) signaling iftar would pierce my senses, from far off, as in a dream, the lilting tones floating and hovering above my consciousness; but the sound of the televised cannon fire booming through the intercom usually woke me up for iftar. Joining the family, it was exquisite to break fast with dates—and thinking happily that a lot of people also broke fast with our dates. That was such a marvelous feeling. At table, we had three varieties: fresh and dried dates from our garden and dried Tunisian dates (dates dried on the stem), which I preferred over our dates because they were not too sweet.

After partaking of the meal, the family prayed together. Iftar could be one big meal or broken into a light meal and main meal. At home, iftar consisted of three parts: the light meal (first course), main meal (second course), and dessert (third course). The light meal was composed of dates, water, laban drink, soup, and appetizers like samboosa (small savory pastries filled with minced meat or cheese or vegetables). The children and I also enjoyed the crispiness of Indian pappadoms, vegetable fritters, mozzarella sticks, or mozzarella on French bread, little meatballs stuffed with olives, and other bite-sized morsels with the soup. My husband on the other hand liked homemade bread with his soup. After praying we ate the main meal, which consisted of traditional fare and other dishes of chicken or lamb and vegetables. In the spirit of brotherhood permeating the occasion, we sent food to relatives, friends, and neighbors, and they in turn sent us food. Some people made big pots of *harees* (pureed wheat and lamb) daily, distributing them to the poor. Our dessert usually consisted of traditional sweets like loqaimat, fruits, and sweets made by my daughters. We ate our dessert in the TV room, while watching the regional TV programs especially made for Ramadan entertainment.

Soon after iftar, the town comes alive as streets and shops fill with people. People stayed up late visiting friends and relatives and praying in the mosques. On almost every street corner impromptu food stalls sold kebabs and shawarma (grilled meat sandwiches). The delicious aroma of grilled meat wafted throughout the night. Invitations were exchanged for *ghabga* (night meal), usually served around midnight. The last meal was before dawn, called suhoor. Traditionally, the musaher, a man who went around town beating a drum, woke the people for the last meal. Sadly, this practice is dying but the tradition continues in Qatar, and we still hear the musaher at dawn on some occasions. Whereas before he went on foot, today he is driven in a pickup truck since the capital Doha has metamorphosed into a city. Patterns of celebrations can evolve with time to accommodate social and environmental changes.

In Qatar, Ramadan was not complete without *Garangaou*, a children's festival held on the fourteenth day of Ramadan celebrating the passage of the first half of the month of fasting. Eyes shining with excitement at the prospect of goodies and a fun-filled evening, children dressed in traditional costumes, hung a special satchel around their necks and went from house to house singing, "Give us something and Allah will bless you." Taking pleasure at the children's excitement, people awaited them eagerly, rewarding them with nuts, candies, chocolates or even money, which the children stored in their bags. The nature of this celebration is changing too. Because cars and traffic endangered the children's safety, civic clubs organized buses to transport them on their rounds under close supervision.

Underlying the festive air about town was an intensely religious and spiritual aura. Ramadan was a time of intense prayer. After iftar, people went to the mosque to pray, usually from 7:30 to 8:30 p.m., or longer, before setting off to socialize. Women prayed in a partitioned section of the mosque, separated from the men. Each night during Ramadan, special prayer services and Qur'an readings were held in some local mosques. The Qur'an has thirty chapters and each day one chapter was read, which completed the entire book by the end of the month. Qur'an readings from the holy city of Mecca were televised. Once, my family was amazed to see me watching and listening to those televised readings. I loved listening to Qur'an readings. I found the rhythm and cadence soothing and touching. Even though I did not understand Arabic, I found that the classical Arabic of the Qur'an when read by a good reader with a good voice was beautiful, for the Qur'an has rhythmic and poetic sounds.

During the last ten days of Ramadan, the religious activity intensified. Laylat al Qadir, or Night of Revelation (of the

Qur'an) falls during one of these nights. The exact date is unknown. Some people practiced *i'tikaf* (seclusion) cutting themselves off from worldly connections by passing the day and night in a mosque, praying. Others contented themselves with *salat-al-qiyam* (midnight prayers) in the mosque, from 10 p.m. to 2 a.m. Still others performed prescribed prayers at home, reading portions of the Qur'an, the aim being to finish it at the end of Ramadan.

Muslims say, "*If salat* (prayer) is the head, *sawm* (fasting) is the heart." Indeed, the ritual of fasting is an Islamic institution, a time-honored custom for refining character and purifying and ennobling the soul. To Muslims, fasting is not a burden but rather grateful submission to God's will. All unanimously commend the spiritual benefits of fasting such as patience, unselfishness, endurance, and sound conscience. There is no authority that compels the believer to adhere to his fast. It is a covenant between the individual and God. There is, however, no way of knowing what percent adhered faithfully to the fast, but an educated guess probably would be in the range of 95 percent or more.

In the beginning, when I started to fast the Muslim way, I found it difficult to completely abstain from drinking fluids. Nevertheless, I remained steadfast, like the date palm, although the temptation to break the fast was great. One Ramadan day, I was dying of thirst on coming home from work. After watering the plants in the veranda outside my study, I sat contemplating the plants; they looked fresh and sparkling, the way plants do after the rain, and so unlike me who was droopy. It was hot but windy, and I thought how nice it would be to sip just a little bit of water, to moisten my parched lips. Finding myself alone, my resolve almost evaporated, like dew in the morning sun. Absentmindedly, I scattered some cookies on the floor to attract the birds to come keep me company but none came although

I could hear them twittering among the tree branches in the garden. Perhaps, I thought, the birds were fasting too. Ramadan was more than just not eating and drinking.

Through fasting I have learned self-restraint and discipline. Muslims say that you gain sensitivity to the hunger and suffering of the poor, but visualizing the plight of the world's poor while in the throes of hunger pangs was not an easy feat. Besides the lessons of self-denial, however, Muslims believe that the person fasting can earn mercy and blessings from God. The intense spiritual atmosphere of Ramadan may saturate your whole being. While fasting, I was inspired to reflect quietly on life.

The holy month of fasting offers Muslims the opportunity to put aside the cares of the physical world and make time for spiritual reflection. In late afternoons, usually about an hour before iftar, I usually found myself sitting in my study, musing and reading by the window while quietly enjoying my view of blue sky and admiring my plants and flowers in the veranda. In the late afternoon breeze, the slender branches of jasmine and hibiscus swayed gracefully while the azaleas and violets fluttered tremulously. Outside, the date-palm leaves rustled. The world was quiet. Those moments, those minutes before iftar at almost sunset time, with the light mellow, birds flying and twittering past, and shadows starting to form, were beautiful.

Muslims believe that the ordeal of Ramadan transformed the individual into one entitled to relish the fruits of victory: God's abundant blessings and paradise. Eid al Fitr, the Festival of Breaking Fast, is an expression of gratitude and happiness at having submitted to and fulfilled God's will: "Fasting is prescribed to you . . . that you may learn self-restraint." (sura II v.183). Having overcome the spiritual trial of Ramadan, strength was needed to return to the real world. Eid was a time of thanksgiving and an opportunity to rest, recuperate, and refuel.

Not surprisingly, its coming was awaited eagerly.

But as any Muslim will tell you, fasting is hard. I know. Yet Muslims also regret the passing of the special month of Ramadan. Until you deny yourself water, food, and other worldly pleasures from dawn to dusk, for a whole month, you cannot appreciate the ordeal. Ramadan is a challenge that tests willpower and depletes energy but it also affirms the strength and character of the individual and his place in the community. There is a certain satisfaction in being able to deny yourself food and drink and an excitement in anticipating iftar.

Once the fast is broken, food tastes so good, and water so sweet.

CHAPTER 16

It Makes Sense to Burn Incense

The burning of incense is still very much a part of social life in the Arabian Gulf. The aroma of incense is always present at ceremonies for weddings, festivals, and other public and social events. Incense is an integral part of the bridal chest, which contains miscellaneous gifts from the prospective groom to his bride. During Ramadan, the Holy Month of Fasting, some families burn incense after breaking fast and before going to the mosque for evening prayers. Burning incense like oudh is still part of the ritual of welcoming guests. It is more often introduced at the end of the visit. An old Gulf Arab saying states, "Departure is good, after the sandalwood."

When I was new to the region, I was fascinated to observe how intimately interwoven incense was in the fabric of daily life. Until then, I had associated incense burning with religious service only and I had never seen it used socially and in personal grooming. When we visited Qatari friends, incense was passed around for guests to perfume themselves with the smoke. The sight of smoke swirling upwards from the incense burner and wafting its sweet fragrance had a spellbinding effect on me. I knew that in antiquity, incense was used as offering to the gods who, it was thought, were pleased by the incense's perfume. On seeing the smoke spiraling upwards and slowly dissipating, it was easy to understand why the ancients believed the fragrant smoke carried their prayers to heaven. In retrospect, the widespread use of incense socially should not have surprised me, since Arabia played a major role in the lucrative frankincense trade in antiquity. In addition to the aromatic food flavorings, the "spices" that the camel caravans transported included resins such as frankincense and myrrh, and syrups flavored with roses and violets.

Seeing how widespread the use of incense was among Gulf Arabs, I was curious where people obtained incense.

"Where do people buy incense?" I asked my husband one day.

"In herbal shops in the souk." He replied. "You remember that little shop, Ibn Abbas, when we went to the old souk? He sells them." He added, "Incense is one of the most important items sold in herbal shops but the tradition of herbal shops is dying."

Nowadays, specialty shops selling incense have mushroomed in Doha. For example, one of the new hotels in the city has a shop that sold incense and kept incense burning in an incense burner, which suffused the lobby with a pleasant smell.

"The only place where I ever smelled incense as a child was in church," I said, remembering the fragrant gray smoke swirling out and ascending from a globular-or elliptical-shaped brass censer and the priest gently swinging it to and fro to perfume the altar during high mass.

"The mosque as a place of worship is considered an inappropriate place to burn incense," Hajar said.

"Fragrance was an essential part of religious ceremony since ancient times," I replied, very much surprised.

"The practice of burning incense, the smoke, probably originated from magic and sorcery, which was condemned by Islam, but fragrance for personal grooming is allowed and that is why its use is pervasive socially." Hajar explained. I recalled that in the story of *Aladdin and the Wonderful Lamp*, one of the

marvelous stories in the Arabian Nights, the genie of the lamp
came out preceded by a thick cloud of twirling smoke, when
Aladdin rubbed the lamp. Illustrations of the genie appearing in
a swirl of smoke to make Aladdin's wish come true had always
captivated me as a child.

No one knew exactly how the ritual of burning incense
originated but its original use was a strong purifying agent—
fumigation. The fumes from the burning were antiseptic or
cleansing in character with some plants being more powerful and
effective than others. The combination of fragrance and smoke
may have had a potent effect on primitive man, making him
believe that the smoke going upwards had magical properties
such as carrying prayers, wishes, and desires to heaven. Early
man believed that incense's perfume was pleasing to the gods
and that scented smoke brought good luck. Archaeologists have
found evidence of ancient incense in many forms and in nearly
every culture and in the ancient civilizations of Mesopotamia,
Arabia, Egypt, India, Greece and Rome. The priests of ancient
Egypt "awakened" statues of deities by passing a censer of
burning incense under their nostrils, preparing them to receive
the many requests of their devotees.

"The incense burned in church was frankincense," I said
thoughtfully. "Is that what people use here?" Frankincense was
held in such esteem that it was included with gold and myrrh as
a gift by the Three Kings to the Christ Child.

"Sandalwood is used in the majilis but it is very expensive
and comes from India. Another variety, what we call bukhor,
is cheaper and used by women." Hajar said, adding, "We used
frankincense resin as chewing gum. I still prefer frankincense
chewing gum to the modern commercial gums; it keeps breath
fresher and it's healthier, without sugar. It was also used to
perfume drinking water containers."

Before coming to the live in the Gulf, my acquaintance with incense was limited to High Mass and Good Friday mass in the Catholic Church and through books, but as a child I remember asking my mother about the fragrant smoke from the censer and she had replied, "Frankincense."

Recently, I learned that frankincense is crystalloid tree sap—a hardened gum or resin produced by Boswellia sacra, a small tree that grows in the coastal regions of the southern Arabian Peninsula and nearby coastal east Africa. Arabian frankincense is the best and the tree—Boswellia sacra—is indigenous to Oman and Yemen. The resin is also known locally as liban, which has two meanings: milk or chewing material.

The perfume exhaled from some spices and gums when burned is called incense in English and is derived from the Latin word incensum, "that which is lit." It was the earliest perfume known to man. The word "perfume" comes from the Latin per fumum, which means "by smoke."

Incense was the most commonly used aromatic product in the ancient Near East and its use spread to other civilizations in the west such as Greece and Rome. In the ancient world, frankincense was most celebrated for its fragrance and used as incense and perfume. It was more expensive than gold. The insatiable demand for it, particularly by Greece and Rome, fueled the lucrative frankincense trade that in antiquity made southern Arabia (Yemen and Oman) the richest place on earth. Greek and Latin authors wrote of an Arabia redolent with spices and aromatics and the Romans referred to south Arabia as Arabia Felix (Happy Arabia). The trade in frankincense flourished for centuries, particularly in the Arabian Peninsula area of Oman and Yemen, and its use can be traced back to the reign of the Queen of Sheba. The zenith of this aromatic heritage is long past but traces can be found in Arabian souks where frankincense is still sold as expensive commodity. Today, however, little frankincense leaves Arabia.

The first time I saw the sweet-scented resins of frankincense was in Oman one summer when my husband took me and the family to spend a couple of weeks in the Omani city of Salalah on the southern Arabian coast. We saw women selling frankincense in small containers along the road. The fragrant gum resins were globular, pear or club shaped tears. They were mostly black or gray, opaque white, or silvery, while others had opalescent hints of rose, green, or topaz. Omani frankincense is considered the finest quality in the world. I learned that the frankincense trees grew in the Dhofar region of Oman, where Salalah city is located. Frankincense was gathered in April and the harvest lasted for three months. I learned that there were different grades of frankincense and the best were called fusus or "gems."

Incense, known as bukhor in the Arabian Gulf, is either imported or made by local Arab women. It is made from a mixture of aromatic substances such as frankincense, ambergris, rosewater, sandalwood, musk, and other types of perfume. The scent of frankincense is rich and exotic—sweet, woody, and smoky. The best and most expensive incense, however, is sandalwood and comes from India. It has a soft, smooth fragrance with a slight hint of rose.

Arabia's pre-eminence in perfumery made scents a part of the fabric of everyday life in Arab and Muslim cultures. Incense was burned in braziers in homes, in palaces, and in desert tents. The burning of incense is not as widespread as before but is still very much a part of everyday life in the Arabian Gulf. My daughters occasionally burn incense (bukhor) at home, especially when some of their friends visit and the sweet fragrant smell would permeate the house. Bukhor has the consistency of fine powder, moist, very dark—black or almost black— shaped either flat like a large coin or rounded like butterball and sold in jars. Only a small amount, a pinch, is used when burning. Because bukhor is made from a mixture of aromatic substances, the bouquet released when burning bukhor is floral, with elusive undertones and overtones that could be spicy, woody, sweet, citrus, or fruity. They are very difficult to pinpoint. I only know that the smell is pleasurable, delicious, and soothing. I, too, occasionally burn bukhor in my bedroom while reading or Internet surfing on my laptop. The sweet scent permeates the room, embracing my consciousness, creating an oasis of peace and luxury around me and inducing relaxation. Fragrance is truly one of the small manifold pleasures of daily life.

Interestingly, researchers from Johns Hopkins University recently found that a Boswellia resin constituent—incensole acetate—relieved anxiety and depression in mice. Incense, therefore, is psychoactive and would explain its continued and persistent use throughout the millennia. Incense has always been used ceremoniously in the past. That there is science behind the ceremony is exciting and underscores the fact that many ancient practices that we think or consider as "mystical" actually have a scientific explanation. As a physician, I am aware that the wisdom behind many folk remedies rests on the accumulated weight of empiric experience throughout the millennia.

But the world of science is not always comforting. I find warmth, comfort, and pleasure in rituals, such as in the act of burning bukhor. I burn bukhor in a mabkhara, a handcrafted incense burner. First, I burn a couple of charcoal until they are red hot, transfer them to a mabkhara with metal tongs, scatter pinches of bukhor over the glowing coals, watch the smoke curl upwards, and leave them to smolder to release their fragrance. There are pre-packed charcoals especially made for burning bukhor.

It had been a pleasant surprise to discover them although

every Gulf Arab seemed to know of their existence. They are sold in cartons of 60 or 120 pieces. The charcoal, cut like chocolate bars, is covered with a shiny paper-thin metallic-colored material that can be broken easily into pieces. I keep my own box of charcoal in my room together with the incense burner. The charcoal box that I have is black and on its cover is a framed picture of a gold mabkhara against a white oval background and surrounded with Arabic writings. On one side of the box reads in English: Easy Ignition, Long Burning, Smokeless and on the opposite side: Made In Japan, information that is also a source of amusement and wonder whenever I burn bukhor.

The mabkhara was traditionally made from clay or soft stone, but incense burners are also made from porcelain, brass or silver. The traditional mabkhara has a distinctive shape: a square cup with outward sloping sides and upward pointed corners and is supported by a square pedestal base, carved out to form legs. It is decorated with patterned combinations of soft metal pegs and brass tacks. The cup is lined with sheet metal and the legs are also covered with sheet metal. The shape and design are characteristic of incense burners in the Arabian Gulf. Since incense is burned in homes to welcome guests, the mabkhara has become, like the Arabic coffee pot, a symbol of Arab hospitality. Such incense burners are ubiquitous items in the souk and I frequently see them standing row upon row in shops there. The sight of them always evokes thoughts of smoke spiraling upwards and wafting magical scents that stir warm, tingly, pleasurable feelings.

CHAPTER 17

Looking For Mother Pearls

The goal—and dream—of every parent is to raise children who grow up to become happy and responsible adults. As parents, we cannot give our children happiness on a silver platter because happiness is something that cannot be given; but at least we can give them the tools to cultivate feelings of well-being and contentment and the keys to leading fulfilling lives. One of these tools is a strong sense of identity—the knowledge and pride of who they are.

Living occurs in the milieu of the family and the community but the family home is where children begin to acquire the values, symbols, and skills of their culture. Cultural identity is important to a person's sense of self and how they relate to others. I have no doubt that a strong cultural identity contributes to a person's well being.

My marriage is bicultural. I was a Roman Catholic and my husband a Muslim. I was Filipina, he was Qatari—Gulf Arab. When we got married, the marriage ceremony was both Christian and Islamic. At that time I did not know much about the many aspects of life in the Arabian Gulf states, but I knew that when we finished our medical training in the U.S.A., we would come to live in Qatar. Early in our marriage, my husband informed me that there were many Qatari men married to non-Qatari women but in the Gulf, as in other Arab societies, bloodline was patrilineal so that children of such marriages automatically assumed the father's nationality. Qatar was also a conservative Muslim society. With such a social environment, I came to realize, in concordance with my husband that our future children would have to be brought up according to his nationality and heritage—Qatari and Arab Muslim.

I love and cherish the rituals of the Roman Catholic Church for they are pieces of my past, and, therefore, part of who I am. Naturally, I would have preferred to raise our children according to the traditions of the Catholic Church but the circumstances were such that it would have been foolish and mad to even attempt it. For sure I did not want to personally increase the already high numbers of dysfunctional children and adults in the world. Besides giving love, I considered it a mother's duty to raise well-adjusted children. Their well being came before any other consideration. I thought it very important for our children to be socially and culturally integrated in the society they would be living in.

That summer of 1978, when we came to Qatar, my husband and I had two small children, a three-year-old daughter, Alia, and an infant son, Tami. In Doha, we had three more daughters—Haifa, Salma, and finally Asma.

Sons are named after grandfathers and daughters after grandmothers or aunts or sisters. Before our children were born, my husband told me that one of his wishes was to name one son after a paternal grandfather and one daughter after a maternal grandmother and the others poetic Arab names. Alia was the name of his maternal grandmother and it means "high" or "noble." The names Salma and Asma have the same meaning as Alia and are common Arabic names for girls in ancient Arabic poetry, whereas Haifa is a more modern name for girls and means "slim." Children are sometimes burdened with irony by the names given them but, fortunately, our daughter Haifa turned out to be slim.

Our son's name, Tami, was a great, great, great grandfather's name, not common, and begins with the Arabic letter "tha," which has no equivalent in the English alphabet. The name Tami means "water rising" or "flooding" and it is a pure Arab name. Common male Arabic names are Mohammed (after the Prophet's name), Ahmed, Hamad, or fearsome names such as Assad (lion) or they begin with Abdul, which means "servant of" and followed by one of the many names of God: Allah, Rahman, or Aziz; hence, Abdulla, Abdul Rahman, Abdul Aziz, etc.

There is no religious connotation or derivation in any of our children's first names. Asma, however, is an old Arab name for girls but happens to be the name of the daughter of Abu Bakr, the first Caliph after the prophet's death and who was a close friend of the Prophet Muhammad.

My husband was proud of his religious heritage and I, too, was proud of mine. We valued the tenets of our faiths but neither he nor I could be described as overly religious. My husband always mentioned that Muslims considered Christians "People of the Book." Through discussions with my husband, I came to the conclusion that the core beliefs in Christianity and Islam were similar: (1) Belief in one God or Supreme Being, (2) life after death, (3) existence of heaven and hell, (4) you go to either heaven or hell depending on how you lived your life on earth, and (5) heaven is a place of eternal happiness—paradise; hell is a miserable place—fire, torture, suffering. The desire of all Muslims and Christians is to go to heaven after death. Both Islam and Christianity teach a way of life that promises heaven in the afterlife.

I read that the ancient Egyptians believed in a life after death.

This belief is clearly illustrated in the famous papyrus painting scene, "Weighing of the Heart." They believed that the heart recorded all the good and bad deeds of a person's life, and was needed for judgment in the afterlife. After a person died, the heart was weighed against the feather of Maat (goddess of truth and justice). If a person led a decent life, the heart balanced with the feather and the person was judged worthy to live forever in paradise. The idea behind the "Weighing of the Heart" fascinated me so much because the Egyptian civilization predated Judaism, Christianity, and Islam, all of which believe in a life after death. I could not help but wonder at the ways in which ideas were transmitted cross culturally through time and space.

With time, it dawned on me that religions are different or alternative ways of life to reach a common human goal—the attainment of paradise, heaven in the afterlife. They are different roadmaps leading to the same place. My readings—and experience living in a Muslim society—led me to believe that although all religions preached the same principles, each religion is a different way of life, i.e., a different culture. I believe religion to be an integral part of human heritage and so does my husband. The cultural and intellectual atmosphere in our home is liberal.

We enrolled our children in Qatari schools where the medium of instruction was Arabic. It was very important that they grew up fully integrated in the society with a strong sense of identity and secure in the knowledge of who they are. Home, school, and society play essential roles in shaping a person's identity and supplement each other. Our children, with the influence of their relatives, the society, and the Qatari schools, grew up with a keen sense of pride in their Arab-Islamic and cultural heritage. They observe Islamic teachings and Qatari social norms and etiquette. They are more sensitive than I am to the signals of their environment. Their acute awareness of the local way of life influenced me to adopt some local social customs and dress. Taking into consideration their sensibilities when they reached adolescence, I wore the Qatari veil when going out with them in Qatar. This little step on my part strongly reinforced my children's sense of belonging, which was essential to their psychological and emotional well being. Wearing the veil did not in any way affect my self-esteem. I was and am comfortable with who I am. In fact I grew to value the privacy and anonymity afforded by the veil when going out in Qatar. When I read in the newspapers or see on TV female celebrities complaining of "losing privacy," the thought would fleetingly cross my mind that if they truly wanted privacy and anonymity, they should veil themselves! For concealment, nothing could rival the veil!

But although parents may have the best intentions in trying to mold their children to become responsible adults with a strong sense of identity, the end result is not always predictable. Sometimes children may express beliefs that surprise their parents in many ways. I had been pleasantly surprised at my children's comments and reactions after they saw the movie, *The Passion of Christ*. Nowadays, movies have supplanted the role good literature had in the past. Movies are especially alluring to the young and also to the general public because they tell human stories and address social issues combined with good entertainment. My children had all gone together to see *The Passion of Christ* on a weekend.

"I wanted to see the movie too. Why did you not tell me?" I had asked when they came back. I had read reviews praising the movie as an "artistic masterpiece . . . restoring the lost dimension of the suffering of Christ in a very graphic manner."

"Mommy, you don't usually go to movies here . . ." they laughed. I used to go with them to the movies when we summered outside Qatar.

"So, how was the movie?" I asked, curious.

"Okay, but too violent. I don't think you would have liked it Mommy, really violent." Asma, my youngest, said.

"Well, Christ was crucified and of course crucifixion is violent but the suffering was only the last two days of his life." I replied.

"The movie concentrated on the last forty-eight hours of his life; that's all it was." Salma said.

"But how would you understand without knowing the events leading to his crucifixion?"

"There was a bit of background and we understood everything," they said.

"I'm familiar with the story of his suffering, crucifixion, and resurrection. Christians commemorate his last days every year during Holy Week. Every year, some Catholics especially reenact his last days carrying the cross. I used to watch the crucifixion processions when I was a child." I said.

"Mommy, you don't understand. I don't mean that. I mean the movie, how he was made to suffer, the violence—you wouldn't like it. It made me cry . . . " Asma continued. I did not tell my children that when I was a little girl, I avoided looking at statues of the Crucified Christ because I found it too unbearable to contemplate: nailed to a cross, blood trickling down his face, arms and feet, a crown of thorns. It was not a pretty sight.

"I don't think the story is true, the violence I mean," Salma said.

"I'm not so certain how much is true of the Jesus story . . ." I mused aloud. My children, familiar with my "anarchic" proclamations rolled their eyes. Here we go again, their faces said. The story was too deeply entrenched in Christian tenets that sifting myth from fact was fraught with controversy. "Truth is one; the sages call it by many names," I read somewhere. The story of Christ resonated with the mystical, timeless cycle of birth, death, burial, and resurrection, recurrent themes in ancient religious thought and philosophy. Such themes touch a chord within our deepest psyche. And the suffering, well, Christians identified with it, for life is filled with suffering. These elements made the story of Jesus so powerful. The movie seemed to be exciting the passion of everyone. The story was just so fascinating, truly "the greatest story ever told."

"You don't know what faith is," Tami declared.

"But the story of his suffering and crucifixion and resurrection is the heart of Christianity. There is a lot of symbolism in the story," I continued, ignoring Tami's remarks.

"Maybe one of you could go with Mommy to see the movie again," Tami suggested in a mollifying tone.

"No need, I'll wait for the DVD," I said.

"Sure Mommy?"

"Yes. Here, I prefer to watch movies at home rather than go to the cinema."

My children had a nodding acquaintance with Christianity. After Islam, Christianity is the most common religion in Qatar. I am a Christian by heritage and they also knew many people who were Christians. As well as being Muslims, my children are bilingual: Arabic and English but Arabic is their mother tongue. I believe that the most important component of culture is language since culture is transmitted orally. Sound knowledge of the oral language of a culture is necessary to understand that culture's subtle nuances and deep meanings. With the exception of my two oldest children who learned to speak English before Arabic, the rest of my children learned both languages simultaneously. At home, we speak English because that is the language common to both my husband and me. It is also the language with which I communicated effectively. My husband and I learned English as a second language but my knowledge of the English language is deeper. Our children spoke Arabic in school, with their relatives, and with their friends.

My country, the Philippines, is one of those countries with multiple languages, and a total of around 170 native languages are spoken in the country. Tagalog was chosen as the national language for reasons that until now are unclear to me. People from different regions in the country, however, speak their own regional language. My mother tongue, Ilocano, is the language spoken in the northern Philippines. I did not think it practical to transmit my lingua maternelle or the official language of my country to my children since learning either had no future value for them, and everyone on my side of the family spoke English as well. I thought it in my children's best interest to concentrate on learning English as a second language since it is the most widely spoken language in the world, the language of international travel, and the de facto language of diplomacy. It is also the second language taught in Qatar and the Gulf.

During my school days, English was the medium of instruction in schools in my country. The Philippines was a colony of Spain and Spanish used to be the official language, even after the revolution against Spanish rule and declaration of independence from Spain. At first glance, it may seem odd for nationalists to continue using Spanish as the official language, but on second thought, at that point in time, it was practical for ease of communication because of the different regional languages. There was no indigenous official language. Then, the United States declared war against Spain over Cuba and U.S. forces occupied Manila, the capital of the Philippines. The United States paid Spain $20 million to cede the whole archipelago to the United States, which found the islands useful both as an economic and military base in the Far East. There followed the Philippine-American War, which officially lasted about four years. After cessation of hostilities, the Americans pacified the population through education—American-style education—and American English became the primary language used for teaching in the schools, and the natives were brainwashed into thinking that American culture was superior over others. Thus, like other colonizers before them, the Americans effectively suppressed nationalism, Filipino nationalism.

I learned American English from textbooks written by American authors and English courses heavy on the works of American writers. I read books and literature in English. My father graduated from a military academy and my mother obtained a degree in teaching. Both of them were educated in English. I still remember my parents reading weekend papers in English on lazy Sunday mornings. I used to love perusing the comic section; my favorite was Superman. As a child I read *Andersen's Fairy Tales* and *Grimm Fairy Tales*. Many children's tales, myths, and legends of other cultures have been translated into English and this explains my familiarity with some of them. Some of these stories I had transmitted to my children by reading to them at bedtime. In retrospect, I regret very much that I was unfamiliar with the thousands of Philippine folk tales, myths, and legends.

Filipino culture is vast and complex because it is made up of different regions with diverse language and cultural practices. The regional stories describe the first Filipino people, their beliefs, their lives, and the way things were before the coming of the Spaniards. These stories were absent from our school curriculum. Knowledge of the folklore tradition of your own country reconnects you to your past, your remote past, and this was sadly lacking in my education. My peculiar background, therefore, was strong on Spanish customs and traditions with heavy overlay of American-isms. This was the atypical cultural brew that I brought into my marriage.

On the other hand, my husband's cultural upbringing was more straightforward—Gulf Arab. He learned to speak English as a second language in Doha first and then in the United States as a college student.

A bicultural family is not unique in the sense that there is an abundance of such families around the world, and I suppose they have been around since way back when Homo Sapiens fanned out from Africa. But interfamily and social dynamics of the family in the context of the society it lives in makes it unique. A mother's persona affects the equilibrium and happiness of the family and this is magnified if the mother comes from a different culture. In the beginning, I had felt like a transplanted organ but with the love and understanding of my husband and support from his family, I was able to cope with my unfamiliar surroundings and live in harmony with the society. I was warmly welcomed and the people delighted in showing and explaining to me their "way"—their customs and traditions. I have always been open to new experiences and I enjoyed learning about their culture. The Gulf Arabs I met were frank, honest, devoid of artifice, and had a refreshing sense of humor. I admired their generosity, hospitality, and refined politeness. They made me feel at home and at ease in their homes. I saw, I listened, and I tried to understand. Gradually, I saw the world from a multifaceted perspective and learned that besides your own heritage, there are other ways of living a life, as varied as the colors of a rainbow. The experience has enriched me.

For my children, having a mother with a different cultural and educational background may have posed some psychological and emotional difficulties but they seem to have dealt with that issue exceptionally well.

It took some time for my children to realize that their mother is a physician, a cardiologist. When they were small and I took them to the hospital for check ups or for minor ailments, they used to ask me, "Mommy, are you a nurse or a doctor?" When I replied, "A doctor," they would smile a little; then they would give me an odd, sideways glance, and say, "Really?" I remember when Haifa was ten years old and I took her to the hospital for check up with her pediatrician. Afterwards I had brought her to my office while I finished up some work. She had gotten bored drawing with crayons in my office and had come out looking for me. She found me in the review room looking at cardiac ultrasound images of patients.

"Mommy, you work in this place?" Haifa asked.

"Yes darling," I replied absentmindedly.

"But Mommy, this is not you. You are surrounded with machines!" Haifa exclaimed.

"Machines? Well, doctors work with machines; doctors need machines to help them find out what's wrong with patients." I replied but Haifa looked troubled.

"What's wrong darling?" I asked.

"It's just that . . . it's just that you look different here. Not like my Mommy at home . . ." Haifa said, her voice trailing. "I like you better at home," she said gravely.

As they grow up, children form a particular image of their mother, most commonly a mother archetype—nurturing, compassionate, generous, and protective; someone who gives them food, takes care of them, and makes sure they grow up properly, safely, and happily. It was distressing for Haifa to see me in the work setting, outside the home and preoccupied with activities that were remote from the traditional domain of motherhood. Nowadays, working career mothers have become common in Qatar but when my children were growing up, such phenomenon was very rare in Qatar. The mothers of their friends were stay-at-home mothers. Children live in a fairytale world where mothers are fairies with magic wands. I had to balance career and motherhood. I tried my best to be around for my children, but there were times when I was not always available instantly, and hence they learned to do things for themselves. I think that having a busy career mother has taught my children to be more independent.

The exchange of cultural ideas and tradition is a two-way street. When there is interaction between differing cultures, absorption of some cultural customs occurs by osmosis, so long as the practice is considered non-threatening. The ability to selectively accommodate practices from another culture is a measure of that culture's tolerance. Through me, my in laws were exposed to non-Islamic and non-religious practices such as birthday celebrations. In the beginning such celebrations were very strange to my in-laws but my children loved birthdays. Seeing how much my children enjoyed them, my in-laws accepted the practice. My youngest daughter, Asma, loved celebrating her birthday and did not leave anything to chance. A week before her birthday, she would drop hints reminding everyone that her birthday was approaching. Her strategy was far from subtle though.

"Tami, what's going to happen tomorrow?" I overheard her ask her brother once.

"Huh? Tomorrow? I don't know. Why?"

"My birthday!"

She would use the same tactic with me with a slight twist. She would call me at work and ask, "Mommy, tomorrow, you know what day is tomorrow?"

"It's your birthday!" I would reply.

"Yes!" She would say delightedly.

"OK Mommy, come home now," she would tell me, giggling. On arriving home, she would tell me to go to my study. There, I would find a bowl of roses with a note: "From Asma to Mommy. Tomorrow is my BIRTHDAY." I thought amusedly that with so many reminders, how could a mother forget?

My children's birthdays were associated with a certain ritual that I initiated a long, long time ago. The birthday child would go to school early in the morning and on coming home from school there would be a basket of flowers, a box of chocolates, and a card arranged on the bed. The non-birthday girls also would find one long-stemmed red rose and a small box of chocolates on their beds but my son, only a box of chocolates. When my children were small, little friends came in the afternoon or evening for the birthday party. In their mid-teens, they tired of parties and the celebrations became private family affairs. The cake and gift ceremony was held after lunch or early evening, depending on their schedules. They were usually fun affairs with much laughter, video clips, and picture taking. The contents of the cards were a source of fun. The cards they gave each other were usually humorous and satirical and these were read out loud before the gifts were opened. Because I didn't have time to go looking for cards, I kept blank cards. So, my cards were usually boring—the Happy B-day-Many Happy Returns of the Day-type. But once, I surpassed myself by plagiarizing a cute little poem, which excited much curiosity. Did Mommy compose it? Not to be outdone, my husband displayed his flair for one-up-man-ship by composing a neat little poem the following week when another birthday came up. Haifa and Salma have birthdays one week apart. My daughters have grown but they still want to keep the old flowers-chocolates-on-bed-ritual.

Nowadays, young Qatari mothers throw birthday parties

for their children like in the West. Birthdays are enjoyable and children have a lot of fun. It is a foreign custom that appeals to young and old alike and it is understandable why families around the world embrace it without reservation.

Children learn by imitating the behavior of their parents and from the experiences provided by their parents. These experiences include nearly every aspect of home and family life. Love and giving are traits learned at home. As they grew up, my children slowly became aware that mothers too, had birthdays and they would surprise me by remembering mine. Before they became sophisticated and gave me store-bought cards, they used to craft birthday cards for me, decorated with hearts and drawings of smiling faces; scrawled over the card in their childish handwriting were the words, *I love you Mommy. Happy B-day!* The cards were usually accompanied with a tiny bunch of flowers from our garden. Those cards—touching declarations of love—I have them still. I still remember the first birthday gift they gave me: a bottle with a ship inside. I had been very surprised.

"Do you like it Mommy?" They had asked anxiously.

"Yes, very. It's very pretty. Thank you, darlings."

"We always see a bottle with a ship inside in the libraries in the cartoons. So, we thought we'd get one for you for your library," they explained. I thought it so endearing that the idea for their gift was inspired by cartoons. That gift occupies center stage on a shelf in my library.

There are many birthdays in a lifetime. I have kept all the cards that my children had given me over the years. From time to time I would read them and they never failed to give me comfort, gentle like warm rain. One of those precious cards reads:

For My Mother On Your Birthday
A mother is one who understands the things you say and do,

Who always overlooks your faults and sees the best in
you . . .
A mother is one whose special love inspires you day by day,
Who fills your heart with happiness in her warm and
thoughtful way . . .
A mother is all these things and more,
The greatest treasure known . . .
And the dearest mother in all the world is the one I call my
own.
HAPPY BIRTHDAY
LOVE: *Alia, Tami, Haifa, Salma, and Asma*

Like most mothers, I wanted to be a "perfect mother" but there is no such thing. The perfect mother is a myth but mothers could certainly try. If at some points in their lives I had been to my children a fraction of the mother described in the card they gave me, then I am content for by then they would have learned to value the things in life that have meaning. By the time they chose that card, the foundations empowering them to become healthy and productive adults had been laid. I felt that my children would be able to handle whatever challenges they may face from having a mother from another culture or whatever life had in store for them.

One other foreign tradition that my children had adopted was Mother's Day. I didn't know how my children learned of Mother's Day. It is celebrated around the world but it certainly was not overtly promoted commercially when I was new to the region. I was not aware when the custom became fashionable in Qatar. It's a lovely feeling though when one's children mark the event. My children usually astonished me by observing the event with flowers or gift and a card. One of the cards had the inscription: *Happy Mother's Day* and below it *Best Mom in the*

World, standard captions for Mother's Day cards but receiving them was always heartwarming.

The cards they gave me over the years underscored the evolution in their development as individuals. Recently they gave me a big card. The face of the card said: *For a Special Mum* and depicted a garden with a funny-looking woman wearing a big sun hat frayed at the edges, watering the flowers, like in a cartoon. They chose that probably because they knew I enjoyed watering my plants. Their intention was humorous and made me smile and I liked very much the picture metaphor of watering plants. Love needs tender care—it has to be watered, just like flowers, otherwise it dies. Inside the card, they had written:

Mommy ☺
With love and thanks for all you do.
It means so much to have a mum like you!
Have a wonderful Mother's Day.
Love ☺

Being a mother, however, is hard. Life is not problem-free but my children always surprised me with their little gestures of love. Sometimes when family life became turbulent, my steadfastness shaky, and my heart heavy with trials, they would invariably surprise me with little acts of tenderness, which touched me. I shall always remember how when they were small, each one of them would sometimes present me with a bunch of flowers from the garden. I always treated the flowers they gave me with the utmost care by putting them in a special vase and placing the vase in a favored place in my room. I shall never forget their radiant smiles and pride on their faces as I bustled about looking for the nicest appropriate vase, displaying them prominently, smelling them, closing my eyes, and murmuring how lovely and fragrant they were. The flowers were usually cut short and uneven but to me they were the most expensive flowers in the world—and they were. They were expressions of love. Then they grew up and life became more complex and complicated, but still they continue to surprise me with endearing little acts when I least expect them. When they were particularly difficult, I would close my eyes in solitude and remember them offering me flowers they had picked.

Mothering requires patience, fortitude, endurance, and sacrifice. The trials, hardships, hurts and pain that a mother goes through over the years refine and polish her heart. She becomes a fountain of wisdom. And it is said that a mother's heart is the child's schoolroom. My mothering experience has taught me many priceless lessons, exquisite like shining pearls.

CHAPTER 18

Love the Child
That Holds Your Hand

A cross cultures and throughout the ages, society has honored and celebrated mothers in proverbs, poetry, art, and song. One of my favorites is a simple folk song with the following lines: Let there be blue sunshine. / Let there be blue skies. / Let there be mama. / Let there be me. That song had always made me smile. Sunshine . . . blue skies . . . mother . . . me. Humming the words makes me think of my beloved mother, long gone now but I still feel a lump in my throat remembering her. I remember myself as a child playing on the floor with my sister in our living room as mother sat crocheting or embroidering, laughing softly as she patiently answered our childish questions. Having mother around is paradise for a child. Mother is warmth and security.

There is no doubt that all mothers love their children, but the style of mothering is very much influenced by the culture, social expectations, level of education, and personality as well as personal goals and ambitions of the mother. I was not a stay-at-home mother. I was—and am still—a working mother, a mother with a career. I had wanted to be good, not only good but to be the best at both.

Children are the same in every culture in the sense that they go through the same developmental stages, and each mother meets those developmental challenges in her own way, her own inimitable way. Every mother has her own ideas on how to bring up children, in every age and in every culture. When I became a mother I had the best intentions, like every mother in the world. I would love my children like no one else could, give them a happy home, teach them, and provide them with enriching life experiences. I wanted them to have the best of everything. I told myself I would be the most patient and understanding mother in the world. I thought I was more than prepared to be a good mother. After all I was a physician and although I was not a pediatrician, I went through pediatric training in my internship and took care of sick babies and children. In my mind, I had the best laid out plan to bring up my children—a foolproof blueprint. But life defies planning and I had not counted on the unpredictability of infants and children.

I had thought that since I was an educated mother in our modern world, I had the advantage. I would familiarize myself with new-age child psychology and they—my children— would have the benefit of being brought up according to the most modern concepts of child rearing. Armed with modern techniques of raising children, I had no doubt that they would grow up to become happy and well-adjusted adults. I thought I had only to follow a "formula" as laid out by experts and voila, my children would turn out perfectly, according to plan. I learned the hard way that there is no foolproof formula for bringing up children. Motherhood has to be experienced and you learn by trial and error. Experience, they say, is the best school. Even so, in retrospect, I think what each mother needs is a crystal ball to look into the future. Perhaps some mistakes could be avoided with such a device.

Motherhood is a universal experience, following recurring patterns and motifs but each mother feels that her own mothering experience is unique and highly personal. No doubt countless mothers have had similar parent-child situations and faced the same challenges that I have experienced. In general though, my mothering experience has been funny, warm, poignant, frustrating, inspirational—and humbling. As it turned out, it was my children who taught me many lessons. One of the most important lessons they taught me was the nature of selfless love and trust. They taught me patience, fortitude, endurance, tolerance, kindness, warmth, gentleness, and courage. One humbling lesson from them was that at home I was not in control, unlike in the hospital where, as a doctor I was in charge. In the hospital, I said, "Do this" or wrote down an order and it was done. At home I told my children, "Do this" and they screamed "No!" I had been told that motherhood is the world's most honored profession, and so I found the discrepancy between what has been said about mothering and reality baffling.

When I joined the exalted ranks of Mothers, naturally, I was thrilled. Everyone talked of the joys of being a mother but no one mentioned fatigue and lack of sleep. Those were facts that each mother had to discover on her own I suppose. Proverbs and poetry celebrated motherhood. That world exists in another dimension, I discovered, a world with its own props and icons: milk bottles . . . sterilizers . . . baby cribs . . . baby cots . . . diapers . . . potties . . . musical toys . . . playpens . . . thermometers. It was another culture, a mother and baby culture, where mother and baby existed for each other; a world of sleepless nights where babies woke up several times in the night hungry and seeking a mother's embrace. I remember those nights: the stillness, the quietness, and the strange peacefulness that enveloped me as I fed my baby while the world slept. Even in that tranquil parallel world, humor would tiptoe in, cheering me up, and banishing fatigue. I would put baby over my shoulder, gently patting baby's back, waiting and softly coaxing for the inevitable bluurp, and when it came, I would laugh softly and murmur, " Ho, wasn't that loud? Did you want to wake up Daddy? Naughty, naughty you," and then gently kissing baby one more time before laying baby back in the crib. I started talking to my children from the time the nurse put them in my arms after they were born.

But I soon discovered that sometimes babies had episodes of prolonged fretful crying that had no apparent cause. Some of my children went through that stage. I used to hug them close, softly humming or gently shushing, while rocking them gently. When the crying was persistent, it was disquieting, frustrating and heartbreaking.

Like all mothers I wanted to do the right thing. I learned that despite going through medical school there were things that medical school did not teach, like how to be a good mother. Anxious, I bought books written by child psychologists and psychiatrists. The experts said that infancy was the easy part and that most parents do quite a good job at that stage, which was most reassuring. The experts, however, had no explanation or solution for the occasional pitiful and distressing cries that had the power to slowly pull your soul out. The books said, remember, your baby can't talk. When he cries, he is trying to tell you something. Well, naturally, mothers know infants can't talk. After all, the word infancy comes from the Latin word *infans*, meaning "without speech."

The failure of child experts to decode the mysterious messages contained within the crying spells was a big disappointment and I felt betrayed by the state-of-the-art science in child psychology. The books, however, outlined some simple rules to follow: 1) be certain your baby is not hungry; 2) check that baby is dry; 3) if neither #1 nor #2, consult a pediatrician to assure you the baby is healthy. If neither of the above, some experts recommended swaddling as a last resort.

Swaddling? My husband told me that he was swaddled as a baby and that this used to be the practice in the Arabian Gulf. It was no longer practiced though. His mother's generation believed that swaddling was necessary for an infant to have a good sleep. They believed that infants were awakened by the movement of their extremities associated with a dream and when awake, they got startled and frightened by the unintentional movement of their hands across their visual field. Data on this theory are lacking but some modern pediatricians recommend swaddling for fussy babies.

Swaddling is an age-old technique practiced in many cultures, particularly eastern cultures and consisted of wrapping a baby tightly in a blanket, like a mummy, to restrict limb movements. It was supposed to keep the baby from flailing his arms around and startling himself. Swaddling supposedly made babies feel snug and secure, and so fall asleep. Some research had shown that swaddling helped some little ones sleep better and longer but about 10 percent of swaddled babies did not. I never did try it because I couldn't bear the idea of severely restricting my baby's movements.

Being a mother with young children can be overwhelming. Like every mother I worried and fretted about my children's high fevers, strep throat, chicken pox, ear infections, and other usual childhood illnesses, my being a physician notwithstanding. A good pediatrician is like chicken soup—comforting and reassuring. In the first four years of my life in Doha, I missed our pediatrician in the U.S.A. the most. She was a very competent and gracious lady who made herself available for consultation at all hours, giving us a number to call anytime, when any of our children got sick and we were worried. She was just a phone call away, reassuring us. One weekend Hajar and I had been worried when our son had a fever and was lethargic. Should we take him to be seen in the emergency room? We had called her, and after listening to the history and asking a few questions, she reassured us that there was nothing to worry about. She advised us to give him acetaminophen (an antipyretic) every four hours, round the clock to keep his temperature down. If he perked up, most likely he was just having a viral syndrome. As she had predicted, after two doses of the medicine, our son was wide-awake and playing. We felt at ease and had good rapport with her, which was important because the relationship between parent and pediatrician may affect the welfare of the child.

I shall never forget the time when, at the age of four months, our son fell off the bed, greatly surprising us. Hajar had hurriedly laid him on the bed after a grocer- shopping trip but he had scooted over to the edge and promptly fallen with a dull thud onto the floor, which was fortunately carpeted. He let out a blood-curdling scream. Perhaps to punish us for leaving him unattended, he held his breath and turned blue. Breath-holding spells usually occur when a young child is angry, frustrated, in pain, or afraid. The spell is a reflex and not a deliberate behavior on the child's part. It is a fairly common pediatric problem but nothing in the world makes a mother's heart stop beating than a hysterical child who stops breathing, staging a color transformation from pink to blue. Fortunately for us, that scary incident was never repeated, so we must have done something right at the right time, like not panicking but projecting a resolute calmness while our hearts were melting like ice on a hot summer day.

Even though my husband and I were certain that the color transformation was a breath-holding spell, we had consulted our pediatrician for reassurance. She said breath-holding spells occurred in about 27 percent or more of healthy children. It was usually benign and self-limiting. The episodes, however, were often frightening to parents, even to parents who were physicians. She had reassured us at the next well-baby visit that our son was in perfect health.

When we arrived in Qatar, there were no Well Baby Clinics. You brought your child to the emergency room when your child was sick or, if you knew a general pediatrician, you brought your child to his office. There was no health education awareness campaign and many mothers were ignorant about immunization to prevent common childhood infectious diseases such as measles, polio, mumps and smallpox. I often wondered, in those early years in Qatar, about the status of child and maternal health in the country. The older generation of mothers were uneducated and lacked rudimentary "health knowledge" (beliefs about disease causation). Several researches have shown that there is a strong and significant effect of education on child mortality. Studies have shown that both primary education and secondary schooling significantly decrease the probability of child death, while literacy played an insignificant role.

With the evolution in health care services in Qatar and with the opening of the modern Hamad General Hospital in 1982, well-trained and competent pediatricians were recruited, contributing to the improvement in pediatric health care services. For me with young children at that time, it was a great relief to entrust the care of my children when they got sick to capable, knowledgeable, and experienced pediatricians. I shall always be grateful to the superbly competent pediatricians who patted my hand and reassured me when any of my children was sick.

Child experts say that each child is unique, each one having a distinctive personality. Right-ho! But experts don't tell you that babies have personalities the moment they're born. One of my children wrecked carefully laid out feeding schedules, crying for milk every two hours instead of the standard three or four-hour feedings. And when he wanted his milk, it had better be there instantly otherwise he would let out a bellow loud enough to wake the dead.

Like all children, my children went through the usual child development stages from infancy to adolescence. I recall well those challenging years and the memorable phases in their personality development when "NO!" was the word of the day along with . . . "I dunno" . . . "Leave me alone" . . . "Mine and don't anybody dare touch it" . . . "Really" . . . "I'm bored."

I found out that the child rearing books I bought were not of much help. I retired them. Countless great—and good—men and women were raised by mothers without the guidance of books on child psychology. For example, Hammurabi, Hatshepsut, Socrates, Plato, Aristotle, Alexander the Great, Julius Caesar, Cleopatra, Jesus Christ, Muhammad, Mozart, Shakespeare, Michelangelo, Leonardo da Vinci, Galileo, Charles Darwin, Louis Pasteur . . . the list is long.

Gradually, I came to realize that a mother had only to love her children coupled with understanding, trust—and a lot of patience. Throw into the brew encouragement, reassurance, and praise, and the kids will turn out just fine. At least, theoretically, they should. Still, with all my good intentions, there were times when I was voted *Worst Mother of the Year:*

"Gosh mommy, why can't you do anything right?"

"There's something wrong with your thought processes."

"Do you always have to say the wrong thing at the wrong time?"

"What's the matter with your hair? You look as though somebody mentally retarded cut your hair."

"Why do you want to watch the news again? You watched

it yesterday."

"I hate it when you tell me to study."

Sometimes though, the pendulum swung the other way, making me *Mother of the Year* and once they anointed me *Mother of the Century*. That was the time when our cook went away on holiday and I cooked lunch and dinner for the family. My first day in the kitchen, I felt like an apprentice at a circus. The children came to look, curious, repeatedly asking, "You're going to cook? What will you cook?" Children's memories were certainly short on good deeds and long on imagined neglect. They had forgotten that long before we employed a cook I used to cook for them, in addition to working full time. After two days my performance was evaluated. All recommended unanimously that I should stay home to cook for them. I had passed the critical scrutiny of the most discriminating taste buds!

They made some earthshaking discoveries too, like, "Did you know Mommy that Daddy is not always right?" And they went through a phase moaning grievances:

"I feel like a prisoner in this house. Nobody ever respects my rights."

"I can't study without the TV on."

"The teachers don't know how to teach!"

"I did not study for this kind of grade!"

"I have no freedom in this house."

"Why must I tell you where I'm going and what time I'll be back?"

From the safe distance of time, I can smile at the memory but those were intensely difficult years. Yet, there are myriad cherished moments in a mother's life. I remember well those precious moments . . . sleepy, dreamy eyes struggling to stay awake as I read their favorite bedtime stories—*Peter Rabbit, Little Red Riding Hood, Jack and the Beanstalk, The Little Mermaid,*

Snow White . . . tiny hands clasping my hand as nightmares were chased away and sleep finally triumphed . . . crying and then beaming as a bump or a bruise was kissed away . . . little faces breathless with excitement, running to me, and clutching a bunch of flowers picked from the garden, "For you Mommy". . . staying up all night soothing feverish little angels . . . little hands ripping through gift-wrapped toys . . . little faces smiling radiantly, on top of the world, on a merry-go-round . . . my youngest telling me with wide eyes "Mommy I love to sleep when it's noisy" when she fell asleep during a folklore dance and drum show . . . a trail of flour on the kitchen floor, tables, and chairs and painted faces shouting, whooping, screaming, intent at playing Indians . . . presenting me with their first wedding anniversary gift, "a vase to put your flowers in" and bought with their pooled pocket money, my youngest clasping my hand and putting it under her cheek at bedtime and telling me, "We wanted to get for you that thing that you get from oysters, what is it called, pearls, but they were very, very expensive" and me kissing her, assuring her that their gift was better than pearls or diamonds.

That's the wonderful thing about children—their love is the purest.

But before children evolve into worldly and all-knowing adult beings, they are filled with wonder at the mysteries of the world and full of questions. They perceive the world differently from adults, and they often ask questions that only a Plato or a Socrates could adequately answer. Parents, especially a mother, must be creative and imaginative. Being endowed with metaphysical flair is a big plus. One of my children, then five years old, was preoccupied with tomorrow.

"Mommy, when will tomorrow come?" She would ask as I put her to bed.

"When you wake up."

"Is it tomorrow now?" She would ask as soon as she woke up.

"Well, yes darling. Today is yesterday's tomorrow."

"Tomorrow Mommy, tomorrow, has tomorrow come?"

"Well, no."

"When will tomorrow come then?

"When you wake up tomorrow."

"Mommy, how come tomorrow never comes?" I had felt helpless, at a loss to explain, and frustrated. Tomorrow was always around the corner, forever out of reach. How do you explain to a child that the concept of time is abstract, that it is relative, and time is an arbitrary invention of man? The poet Khalil Gibran expressed it beautifully, "Yesterday is but today's memory, and tomorrow is today's dream."

Another of my children had a different sort of dilemma at the age of four. When told that I wanted privacy while I was taking a bath, my son went searching for privacy from room to room and opening drawers. Not finding privacy, he came back and called through the door, "Mommy, I can't find privacy. What does it look like?"

Such are the imponderables that children grapple with. But if children have difficulty with abstract thinking, they seem to instinctively understand feelings and emotions.

One day, my husband accidentally broke one of my favorite Chinese jars. It happened when we had guests over for tea. He was having such a good time, talking to our guests and gesticulating energetically. The jar was perched on a table behind a two-seater sofa where he was sitting. At one point during the animated conversation, he laughed, threw his head back, and flung his arm wildly over the back of the sofa. The jar fell to the floor with a loud crash, breaking into big and small pieces. I paled, and then quickly collecting my composure, smiled and said, "It's all right. It wasn't expensive anyway," as I collected the broken pieces. True, it wasn't expensive. My husband took one look at the broken jar and pronounced, "It shouldn't have been there in the first place," aggravating me but I had to smile through my distress.

On learning what happened, my children had gasped with disbelief. It was the very same jar over which, when they started trading blows at each other near it, I would yell, "My jar, oh my beautiful jar! Don't break it. Go and do your fighting somewhere else." They would invariably stop their fight and turn to me, saying, "You care more about that jar than about us. You don't even care if we get hurt." They judged me a "heartless mother" not realizing that distraction is one of the strategies that a mother employs to abort a war among her children. For days after the smashing of the jar, they followed me around the house, whispering and giving me queer glances. When I closed my door more than ten minutes, one of them rapped on the door loudly inquiring, "Mommy, are you all right?" There was always one of them following me around. As soon as they were certain their mother was not going to hang herself from the ceiling, they gaily deserted me to join their father's camp, maintaining, "It was in the wrong place from the beginning." Still, they darted furtive glances at me from time to time. More than their father, my children knew how dear the jar was to me.

The breaking of the jar happened when two of my children were going through adolescence, a difficult time in any family. Life, of course, is not always harmonious, even in the best of families and particularly in a family with many children. There are times when we break each other's hearts without meaning to.

Many days, weeks, and months passed. One Friday afternoon, I took out the broken jar from storage and started putting the pieces back together. While I was fixing it on the kitchen table, all my children came to watch. They seemed fascinated. Luckily, some of the pieces were big and it was easy to superglue the pieces together. They helped me figure out the parts like in a puzzle.

"Will it be the same as it was?" they kept asking anxiously.

"With superglue anything is possible," I replied cheerfully.

Like me, they seemed to take comfort in the process of repairing the jar, of trying to make it the same as it used to be. But there was something sad about the process of gluing the pieces back together because we all knew the jar wouldn't look exactly as it did before it was broken. Some pieces were too tiny to glue back, so the jar had a tiny hole, though almost invisible. Nevertheless, we were delighted with the result. It was almost like new. My children felt a sense of accomplishment in helping me mend the jar. They argued over who helped most, each one claiming the lion's share. Haifa pointed out that the lines of breakage could be seen on closer inspection.

"It's all right" I said. "Once broken, a thing could never be the same, though hearts could heal."

When we are busy with life, we do not notice the passage of time. This is true whether you live in New York, Doha, or Timbuktu. Time passed like a dream. My dream that my children would grow up, have college degrees, have careers and jobs, marry and lead meaningful lives came true. But they live, play, laugh, and cry in my heart still as children.

I have two small grandsons now, two-year-old Aziz and baby Saud. I dream of many, many grandchildren in the future, God willing. My dreams are filled with the sound of children laughing and playing; the pitter-patter of little feet running; and splash and screams in the swimming pool.

As I play with Aziz, my first grandson, I see in him his mother, my daughter Alia. When Aziz is around, the house again resounds with that unique and age-old word, NO! When he plays in my room and sees my attention focused on my work or my laptop or reading, he calls to me, "Grandma, come play with

Aziz." He pronounces his name Athith because he can't say the letter "Z" very well yet, but I love it. He'll grow up soon enough and his diction will be better than mine, like his mother. So I interrupt what I'm doing and get down on the floor to play with him, with his cars, trains, and Legos and sing nursery rhymes. Playing with him, I remember myself playing with each of my children when they were small. How like Aziz they were! In such moments I could not help but think how the cycle of life repeats itself. I am reminded of the Babylonian epic, Gilgamesh. The hero, Gilgamesh, went in search of eternal life and a wise man advised him: "Gilgamesh, live each day in joy . . . love the child that holds your hand . . . delight in your wife's embrace . . . for these alone are the concerns of mankind."

Part Four

LIFE IS AN OCEAN

CHAPTER 19

Arab Love Song

always remember how my husband and I met for the first time. I met him during my residency in Kansas City, Missouri.

I was full of dreams when I graduated from medical school. I was young and youth is a temple full of dreams but all I remember now of the dreams of that period is that I wanted to be a good doctor, a modest goal. I recall that all my friends in medical school had left for America and I did not want to be left behind. So, to America I went for postgraduate medical training. It was the dream of young physicians in my country, the Philippines, to go to the U.S.A. for postgraduate medical training. America has a well-deserved reputation of providing excellent professional and advanced medical training for physicians. Like shifting sands, world renowned centers of learning in medicine move from one region to another throughout history: Greece and Alexandria in antiquity; Cordova and Baghdad in the Middle Ages; Europe, in particular Italy, during the Renaissance; Germany in the nineteenth and early part of the twentieth century; and the United States over the last fifty years. Who knows, perhaps, in the coming century, China might become preeminent. Physicians have traditionally flocked to such centers in search of knowledge—and opportunity.

The perception before the 1990s was that the United States had a shortage of physicians and accepted foreign doctors to work in its hospitals. Such doctors were known as Foreign Medical Graduates (FMG) or International Medical Graduates (IMG). Quality of medical education, however, varies from country to country and to ensure fitness to enter residency or fellowship programs in the United States, foreign graduates must pass an examination and be certified by the United States' Educational Commission for Foreign Medical Graduates.

In the Philippines, medical education is patterned after the American system. After the Second World War, there was a lack of adequate health services in the country. Morbidity and mortality rates were high. There was only one physician for every 2,000 individuals. There were only five medical schools graduating a little over a thousand physicians annually for twenty million people then. Clearly, more medical schools were needed to graduate more doctors to meet the health needs of the country. There was great concern, however, for the quality of medical education and in 1957, the deans of medical schools and two government officials went to the U.S.A. to study the system of medical education. Consequently, a system similar to the American medical school system was implemented. To qualify for an M.D. degree (Doctor of Medicine), you must have a Bachelor in Science degree (B.Sc.) and then complete four years of medical school as well as one year of rotating internship. To be licensed to practice medicine, you must pass the National Board Examination in medicine after obtaining an M.D. degree.

I obtained my B.Sc. degree from the University of Santo Tomas, the Catholic University of the Philippines (UST). It is one of the oldest universities in Asia and was founded by Dominican priests in 1611. It is old but not the oldest; the oldest university in the world is Al-Azhar University in Cairo, Egypt, which was founded in 969 AD. I have warm memories of my university days in UST. It was a sheltered life and I was happy there. Classes for male and female students were separate and there were separate stairways for the sexes. In the old building— the Main Building—there was a central stairway that enabled students to bypass the long corridors leading to the different classrooms. It was a convenient stairway to use when you were late for class and girls and boys gravitated to that stairway. But there was always a priest there at 8:30 in the morning guarding, turning students away, and pointing to the appropriate stairways: this stairway for boys; that stairway for girls. That system of segregating the sexes in my university probably prepared me for the basic social structure of separation of the sexes in Qatar!

Sometimes, when I have flashbacks of my pre-medical student days, I see myself hurrying for class to the main building through the Arch of the Centuries, a fine monument on campus with Doric columns and baroque details. On the sides and at the top of the Arch, there were panels depicting the life of Saint Thomas Aquinas, the patron saint of the University. I remember reading the following inscription on the arch: "Gateway to the history of the finest breed of Filipinos." The university claims many notable alumni, among them Jose Rizal, the Philippine national hero honored with a commemorative plaque on the left pillar of the Arch and Manuel L. Quezon, second President of the Philippines from 1935 to 1944, honored with a commemorative plaque on the right. And then of course there is me . . . I graduated despite an old superstition that while studying at the University, you must never pass through the Arch until your graduation. If you do, an event will happen that will not allow you to graduate at the school.

I would have loved to have continued my medical studies in

UST but its location required me to commute more than an hour with heavy traffic, too long for a medical student who wants to sleep "five minutes more" in the mornings. So for convenience, I attended another university situated nearer our house, the University of the East Ramon Magsaysay Memorial Medical Center for my M.D. degree.

Musing over my life as a medical student, it seems now like one long series of examinations. I remember the long hours of study . . . everyone in class on exam morning afflicted with a syndrome and saying, " I did not study. I fell asleep. I am not ready" . . . the butterfly feeling in my stomach before an examination. No medical student could have been spared the butterfly sensation on such days. Looking back now, I frequently wonder how I survived. But always, after passing each year of medical school, there was that nice, warm feeling of accomplishment.

After obtaining my M.D. and passing the national board examinations in medicine, I also took and passed the examination given by the United States Educational Council for Foreign Medical Graduates (ECFMG), qualifying me to enter residency and fellowship programs in the United States. Foreign medical graduates from all over the world go to the United States, like waves. Studies analyzing physician demographics in the United States reveal that about 25 percent of active physicians are foreign graduates and that 20 percent of these physician foreign graduates are US citizens. These doctors, escaping from the social and political conditions in their countries, are seeking opportunity and stability, partly for themselves and largely for their children. So, many choose to stay in the United States rather than return to their country after completing training. They serve ably, often working in areas of great need.

Kansas City was the first American city I set foot in. My entry was not at all like the triumphal "I came, I saw, I conquered" style of Julius Caesar even though the airport had a small town feel, unlike the international and cosmopolitan aura of Los Angeles Airport through which I had transited. When I arrived in Kansas City, it was snowing. My brother, who was living in Chicago, had flown in to Kansas City Airport to meet me. I was glad and thankful that my brother had come to welcome me. The sight of him warmed my heart. He has the kindest and biggest heart. My brother was bundled up in a quilted parka with a hood and he wore gloves. I lightheartedly told him he looked like an Eskimo in his getup. He smiled and gave me a pair of winter gloves to wear, because he told me it was very cold outside. He made sure I was warm enough in my winter coat before we went out to look for a taxi. An airport minibus was parked just in front and after speaking to the driver, my brother told me to get in the bus. We were the only passengers.

Through the bus window I looked at the scenery with excitement and eagerness. It was still snowing and the streets and pavements were covered with snow. It was my first time to see snow. The falling snowflakes seemed as light as floating feathers softly falling on the ground, like a whisper. I wished to touch— and taste them. I found them beautiful. The trees, bare of leaves, were heavy with snow and icicles hung from some of them; the roofs of houses and buildings were covered with snow. The winter landscape before my eyes was like a scene from a pretty winter postcard. The houses had sloping roofs, some gabled, reminding me of the gothic romance, *House of the Seven Gables* by the nineteenth century American author, Nathaniel Hawthorne. But unlike the dark foreboding exterior of Hawthorne's seven-gabled-mansion, I found the sloping roofs and gabled houses in Kansas City quaintly charming. Being used to monsoon rains, lush green trees, and exotic flowers as well as city crowds and pollution, the whiteness of snow captivated me. Everything was so different from what I was used to and my brother smiled indulgently at my obvious pleasure with the snow.

My brother and I were pleased to find that my accommodation was a comfortable two-bedroom flat in a six-story apartment complex and located conveniently across from the hospital where I would be working. I had always lived with my family, never alone. I was excited at the prospect of being on my own—free and independent, qualities pursued by the young with passion. I had thought then that I had my life planned: five years of postgraduate training and then back to my country to practice my profession, and perhaps join the faculty of my medical school. Fate however, had other plans for me. I did not know then what was in store for me. I had no crystal ball and I had been too tired from the long flight to speculate on my future. *Que sera, sera . . . what will be, will be.*

The total flight time from Manila to Kansas City was twenty-four hours, excluding waiting time in airports, so I was worn out. I had changed flights twice, in Honolulu and Los Angeles. The flight from Manila to Honolulu via Guam took more than twelve hours; from Honolulu to Los Angeles five to six; and from Los Angeles to Kansas City also about six hours. I don't remember much about that long flight from Manila to Honolulu except that I forgot my graduation ring in the bathroom. When the stewardess announced that a ring was found in the bathroom, I suddenly realized that my ring was missing and it had disturbed me. To me, the ring was like a trophy, the culmination of years of study to become a physician and hence, important. Throughout history, rings have been symbolic and the iconography of rings can be found in art and literature. Rings are powerful symbols and in the world of books, they confer special magical qualities such as in the popular and enduring epic fantasy trilogy *Lord of the Rings* by J. Tolkien. Whereas it is true that rings are worn simply for ornamentation, often there is a deeper meaning. An outstanding example is the wedding ring, a symbol of love and commitment to another. On the other hand, the class or graduation ring signifies that one belongs to a group, like distinctive plumage.

When I went to claim my ring the stewardess asked me to describe it. In the manner of class rings, it was a clunky 14-carat gold band engraved with my name and the name of the university. It had my year of graduation from medical school, and the staff of Aesculapius—a rod with a snake coiled around it. Each profession has its symbol and the Staff of Aesculapius is the symbol of medicine. I was attached to my ring and wore it with pride, relishing and basking in the silent message of Aesculapius' staff: *I belong to the honored guild of physicians.* Aesculapius was the legendary Greco-Roman god of medicine and Homer in the Iliad refers to him as "blameless physician," a heartwarming and welcome phrase in our current era of litigation where physicians are blameful. Aesculapius' attribute was a staff with a single snake coiled around it. In classical antiquity, snakes seem to have played an important part of the healing ritual and were held to be the sacred servants of Aesculapius.

The Staff of Aesculapius adorned my clunky graduation ring and was dear to me for sentimental reasons—and for its symbolism. I was happy to get my ring back.

My destination when I arrived on American soil was Trinity Lutheran Hospital in Kansas City, Missouri. The hospital had a residency program approved by the American Medical Association and affiliated with the University of Kansas. It was in this hospital that I met my husband, but he was not waiting for me in the hospital on the day I arrived. I met him a couple of months later.

After finishing one year of residency in Kansas City, I went to the University of Oregon Health Science Center (UOHSC), where my husband had gone on to complete his medical residency and fellowship in cardiology. I had applied for and was accepted as resident in the same institution and then also joined cardiology with special training in echocardiography. The field of echocardiography was a new subspecialty in cardiology then. Echocardiography is a cardiac diagnostic procedure that uses ultrasound to study the structure and motions of the heart. It does not require insertion of wires or catheters to image the heart hence it is called non-invasive. At that time, at UOHSC, we were using an instrument that provided time-motion records called M-mode echocardiography that required pattern recognition of images, which bore no resemblance to actual cardiac structures. This prompted the fellows to joke, "Non-invasive, non-diagnostic." Since then, however, with technical advancements, echocardiography has become a powerful tool to study the anatomy and physiology of the heart. For more than thirty years, echocardiography has been the most important and cost effective diagnostic imaging modality in clinical cardiology.

In 1976/77, we were fortunate that Dr. Jos Roelandt of Thoraxcentre, Rotterdam, Netherlands was at the UOHSC on sabbatical from his institution. Professor Jos Roelandt is one of the pioneers in echocardiography. He tirelessly promoted the development and use of real-time cross-sectional imaging in clinical practice and is considered the godfather of clinical echocardiography in the Netherlands. In 1974, Professor Roelandt stated: "Non-invasive ultrasonic examinations should be increased in order to reduce the number of potentially hazardous angiograms and avoid these invasive studies entirely in specific groups of patient." At that time, that was a radical statement but since then echocardiography has evolved into a very sophisticated and accurate diagnostic modality and in valvular heart disease and prosthetic valve disease, cardiac catheterization is rarely done anymore. Dr. Roelandt is the recipient of numerous awards for his pioneering work in cardiac ultrasound. He has authored and co-authored over 1000 scientific papers and 19 textbooks. He was the chairman of the Department of Cardiology of the Thoraxcenter, Rotterdam from 1987 to 2004 and is presently editor-in-chief of the European Journal of Echocardiography. When he became editor-in-chief, he invited me to be a member of the editorial board as well as reviewer for the journal, an invitation that I accepted with pleasure.

The fellows at UOHSC learned echocardiography from Dr. Jos Roelandt. I have fond memories of the echocardiography sessions with Dr. Jos Roelandt, me sitting on his left and Hajar, my husband, on his right. For some reason, I remember the room. It was narrow and rectangular and at one end was a window with a rectangular table, where we sat reviewing. On the table, rolls of dry silver papers individually tied with thin rubber bands were scattered. They had reminded me of the parchment rolls of antiquity, before the invention of printing.

Dr. Jos Roelandt peppered our echocardiography lessons with historical vignettes in cardiology. For example, while scrutinizing, m-mode recordings of the aortic valve, he would mention that the human anatomical drawings of Leonardo da Vinci in the fifteenth century accurately depicted the tricuspid aortic valve, which had surprised me because I knew of Leonardo da Vinci only as a celebrated master artist who painted the famous portrait of the Mona Lisa. He further informed us that Leonardo, based on his observations and experiments, considered the three-cusped valves of the heart as a perfect example of a mathematical necessity in the workings of nature. Three was the optimum number and that is what nature had provided. All the valves in the heart except one valve—the mitral valve—have three cusps. Leonardo correctly deduced the mechanism of closure of the valves. Leonardo's illustrations in cardiac anatomy, his experiments and observations are extraordinary for the age in which he lived.

The best teacher I ever had was Dr. Jos Roelandt. I still see him in my mind's eye, thoughtfully perusing dry silver papers on which were inscribed ultrasound messages from the heart, highlighting a diagnostic point, clarifying and explaining the grammar and syntax of cardiac ultrasound, and narrating fascinating anecdotes from the pages of history. I often think of those wonderful sessions with Dr. Roelandt.

After finishing our training, my husband brought our small children and me to live in Qatar. My knowledge of the Arab Islamic world was almost non-existent when I married my husband. Over the years my husband tried his best to fill the gaps in my understanding of his world. The difference in our religious belief was never a problem since neither he nor I are religious zealots and we respect each other's religion. It was the different socio-cultural aspects of his society that I had to get used to a different way of life, a different way of doing things, a different way of thinking. The Arab Islamic world was heir to the rich cultural traditions of the civilizations of antiquity: Mesopotamia (Iraq), Egypt, Persia, Greece, and Rome. Building on the legacy of the great civilizations of antiquity, the Arab empire developed a high level of cultural, scientific, and technological advancement, a refinement of thought, manners, and taste and a unique and distinctive civilization known as Islamic flowered. The zenith of scientific and technological achievement is long past, but the people still live the thoughts, manners, and taste of that period.

It was a pleasure to encounter—and learn—about old customs and traditions that are still kept very much alive by the people. I found the people courteous, polite, sociable, gregarious, and hospitable, qualities that seem encoded in their genes. In the society, a premium is put on appropriate public behavior and privacy. Certain social rituals are adhered to strictly, especially the little courtesies they accord each other when they meet.

I enjoyed learning the different way of life in my new society. But there were moments of melancholia in my life in this part of the world; it was inevitable. I found, when I came to live in Qatar, that the vastly different customs and unfamiliar language occasionally gave me feelings of isolation. Part of me lived in my dreams of going home, smoldering like glowing coals. My work gave me solace and I continue to find consolation in my career, for work defines and validates us and gives some purpose to life. Furthermore, the practice of modern medicine has no boundaries and is worthwhile.

A few months after starting work in Qatar in 1979, in Rumaillah Hospital, I was made Director of Non-invasive Cardiology but there was no staff except me. My mandate was to establish a non-invasive cardiac laboratory section. There were no trained technicians or nurses to assist and I had to start from scratch and train people to assist me and other doctors in performing non-invasive cardiac diagnostic testing such as treadmill stress test, holter (ambulatory monitoring), and echocardiography. In many hospitals, nurses are trained to assist the doctor for such procedures. The first person I trained as a technician was Hassan, a Somali nurse. He became quite good but he was arrested for drunk driving and jailed. My husband, who was chairman of Cardiology, got him out of jail but a couple of months later, he was again arrested for drunk driving and possession of alcohol, a grievous offense in an Islamic country. As it was his second offense, the chairman could not help him and he was flogged eighty times. He was finally deported by the police for repeated drunkenness.

In 1982 we moved to the new hospital, Hamad General Hospital and there was room for expansion. Non-invasive Cardiology, through my efforts, evolved into a very sophisticated, fully digital laboratory, providing the latest diagnostic facilities in the evaluation of adult and pediatric patients with heart disease. Non-invasive cardiac laboratories traditionally have four sections: EKG, Holter, Stress test, and echocardiography and I developed the laboratory accordingly. There has been rapid progress in non-invasive testing, particularly in echocardiography, and I am quite proud that the laboratory is equipped with the latest technology and has kept pace with sophisticated advances in the field. The non-invasive cardiology section in our hospital is a showpiece in the Gulf region.

When Doppler echocardiography and color Doppler flow mapping burst on the cardiology scene in the mid-1980s, Professor Jos Roelandt was kind enough to come to Doha and teach me that new modality. Dr. Jos Roelandt first came to Doha in 1979, soon after I was appointed Director of Non-invasive Cardiology. He was invited to help us with the logistics of setting up the laboratory. It was almost impossible at that time to attract cardiac ultrasound technicians to come and work locally and he had advised us to train technicians, saying "you could teach anatomy to anyone with a high school degree." It seemed an enormous task then, requiring patience and dedication. I remember that during that visit, while sitting next to Dr. Jos Roelandt and discussing the logistics of setting up the laboratory, I had suggested to my husband that perhaps someone else with a lot of experience should be hired to head Non-invasive Cardiology. For some reason, Jos and my husband found my suggestion hilarious and they both burst out laughing with my husband sputtering, "Rachel, you are just feeling inadequate because you're sitting next to Jos!" And Jos, his shoulders shaking with mirth, said, "Rachel, you're fine!"

In the early 1980s, Dr. Jane Sommerville, the well-known pediatric cardiologist from London, came to Doha to see patients with congenital heart disease. Most congenital heart disease patients in Qatar were sent to Dr. Jane Sommerville then. I had reservations doing congenital echocardiography in those days because I had no background in pediatric cardiology. The echocardiography of complex congenital heart disease is not simple. Dr. Jane Sommerville invited me to join her fellows in London but due to family considerations, I could not go. So, she arranged to send her best fellow, Dr. Horacio Capelli who was from Argentina, to Doha to teach me congenital echocardiography. When I asked Dr. Capelli how long he would be staying, he said with a shrug, "As long as it takes for you to learn congenital echo, three months, six months . . ." Like most adult cardiologists, I lacked sufficient background in complex congenital heart disease and the aim was not to train me to become a pediatric cardiologist but to help me understand the anatomy and physiology of congenital heart disease which would enable me to perform and interpret with confidence the echocardiograms of children with complex congenital heart disease. Early diagnosis can be life saving when appropriate management is instituted early. We had no pediatric cardiologist at that time and echocardiography is a valuable non-invasive tool, especially in congenital heart disease.

Dr. Horacio Capelli, very good and very professional, stayed three months. I learned the logical steps and segmental approach in the echocardiographic evaluation of patients with congenital heart disease. For a time, before a pediatric cardiologist joined our team, we sent patients to Dr. Jane Sommerville in London for surgical interventions or consultations, relying mainly on my echocardiography findings. I shall always be grateful to Dr. Jane

Sommerville for making it possible for me to be involved in the care of congenital heart disease patients during that period. The knowledge gained gave me special clinical perspective and insight into the world of children with heart disease.

In 1984, an American pediatric cardiologist, Dr. Gordon Folger, joined our team and I worked with him closely. Dr. Gordon Folger established the Pediatric Cardiology section in our hospital. Before he came to Doha, he was Professor in Pediatrics at the University of Michigan and from 1972 to 1984 he was Director of Pediatric Cardiology at Henry Ford Hospital in Detroit, Michigan. He also established the Division of Pediatric Cardiology at Medical College of Georgia as its director from 1964 to 1972. He trained at the Johns Hopkins University, under the tutelage of Helen Taussig, the founder of pediatric cardiology. Dr. Taussig devised the subclavian-pulmonary anastomosis, a palliative operative procedure that dramatically transformed the lives of "blue" babies (cyanotic congenital heart disease patients), making her the most important pediatric cardiologist of her time.

Dr. Folger had fond memories of Helen Taussig, referring to her as Dr. "T," chief and mentor. "She was a great teacher," he said and remembered patient presentations to Dr. Taussig as "dramatic productions that required preparation and great attention to detail." He said that during those presentations, the parents and other family members of the child were often present as well as other members of the staff. Dr. "T" would examine the child using her special electronic amplifying stethoscope (she was partially deaf). If she disagreed with the assessments of the presenter, she would commence quizzing the presenter trainee. "The experience" he said, "was often embarrassing and even humiliating but one rarely forgot the exercise." Dr. Folger recounted an occasion when Dr. "T" believed he had missed an auscultatory finding. Dr. T had insisted that Dr. Folger listen with her amplifying stethoscope. The heart sounds were so loud that he never heard what she seemed to have heard and he thought he would never recover his hearing!

As well as regaling me with anecdotes about his time with Dr, "T," Dr. Folger also entertained me with his observations about patients and fellow doctors. He was a colorful personality to work with. He is retired now but was an excellent pediatric cardiologist and did not like subjecting his little patients to catheterization unless necessary. Dr. Folger has authored and co-authored numerous scientific publications, fourteen of which were from Hamad General Hospital. One paper, which I co-authored with him, showed that color Doppler echocardiography was useful in identifying subclinical valvular insufficiency in patients with acute rheumatic fever. The paper had important therapeutic implication and has been frequently cited.

One of the pleasures of working in a highly specialized and innovative field like cardiology is introducing new techniques as they evolve and become accepted. I have sought to keep our laboratory up to date by introducing new modalities in my subspecialty as they became available: transesophageal, intraoperative, dobutamine, myocardial contrast and fetal echocardiography, tissue Doppler, and three-dimensional echocardiography. I remember when I introduced transesophageal echocardiography in our hospital. Transesophageal echocardiography is one of the exciting advances in cardiac ultrasound technology. The technique is semi-invasive since it requires passing a scope through the esophagus to image the heart. The procedure is low risk but still, to ensure safety, I sought help from our gastroenterologist with the technique of passing the scope, and he helped me set up a conscious sedation protocol. After that, I trained the rest of the staff in using the technique.

My work has kept me busy, helping much in allaying feelings of anxiety and culture stress. I find satisfaction and fulfillment in my work. Another activity related to my work that I find rewarding and satisfying is teaching. Recently, our Cardiology Department has started accepting fellows for training in cardiology and the fellows rotate in my section. When I am teaching the fellows, I remember myself at that stage in my life. During those times, I would remember the day when I arrived in America for the course of my life changed, I suppose, at the moment I set foot in America. But I did not know it then.

Medicine is exciting but it can become tedious. Physicians like other people need relief from the monotony and repetitiveness of daily life. I was inspired much later in my career to start a cardiovascular journal, *Heart Views*, devoting a few pages to the history of medicine, art and medicine, and a special section dealing with doctor/patient relationship/interaction. I felt and still do that awareness of such themes—what I call "medical culture"—is integral to giving a sense of "well being" to physicians. In addition to international scientific contributions, the journal seeks to stimulate local and regional cardiologists to do research and write papers for publication.

I conceived *Heart Views* on a wearisome evening while reading one of the mainstream cardiology journals. Idly turning the pages, I had paused and plucked from the shelf one of my art books for consolation, then spent a happy hour or so looking through its contents. Art and history provide intellectual pleasures not found in high-tech medicine. The arts soften the hard edge of medicine. I had thought then, *wouldn't it be nice if there was a cardiology journal that combined scientific papers with art and history?* And with this in mind, I founded *Heart Views*. Using my office computer and working with a graphic artist in the hospital, I printed out a thin 18-page issue using my printer. In our cardiology staff meeting, it was endorsed unanimously as departmental journal. I sent sample copies to my colleagues in Doha and abroad asking their opinion on whether the style of the journal would have a viable readership. Surprisingly I received very warm responses.

The then Media Director of our hospital, Mr. Jassim Al Fakhro, saw the sample copy, became very interested and quickly got sponsors to print the journal professionally. The second issue, which was printed professionally, came out in winter 1998. It was launched under the auspices of the cardiology department in our hospital. Since then the journal has acquired a following and has spread through word of mouth also. The journal is distributed without charge to interested physicians worldwide. Through special arrangement with Qatar Post, postage is free. This, and the fact that printing is paid for by companies who advertise in the journal have enabled us to distribute the journal without a fee. In January 2002 the Gulf Heart Association was founded and *Heart Views* was designated as its official journal.

Does an interest and appreciation for the arts and history make one a better doctor? I don't know, but I think it gives one better insight and understanding of patients, doctors, and human nature. The most flattering comments I have received about the journal were from a colleague who said he kept a copy of *Heart Views* on his bedside table and a letter from far-away Cleveland Clinic Dr. James Young, Professor and Chairman, Division of Medicine, informing me: "It holds a special place on my shelves because it is such an extraordinary publication that truly spans the spectrum of clinical and academic interests. Particularly important are your efforts to fan the flames of humanism in medicine. This in particular relates to the wonderful historical vignettes and extremely personal commentaries made in this publication. Please know that I truly appreciate it . . ." I deeply appreciate and cherish Dr. James Young's comments and thank him for eloquently encapsulating the spirit of *Heart Views.*

I am still actively involved in the journal as its editor-in-chief, a designation which sounds stern and serious but it's not really, for I find relief and a bit of magic in the medical culture section

A bit of magic . . . we all need magic in our lives, once in a while, especially when the details of life crowd in and threaten to overwhelm. Then, we need a magic wand to touch ordinary life, to light the flame that makes ordinary aspects of the world become extraordinary, light and fleeting as an occasional piece of music. It could be a hobby . . . a passionate interest . . . seeing beauty in a flower . . . a strong emotion, like love. I remember an incident long ago, before my husband and I were married. I had borrowed his pen, heard my name on the hospital pager and then started to walk away, to find a phone, to answer the page. He had called out, "My pen, my pen" as though I was stealing it. Smiling, I had turned back to give him the pen, reassuring him, "Don't worry. I'm not going to run away with your pen." And he had replied, "No, but you are running away with my heart." His reply had been so quick and unexpected, so poetic in a thrilling kind of way, and gave me a warm glow that lasted for days . . . and days. Did I fall in love then? I don't know but even now, decades later, I still find the phrase "running away with my heart" enthralling . . . a bit of magic, and he has been the magic in my life ever since.

There are unforgettable moments in life; there are humorous ones too. Many would say that meeting your love is a special event, and it is. Meeting my husband was a special event, and unforgettably humorous too. On a wintry day, in the hospital where I used to work as resident, I was in the medical records section busy dictating patients' medical histories when I heard my name paged to call Dr. Earnest's office. I was in my cardiology rotation and Dr. James Earnest was my attending. I had liked Dr. Earnest; he had warm brown eyes and sometimes he shortened my name to Rach, which I did not favor because I did not find it graceful or lyrical, but I was too shy to tell him. Once, I was walking with him during rounds, listening to him talk about patients and bits of news when I looked down and noticed that he had on a pair of Hush Puppies that had seemed so comfortable. Without thinking I had blurted, "I like your shoes. Where did you buy them? I'd like a pair for myself." He had stopped dead in his tracks, glared at me, and then threw back his head and laughed. He never told me where he bought his shoes but news of the incident had spread fast and it was "the talk" among the residents for days.

When I called Dr. Earnest, he asked me to stop by his office to discuss a patient who was to undergo cardiac catheterization the following morning. Cardiac catheterization is a medical procedure whereby a long, thin, flexible tube called a catheter is put into a blood vessel in the arm or groin and threaded to the heart. Through the catheter, doctors can perform diagnostic tests and treatments on the heart.

When I arrived in Dr. Earnest's office, he was talking to a young man, in a white coat, with dark curly hair and dark eyes. Dr. Earnest sat behind his desk and the visitor sat in front. They both looked up when I arrived.

"Rachel, this is Dr. Hajar. He is my friend," Dr. Earnest said. I nodded towards Dr. Hajar greeting him in a low voice, "How do you do?" In those days, I was very shy and did not talk much.

"Please sit down Rachel. Dr. Hajar is a resident at Kansas City General Hospital. He is here to discuss with me his rotation in cardiology next month," Dr. Earnest continued. I sat down feeling slightly disconcerted and wondered what my role was in the discussion. *Is my arrival ill timed?* I thought.

"Are you still going to be with me next month?" Dr. Earnest asked. I shook my head, informing him that I finish my cardiology rotation at the end of the month.

"Dr. Hajar and I graduated from the University of Colorado. I was three years ahead of him." Dr. Earnest informed me. There was some dispute between Dr. Earnest and Dr. Hajar as to the number of years Dr. Earnest was ahead. I smiled a little, uncertain what to say, while looking down at my shoes and wiggling my left ankle a little. I was relieved when Dr. Earnest finally discussed the patient who was to undergo cardiac catheterization in the morning.

"Where will you change?" Dr. Earnest asked as I got up to leave. I had to wear a sterile scrub suit in the catheterization laboratory, just like in the operating room. Since I was going to be on call that day I thought it would be more convenient to change in the intern's room.

"Will you need help? I'll be glad to help you." Dr. Hajar said, smiling, before I could reply to Dr. Earnest. Dr. Hajar had stood up and was standing near me.

"No, thank you. I can manage very well." I replied frostily.

"Don't mind him Rachel. He's just teasing you." Dr. Earnest said, laughing and adding as I took my leave, "I'll see you tomorrow then Rachel."

I had left his office feeling incensed. I did not know Hajar's brand of humor at that time. I was aggrieved that Dr. Earnest did not reprimand his cheeky friend. Every day after that meeting, much to my annoyance, Dr. Earnest would ask me if I had heard from his friend, Dr. Hajar. Certainly, on that first meeting, Dr. Hajar was not the magic he later became.

That incident, however, receded in a blur of night calls, rounds, seeing patients; taking histories, doing physical exams; looking for a vein to insert an IV or an artery for blood gases; running around answering incessant pages to the emergency room . . . wards . . . intensive care unit; rushing to code blues, conducting resuscitations, looking at the face of illness . . . the face of death . . . death was inevitable, omnipresent. Days passed, each day monotonously indistinguishable from the day before. Cold, dark, somber days . . . rainy, cold, windy days . . . white snowy days . . . days without the sun . . . days missing the sun . . .

One day, after rounds, Dr. Earnest called me to a window at the end of the hallway. "Come and look here, Rachel," he said, pointing to the garden below at a little tree with white blossoms. The other trees were still bare, their branches still laden with snow. To see a flower in the midst of winter is a sight to behold.

"Ain't it pretty? It's a flowering dogwood tree announcing spring," he said thoughtfully. Seeing the lovely flowers made me think of warm weather and blue skies. There was something holy about seeing a tree or shrub flower in winter. Soon after, the cold days melted, the sun returned from its travels, giving warmth and blue skies, trees dressed up in leaves, grass blanketed the ground, and the landscape bloomed with flowers. It was during the time when nature was in a celebratory mood that Hajar came for his cardiology rotation with Dr. Earnest.

Meanwhile, I had moved on to another rotation; on the same rotation was Dr. Robert Collier (Bob), who was one of Hajar's best friends. Through Bob, I got to know Hajar better and the three of us frequently ate lunch together. Hajar was intelligent, witty, and very entertaining; he was enjoyable to be with. He was the most fascinating person I had ever met. He had a refreshing sense of humor and his comments, observations, and jokes lightened up our days. Laughing is good and we laughed a lot when he was around. For a medical resident, laughter is a matter of survival. Research has shown that humor reduces stress, enhances the immune system, helps people cope better with pain, and even increases longevity. Laughter is an essential component of a healthy, happy life. Hajar frequently amused us with hilarious narrations of his on-call experiences.

I remember a hilarious incident that he narrated when he was on-call in the emergency room. A young black man had been brought to the ER claiming he was "paralyzed" and had no sensation from his knees down. Hajar had performed a complete neurological examination but could find nothing wrong. When he tested the sensation of both legs with pinpricks, the young man claimed he could not feel pinpricks below both knees but could feel them above his knees, which did not follow a particular dermatome distribution. Dermatome is a Greek word, which literally means, "skin cutting." In medical parlance, it means an area of the skin supplied by nerve fibers originating from a single nerve root. In diagrams or maps, the boundaries of dermatomes are sharply defined, but in real life there is considerable overlap of innervations between adjacent dermatomes. Thus, if there is loss of sensation due to pathology of a spinal nerve, sensation in the region of the skin, which it supplies, is not completely lost as overlap from adjacent spinal nerves occurs; however there will be a reduction in sensitivity.

That young man's sensory loss had been too sharply demarcated and Hajar suspected that he was acting or pretending. So, Hajar had told the nurse to bring an angiocath needle (a big, long needle usually used for medical procedures such as aspirating fluid from the chest, abdomen, or heart). The patient had been laying on the stretcher. Hajar had shown the big needle to the patient, explaining that he would poke him with the needle deep in the sole of his foot to stimulate the nerves and cure him. Then, Hajar had raised his arm with the needle high in the air, ready for the poke. And the young man had quickly jerked his knees up and jumped out of the stretcher, cursing, "Son of a . . . . .! But Hajar had replied, "You're not grateful. You should thank me for curing your paralysis."

Another highly amusing story he told us was about a drunken man who had gone to the emergency room because his tongue was sore. He had told Hajar that he had been kissing his pet snake and the snake had bitten his tongue! Fortunately, his pet was not poisonous but his tongue was painful and he just wanted to make sure everything was fine.

Hajar's amusing and interesting anecdotes were like bright plumage in the often dull, occasionally bleak days of a medical resident. He had a wide network of friends whom he could call on to lend a helping hand. One morning after a night call, I found that there were a lot of admissions in the non-medical and non-critical wards of the hospital and I had to do the history and physical examination of those patients. There were more than a dozen of those patients admitted for minor procedures. Hajar called Bob and other friends and each one helped me by taking two or three patients. The job was done in no time! Over lunch, in the doctors' lunchroom, the guys were laughing, talking about it, and joking with me. Anita, a female Indian resident overhearing the incident lamented, "How come no one ever helps me when I have a lot of those admissions?"

So, my residency days in Kansas City went by . . . days tumbling one upon another, like falling leaves. Glorious spring days gave way to summer . . . longer days . . . sunsets at nine . . . lazy days . . . after work outings with friends . . . picnics . . . pizza days . . . dinners . . . weekend tennis, watching from the sidelines . . . Hajar left to continue his residency in Portland, Oregon . . . Autumn came . . . Winter came, and I finished my first year residency in Kansas City. But Hajar in Oregon beckoned with a poem:

O' my lovely girl
My dearest one
Dark and loneliness
Without the sun.
Everyone has a lover
Everyone has gone
And alone I fell down
Like a broken gun.
Breathless and full of tears
I can no longer run
From ashes of sadness
Ton over ton.

O'my lovely girl
My only one
You are my life
You are not any one.
Fly to Portland
And replace the sun
And shine over my heart
With all the fun.

To Portland, Oregon I flew, to replace the sun . . . and we were married on February 1, 1975.

I remember my wedding with nostalgia. On that special day, I woke up to find it snowing. Softly, softly the snowflakes fell from the sky . . . so white, so pure; gently, gently, they landed, blanketing the ground in white; white—the color of truth, symbol of light, innocence, and purity. It was beautiful to watch the snowflakes fall through my window the morning of my wedding day – a new page in my life, a new beginning. People usually get married in spring or summer when the weather is warm and nice but Hajar and I didn't think of the weather when we chose our wedding date. It seemed immaterial, unimportant. *How long will the snow last*, I wondered, *Will the snow stop falling for my wedding?* I closed my eyes and made a wish. The wedding was in early afternoon and after noon, the snow abated. The sun came out, shining, smiling, and conjuring an exquisite rainbow in the sky to celebrate.

Weddings are usually elaborate family affairs but ours was very simple since neither his family nor mine could attend. My brother who was living in Chicago was supposed to give me away but he could not come because his wife was hospitalized at that time. The rest of my family was far away in the Philippines and Hajar's family was in Qatar. That situation had made me sad but I was happy on my wedding day. The medical staff of the department of medicine in UOHSC substituted for our families. The absence of our families threw into sharp relief the essence of the nuptial ceremony, of two people vowing to love and cherish each other, "to have and to hold, from this day forward, for better, for worse, for richer, for poorer, in sickness and health, until death do us part."

The marriage ceremony and reception was held in the home of our gracious friends, Dr. Dennis Koukol and his wife, Linda. Dennis was a very good friend and at the time, he was medical chief resident at UOHSC. Dennis gave me away. Walking slowly to the tune of "Here Comes the Bride" and holding onto Dennis' right arm as we walked towards the makeshift altar, I remember becoming nervous and he patted my hand kindly and affectionately. Dennis' son, Brent, was the ring bearer. Brent wore an Arab costume, complete with flowing red-checkered Arab headdress called ghattra and he carried the cushion on which sat the wedding ring like it was the most precious thing in the world.

The wedding ring . . . yes . . . my wedding ring. It still fits my ring finger. I remember the day when Hajar took me to a jewelry shop to buy the wedding ring. It was on a Saturday and Dr. Nizar Feteih and other friends came along. Dr. Nizar Feteih was the best man at our wedding. Nizar was Hajar's best friend. Hajar often turned to him for help and advice. He was an old colleague of Hajar's from the University of Colorado Medical School. He was a cardiologist who became the managing director of King Faisal Specialist Hospital from the 1970s to the 1980s. He was also physician to the Saudi royal family. Nizar died of brain cancer in 2007. I shall always remember Nizar with affection, and he will always occupy a special place in the garden of my memories.

When we entered the jewelry shop, a man with glasses and a slight stoop pleasantly greeted us. The guys, greeting him jovially, said, "We'd like to look at wedding rings" and the man took us to a glass counter filled inside with trays of glittering rings. "Rachel, choose what you want," Hajar said. I looked at the array of sparkling rings and tried on some models. Most of the rings were too sparkly for my liking, but finally I chose a baguette diamond ring set in white gold, a rectangular center diamond flanked with four smaller tapering baguettes. It didn't twinkle but I had liked its quiet glow. Nizar pointed out, "Rachel, it doesn't sparkle and catch the light" and directed my attention to the flashy, glitzy rings. But I had my heart set on the baguette. "Let her have what she wants," Hajar said. Much later after our marriage, Hajar told me that Nizar had whispered to him, "Don't buy it. It's too expensive."

Hajar's Arab friends provided roasted whole lamb for the occasion, which was a sensation and a novelty among the guests—and for me! A Catholic priest, Father Paul from Lebanon and an Islamic sheikh, Mr. Nouri Alkhalidy, also from Lebanon, officiated during the ceremony. Before the actual wedding, we had met with the Mr. Alkhalidy. During that meeting he had asked me to set the dowry amount and I had been deeply insulted. Hajar and Mr. Alkhalidy then spoke in Arabic and then we had left. I did not know it then but during that meeting, the Islamic marriage contract was supposed to be signed. The dowry was central to the contract. In the marriage context, dowry is the money paid to the father or senior male relative of the bride. The father of the bride sets the sum. The dowry is the bride price, hence my revulsion—and horror.

Over subsequent days, Hajar explained to me that before any marriage could take place in an Arab society, a marriage contract must be signed and that the dowry was an integral part of the contract. The signed contract and ritual associated with the signing is called *milca* (pronounced milcha) in Arabic.

"The problem is that no Islamic marriage could take place without the dowry part." Hajar explained.

"We could do without the Islamic marriage part, just the Christian part." I replied, having formed the opinion that an Islamic marriage had some preconditions that I considered offensive. The dowry stipulation was a dilemma. I considered it a big obstacle and it had weighed me down. It was a matter of pride and self worth, weighed against a marriage ritual that was different to my way of thinking and what I was used to.

"We must have an Islamic marriage too." Hajar said firmly.

Despite my agitation, I understood his position. He was after all a Muslim. He had the right to want an Islamic marriage as much as I wanted a Catholic marriage. Besides, the milca (marriage contract) is an official document of proof of marriage. All of us live within our heritage even when we think we have outgrown it.

"Why don't we just put $1.00 as token?" He suggested.

The $1.00 token seemed a solution to an otherwise delicate

state of affairs. In the Islamic marriage contract that Mr. Alkhalidy drew up, the amount of dowry was not mentioned but to this day, Hajar, whenever he has the opportunity, tells me with much glee, "I bought you for $1.00!"

In the Arab world, the dowry is called mahr—gift. I no longer consider the dowry, as "bride price" and I no longer regard it with as much horror as on that day long ago when Mr. Alkhalidy asked me to set my dowry. This modified perspective comes from the knowledge of hindsight. Arab Muslim customs, especially those of the Gulf have two mahr: one given in advance and the other deferred, which involves a larger sum of money or gold to be paid to the wife in case of divorce. It is meant to discourage the man from divorcing the wife and gives the wife some financial security.

Marriage customs go straight to the heart of a society. It is the inner core that contains many dearly held beliefs and each culture evolved a distinctive set of marriage customs and rituals. The institution of marriage is old, very old, and marriage customs, as practiced today, originated in ancient cultures. We do not know the origins of many rituals, practices long forgotten and mantled in swirling mists. As I had so often done in the past, I looked to history, to better understand the society in which my husband lived and which I came to share. I found that what I thought was an anomalous ritual is a custom steeped in the traditions of antiquity and had not much to do with religion. The dowry marriage tradition is found in many cultures around the world. What was a simple quest into the origins of marriage customs became a fascinating romp into the realm of biology, culture, science, genetics, evolutionary psychology—and who we are.

Central to marriage is procreation, the biological urge to perpetuate the species, the language of the genes. In the beginning, male Homo sapiens secured a wife through capture, and sometimes as a present. The custom of giving wives as gifts to other men was rampant in Greek and Roman culture. A man could have as many wives as he wanted. But even though female Homo sapiens are supposedly naturally faithful, there were no laws to prevent them from running away with a more attractive and more desirable partner. However, male Homo sapiens, being brainy, came up with the idea of the marriage contract, a document with the force of law, which allowed a man and a woman or women to cohabitate and procreate, in peace, without interference or competition from other males. The ancient marriage contract stipulated that the woman belonged to the man, in other words, she was his property, and to underline this, there had to be payment—a "price," that was set by the father of the bride. It was a very clever way to protect the male's bloodline, his genes.

The dowry marriage contract eliminated or reduced stress concerning rivalry over genetic perpetuation. Gender roles were defined, with males dominating and females subservient; man the breadwinner, woman the nurturer of his genes. Thus, the patriarchal society came into being across many cultures.

In the Code of Hammurabi, one of the most ancient written legal systems in history, we learn that the custom of giving dowry to the bride was a well-established tradition and clarifies how it was to be handled under several circumstances. The basalt stele upon which Hammurabi's law code has been inscribed is at the Louvre Museum in Paris. When I first saw it during a visit to the Louvre, I thought it was grand for what it represented and beautiful in its simplicity: black polished basalt, 8 feet high and 6 feet in circumference, conical in shape and covered with beautifully engraved Babylonian writings. Carved on the upper part of the stele is an engraved picture of a seated sun god on a throne handing a scepter and ring to Hammurabi (1792—1750

BC), King of Babylon and known in history as "the lawgiver." The composition served to symbolize the divine origin of the great code of laws, which King Hammurabi received.

The Code, which contains 282 laws encompassing nearly every area of ancient life: social, moral, religious, commercial and civil law, is considered by historians and archeologists as the most comprehensive and well-preserved law code of ancient history. The laws give us insight into the society and civilization of Sumer (Ancient Iraq).

The contents of Hammurabi's law code are available on the Internet and anyone reading a sample of the laws will realize that the ancient people for whom those laws were written were sophisticated and humane and not barbaric and uncivilized. In that society, the dowry marriage system was an integral component of social and family life, and Hammurabi passed laws prescribing regulations for its proper use. The laws make clear to us that one of the basic functions of a dowry has been to serve as a form of protection for the wife against the possibility of ill treatment by her husband and his family. It was a form of financial security for the wife in case of divorce or separation. Code No. 137 of Hammurabi's law states: "If a man wishes to separate from a woman who has borne him children, or from his wife who has borne him children: then he shall give that wife her dowry, and a part of the usufruct of field, garden, and property, so that she can rear her children. When she has brought up her children, a portion of all that is given to the children, equal as that of one son, shall be given to her." So, I believe that the origin of dowry marriage as practiced in Arabia may be Babylonian.

In societies where marriages are arranged, the dowry is a central part of the marriage contract. Through time and across cultures, marriages have always been arranged. It was a form of alliance between families or kingdoms in the case of the aristocracy. It was based on practicality, stemming from considerations of property, duty, politics, and religion. The fathers of the couple had the legal right to give or withhold consent, and they frequently entered into economic negotiations before the engagement was formally concluded. From my readings, I have come to the conclusion that in its original context, the dowry served to protect the interests of both parties: the male his bloodline and peace of mind and the female her financial security.

Studies have shown that married men are the happiest, followed by single women; whereas the most miserable are single men with married women close behind. So, why do women ever want to get married? For many women, it is an economic necessity. For financially independent women, it is a mystery and can only be explained by love, I suppose.

In my case, I married for love, and so did my husband. Why do we love? No one knows. My husband believes in romantic love, and so do I. The notion of romantic love, i.e., love before marriage, is fairly recent. It was only in the mid-eighteenth century that marriage came to be based increasingly on love and affection. This trend intensified steadily, and by the nineteenth century the sentimental doctrines of romantic love had come to prevail in the West and in distant colonial lands. It has been mentioned that the twelfth century troubadours brought the notion of romantic love from the Arab lands (ironically) during the time of the crusades. Of interest, a married woman in a Christian love marriage lost the right to own property and she assumes her husband's name. In the Arab Islamic marriage, which is arranged, she retains the right to own property and she keeps her maiden name. What intriguing contradictions!

In my husband's society, marriages are arranged. After our marriage, he told me that while a student, his family had attempted to arrange a marriage for him three times. His condition always was that he must see the girl first. On each occasion, the father had refused. On the second attempt, Hajar had arranged a meeting with the father of the girl. Hajar always believed in his own powers of persuasion. He had tried hard to convince the father to allow him to meet his daughter. The father steadfastly refused but was agreeable to Hajar seeing a picture of his daughter. That had been a big concession but a picture was not good enough for Hajar. He had refused the picture offer because he "had to see the real thing!"

During the 1960s, when Hajar tried his bid to meet a potential bride, the groom never set eyes on the bride until the wedding night. Since that time, there have been slight concessions, but even now, no respectable family would allow a face-to-face meeting before the milca (marriage contract). I had found it extraordinary that Hajar tried to go against tradition. Life's choices are frequently dictated by the prevailing or existing social conditions of the particular society we live in. There are some individuals, however, who question certain social customs and will defy certain traditions if such is not to their liking. Hajar is one of them.

When I asked Hajar if he would ever consider marrying someone chosen by his family, he unhesitatingly answered, "No." My husband believes that the choice of a wife is the prerogative of a man and no one else.

After living in Qatar for many years and meeting and talking to couples in arranged marriages, I have come to believe that love could come after marriage. As to which is better, I am not sure. Many love marriages have ended in divorce; so have many arranged marriages. As reported by the Qatar Statistics Authority in 2007, the divorce rate among Qataris was 35.8 percent. In the U.S.A., the divorce rate is about 40—50 percent.

So, it would seem that the risk of divorce is high in both types of marriage. I suppose the success of any marriage boils down to personality and temperament as well as the commitment of both parties—and a certain maturity. Since my husband and I come from different cultures, the odds of divorcing were very high but fortunately it didn't happen.

Intercultural and inter-religious marriages are not uncommon in the Arabian Gulf. The governments send their students on scholarship to pursue higher studies abroad in Western colleges and universities, mainly to the United Kingdom, U.S.A. and Canada. It is inevitable that some of these students would meet and marry foreign women as in the case of my husband. At the time we got married, it was against the law in Qatar for a student to marry a foreigner. I did not know of the existence of such a law until one day in the autumn of 1977, when my husband informed me that the Qatar ambassador to the United States had called him.

"Oh, why did he call? Do you know him?" I asked.

"No, I don't know him personally. He told me that there is a rumor that I'm married to a foreigner." He replied.

"Is that a problem?" I asked lightheartedly. "It's strange that he should call you just for that," I continued, puzzled.

"It is not so strange. You see there is a law that no Qatari student could marry a foreigner."

"What do you mean? I don't understand." I said, stunned.

Hajar explained that to marry a foreigner, a Qatari student had to obtain the permission of the government through the Interior Ministry. The punishment for marrying a foreigner was being kicked out of the scholarship and refund what the government had spent on the student. The Amiri Diwan (Office of the Amir) had heard a rumor that Hajar was married to a foreigner, hence the call from the ambassador. Hajar further explained that he had good standing with the government, being one of the best students, and that he had a letter from the minister of education that he was proud of him. He further informed me that before the government sends a student abroad on scholarship, that student had to sign a form agreeing not to marry a foreigner. My husband had not signed that form.

Hajar told me: "The ambassador told me the following: 'The Amiri Diwan wanted me to spy on you and find out if the information that you are married to a foreigner is true or not. I thought I'd call you and find out what answer do you want me to tell the government. What do you want me to say? Tell me what you want and I'll put it to the government just as you want.'"

"What did you tell him?" I had asked wonderingly.

"I told him, 'The answer is: It is true and I have two children. If the government wants to make trouble for me because I married a foreigner then I will not go back and they will lose a trained doctor. If they agree they will gain two doctors because my wife is a doctor. If you obtain no objection from the government I will send you my passport to add my wife and my children in my passport so I could go to visit my family.'"

The ambassador, Mr. Abdulla Al-Mana, had called him again a few days after that conversation and told him: "HH the Amir has no objection and he ordered us to issue you the passport for your family as you wish." The Amir of Qatar at that time was Sheikh Khalifa. Many years later, when we were already living in Qatar, my husband told me that the then Amir Sheikh Khalifa had suggested to him, probably in a teasing manner: "Marry a Qatari and I will pay for all the expenses and give you a house for her." I told my husband, "The Amir was not joking and he was serious." I thought then, *with so many incentives to marry a second or third or fourth wife, how could our marriage survive?*

At first glance, the law against marrying a foreigner seems

like an infringement of basic human right but there may be mitigating circumstances on closer inspection of the society and existing social conditions. Qatar probably does not want to lose its young and educated men through emigration to foreign countries. Foreign wives may encourage them to emigrate.

We spent our honeymoon in Cannon Beach, on the north coast of Oregon, a two-hour drive from Portland. We drove there in his orange Camaro over snowy mountains. The tall pine trees covered with snow and the road snaking up and down wintry mountainsides was picturesque. I remember that we stayed at a place called Tolovana Inn, a resort that was right on the beach. We had a suite with a fireplace and spectacular views of the Pacific Ocean. It was not a vibrant place but the breathtaking views more than made up for the deserted ambiance. The weather was cold, rainy, and cloudy but it was nice walking by the beach, watching birds flying and swooping into the ocean, and admiring their silhouettes against the sky. I wished I were a painter. While walking, I had asked Hajar, "Do you like animals?" And he replied, "Yes, that's why I like you." I remember being offended and looking back now, it sounds very funny.

One aspect of Hajar's personality that I always admired is his eloquent way with words, when he is not in a teasing mood. Hajar is a poet and his poems have been published. He enthralled me by translating to me Arabic poetry by a blazing fireplace. It was beautiful. I learned that poetry and eloquence were cultivated by the ancient Arabs and poetry was an integral part of desert social life. In pre-Islamic Arabia, great contests in poetry were held at the marketplace of Ukaz near Mecca, where poems were recited and remembered. The best of these poems are known as The Seven Ancient Arabic Prize Poems or *Mu'allaqat*. These poems were written down upon silk, the words embroidered in golden letters and suspended on the Ka'aba, the "House of

Allah," a cube-shaped ancient shrine in Mecca and site of the annual Islamic pilgrimage. This custom continues in Islamic times and every year a new shroud is made and embroidered with the *Mu'allaqat.*

To this day, a poet commands great respect in Arab society. In the years that I have been living in Qatar, I observed how Arabs love poetry and how they admire their poets. The adoration of beautiful words is so deeply ingrained and pervasive in the society that I suspect every Arab is secretly an aspiring poet.

One poem that Hajar read to me was his English translation of an old Arab poem, which had greatly captivated me. "The poem," he said, "was sung by Umm Kulthum." The singer Umm Kulthum (1908—1975) was his favorite singer. She was Egyptian and is considered the greatest singer in the Arab world. He further informed me that the poem was part of a long poem and was written by an Arab poet, Abo-Faras Al-Hamadai, who lived in the tenth century. The poet—a prince and warrior—was captured by the Romans and imprisoned in Constantinople where he wrote his beautiful poems of love and homesickness.

As I listened to Hajar read his translation, I could not help but be swayed by the poem's rhythm and tempo. It was titled

Arab Love Song:

> *Patient man with no tears I see*
> *Does love have no word*
> *Or order on thee?*
> *Yes, I am in love and my heart would flee*
> *But secrets are not to be told*
> *Of a man like me.*

With the hand of love I reach,
When night comes by,
And down let my tears
Which always were high.

Between my bones
Fire could light,
With the flame of love
And memories of night.

I am alone,
While all my folks are present,
Any place away from you is like a desert.

Death will meet
Before I reach your side,
Later rain will not help
If thirsty I died.

CHAPTER 20

Dancing With Flowers

I sit by the window in my library, at sunset, listening to the soothing cadences of the adhan, the call to prayer. In the silence that follows, I contemplate the plants and flowers in my little balcony, reflecting how far away I am from my childhood home. I smile a little at the recollection of my early days in Doha, when the call to prayer at dawn used to wake me up.

The adhan is now part of the pressure wave repertoire in my mind. I marvel at the distance I have travelled. My eyes fall on the hibiscus plants; there are two pots, one of them had bloomed gorgeously at mid-morning, its red petals delighting in the warm kisses of the sun, but with the day ending, the flower faded, dying away. Hibiscus flowers last only one day. I remember spectacular hibiscus blooms in far away gardens, in my homeland—the Philippines: red, pink, white, yellow, orange, apricot, and multi-colors. We call it *gumamela*, softer and more melodious. It is a happy flower but it needs the sunlight to blossom. Light is the key to unlocking its blooms, and there is light aplenty in Arabia, all year long. Tomorrow my hibiscus will greet me with another stunning and happy blossom, dancing flirtatiously in the sunlight. I look forward to tomorrow.

Simple pleasures are the best, and in Arabia my three sacred spaces are my library, my little terrace, and the swimming pool.

274

I love to swim in the glow of moonlight and listen to the distant summer laughter of my children's shouts of "Mommy, look!" as they jump and somersault in the air, and the sound of splashing water as their little bodies hit the water. I savor the quiet moments in the terrace communing with my plants, silent sages. I delight in the time spent in the company of my books, reading quietly. In my sacred spaces I distill my emotions, try to make sense of life and gain valuable insights about life. In my hallowed spaces I become aware of the spiritual, the sacred. The word sacred for me does not mean religion but rather universal human values in their pure form: love, honor, integrity, honesty, family, kindness, respect, responsibility, and identity—individual and cultural. These values are unchanging throughout time because they are sacred. Everyone needs a sacred space to gather, focus, and clarify thoughts and intentions, to ruminate on the direction of life and to connect with one's inner self.

When life becomes tiresome and life in a different culture overwhelms me, I commune with myself in my sacred spaces. I realize that the values I cherish cuts across cultures; they are universal. We all hold dear in our hearts the same values. The realization does not, however, prevent me from feeling homesick. The values may be the same but environment, social ethos, and perspective are different. I learned that silence is a virtue and take comfort in little pleasures that come my way. Such little delights abound and come in the form of quiet pursuits such as reading, sipping a cup of tea, looking out at nature, gardening, listening to music or just taking pleasure in simple things. When life is busy or heavy, pausing for a minute or two and looking at the world from a detached plane shifts my perspective.

The sun has dropped below the horizon; it is twilight. I play music, "Ave Maria," in my computer; sometimes I also like listening to Gregorian chant or classical music but this evening

I'm in the mood for "Ave Maria." I open the French window of my study. It is the end of October, the tail of summers in Arabia. The searing heat has mellowed but it is still warm and humid. It is still not comfortable for me to sit outside. The sweet, fragrant, and heady scent of jasmine fills the air. Down in the big garden of our house there are many flowering jasmines—Arabian jasmine. My husband has potted two for me, and the flowers perfume my balcony. The strongly scented and delicate pure white flowers open at night and close in the morning. Arabian jasmine can bloom all year long in warm climates. Sometimes our gardener puts a bunch of jasmine in my husband's car, scenting the interior, making the ride to work pleasantly fragrant. Arab perfume makers have used jasmine oil as early as the ninth century AD and its oil is among the most important of all fragrances used in perfumery, even today. Its bouquet is unique and cannot be effectively imitated by synthetics.

Arabian jasmine is the national flower of my country and we call it *sampaguita*. The flowers are gathered and strung into garlands and corsages and its oil distilled and sold in stores, streets and outside churches. The flower symbolizes purity, eternal love, and nobility. In China, as early as the third century AD, the unopened buds were used by ladies to decorate their hair and were also used to give fragrance to tea. Jasmine tea is available in Doha. Commercial jasmine tea is green tea leaves scented with jasmine flowers and comes from China and Taiwan. The jasmine flowers are harvested during the day and stored in a cool place until night. During the scenting process, the flowers are layered over tea leaves at night when the flowers bloom with full fragrance. I like jasmine tea. Jasmine imparts a very delicate flavor to tea and the bouquet is divine. I keep a can of jasmine tea in my office and occasionally prepare jasmine tea for colleagues and friends who drop by my office. Sometimes in the middle of the day when work slows down, I take a break. I brew jasmine tea, and then sit back, sipping it slowly and savoring its flavor and fragrance. Just sipping it and smelling its heavenly scent is relaxing.

Gumamela (hibiscus) . . . *sampaguita* (Arabian jasmine) . . . "Ave Maria" . . . Gregorian Chant . . . they are part of my heritage, part of my past. It is comforting to see the nostalgic flowers in my terrace, in my husband's country Qatar, and now mine too. My husband has planted them for me. He narrated to me once a touching story about Abdul Rahman I, ruler of Arab Spain in the eighth century. Abdul Rahman I was a prince of romance. He was a descendant of the Umayyads who ruled the Arab Empire from Damascus, Syria. At that point in history, the Arab empire stretched from the Atlantic and the borders between Spain and France in the West to the borders of China in the East. The Umayyad Dynasty came to an end in 750 AD when they were deposed and massacred by Es-Seffah, "the Butcher," who founded the Abbaside dynasty based in Baghdad. The Umayyads were hunted down in all parts of the world and killed mercilessly. Abdul Rahman fled to Spain, to Cordoba, where he established an Arab kingdom separate from the Abbasides in Baghdad. He was a poet too. He imported a date tree from Syria, as a reminder of his homeland, and to it he dedicated a sad little poem expressing his loneliness and sadness away from home: "Like me, thou art separated from relations and friends; / thou didst grow in a different soil, / and now thou art far from the land of thy birth." Sometimes, in the quiet moments of my life here, I share the sentiments expressed by that poet in the distant past and feel a kind of kinship with him.

The house is quiet, being a weekend, and my thoughts roam freely. . . Many Octobers, fall, winter, spring, and summer have come and gone. I have watched the passing of the seasons in my little terrace. Through a French window my library opens into a small terrace, my tiny garden—my little corner of paradise in Arabia. The English word "paradise" is derived from Greek "paradeisos," which means enclosed garden but Merriam Webster traces it to the Iranian word: pairi-daeza (enclosure), from pairi (around) and daeza (wall).

My paradise is enclosed by concrete mineralite-covered walls on three sides, but open to the sky. When I sit in my library, I see a bit of blue sky—my own little piece of blue sky—through the sliding glass door. And I see my plants and flowers—splashes of green, dashes of reds, pinks, yellows, and violets. The tiling is in the style of Sevillan or Cordoban courtyards—large, plain off-white colored tiles with just the merest hint of design and texture. Decorative floor tiles run along the walls. Hajar had wooden grills mounted around the concrete parapet considerably cutting down the intensity of light and making the area look cool, tranquil, and intimate—and elegant too. It is where I sit in the evenings and on weekends when the weather is pleasant, listening to the sounds of life: the swishing sound of water as the garden around the house is watered, dogs barking, cats mewing, screeching, children playing, the distant sound of cars passing, and birds twittering on the date-palm trees in the garden around the house.

Years ago, Hajar had planted an evergreen tree beneath the western side of the terrace when I complained at the intensity and harshness of the afternoon sunlight filtering through the glass door of my library. "A tree will last and give you shade as well as greenery," he said. The tree grew, reaching the parapet of my balcony's front wall with the top part peeping through the wooden grill, and marked the passage of time. Sadly, that tree didn't last; it was sacrificed when the front garden was re-landscaped, underlining the fact that the only permanent thing in life is change.

As yet, because of the weather, there is not a profusion of flowers in my garden. We are waiting for the weather to improve before putting in more plants and flowers. Hajar says "a couple of weeks more." Now that it's planting season in Arabia, I look forward to having more flowers, a repetition of previous pleasant seasons: violets, geraniums, roses, dahlias, petunias, azaleas, and other varieties. Soon I shall hang on the wooden grille small pots with cascading flowers, hoping to recreate the remembered lovely *Calle de las Flores* (Street of Flowers), a little street behind the Great Mosque in Cordoba, Spain. Hajar, however, prefers larger containers because "the plants will last longer." But I am not after longevity. Flowers bloom . . . fade . . . wilt . . . die . . . bloom . . . just like everything in nature: birth, death, and rebirth—a physical law that is embodied in the religious and philosophical corpus of Eastern and Western civilizations.

The thought of more flowers in my little garden sets my heart pulsing with anticipation. Sometime ago, coming back to Doha after the family summer holiday in Switzerland where flowers abound, Hajar had gone to a nursery and saw "a plant with delicate white flowers" that he wanted to get for me but "it won't survive outside." He was told they were orchids and he wondered if I knew about orchids. I told him that we had orchids in our garden when I was a child. My father used to graft them on trees. Before my mother became bedridden, she tended in our garden some white orchids. All I know about caring for orchids, however, is that they need humidity. Orchids have a delicate beauty, and I would love some in the terrace but I don't know if they would survive in the desert.

I cannot imagine a world without flowers. One evening, I came back from a vacation in the Philippines and after freshening up I had eagerly peaked at my balcony—little paradise—curious how my plants had fared while I was away. I had been delighted

at the profusion of flowers. Hajar found me in little paradise
and told me he was planning to show me the flowers in the
morning "to surprise you." I thought it was so sweet of him to
fill up little paradise with flowers on my return. The climate in
my own country is tropical and flowers bloom all year round.
During that vacation, I used to sit with my sister by the window
in her living room, sipping tea, looking out into her garden, idly
chatting, admiring the flowers in her front lawn, listening to her
floral plans, and reminiscing of the flowers in the garden of our
childhood home.

In Doha, the variety of plants and flowers is limited, but the
palette of colors in little paradise is more than enough to drench
a watercolor canvas of my life here: green leaves, blooming
fragrant flowers with colors varied as the rainbow, and clear blue
sky; occasionally cloudy skies but the rays of the sun stubbornly
and fiercely pierces through and proclaims that here in Arabia
the sun reigns supreme.

On weekday mornings, I don't have time to look at my
garden but on coming back from work, I would immediately go
to the terrace to check on my flowers. When I see the hibiscus
blooming, dancing and flirting with the sun, the roses flowering,
or the violets quietly flourishing, I feel such joy. At such times I
muse, what can a heart desire that cannot be had in a garden? And
I remember the summer of my arrival in this part of the world, so
long ago it seems, and seeing the dying flowers in my husband's
family courtyard home. It is like that here still in the summer:
Plants and flowers wilt and die or at least appear to. I remember
the Syrian rose bush. When summer came, we had transferred
it down to Hajar's garden where it was put in a shaded area
and when October came around, we transferred it back to my
terrace. It had come back looking as dry as a mummy's bone,
and I thought it was dead. Hajar said, "Let it be and see what

happens in a couple of weeks." I had tended it without much hope. Then three weeks later, I had been startled to see it sprout a profusion of young tender green leaves. It had made me so happy, and reminded me of the practice of medicine. Physicians frequently take care of patients whose condition seems hopeless but as physicians we do the best we can, utilizing new-age medical knowledge, and miraculously the patients rally in spite of the odds. Life is like that . . .

I water my plants in the evenings. Watering my plants is a quiet and relaxing pursuit, hearing the soft swish of water, smelling the merest hint of flowery fragrances: sweet jasmine, woody and mossy violet, and the enthralling scent of roses. It is especially lovely to perform the plant watering ritual under the moonlight. In Arabia, moonlit nights are gorgeous: sickle moon . . . quarter moon . . . half moon . . . full moon. Alone, watering my plants in the moonlight, I laugh softly sometimes as I remember a playful Chinese poem:

> *Among the flowers, with a whole pot of wine,*
> *– A solitary drinker with no companions –*
> *I raise my cup to invite the bright moon:*
> *It throws my shadow*
> *And makes us a party of three.*
> *But moon*
> *understands nothing of drinking,*
> *And shadow*
> *Only follows me aimlessly.*
> *For the time*
> *Shadow and moon are my fellows,*
> *Seizing happiness*
> *While the Spring lasts.*
> *I sing:*

the moon sails lingeringly,
I dance:
my shadow twirls and bobs about.
As long as I'm sober, we all frolic together;
When I'm drunk, we scatter and part.
Let us seal for ever
this passionless friendship –
Meet again
by the far-off River of Stars!

Drinking Alone Under the Moon
By Li Bai (Li Po) (701-62)

I read the poem to Hajar one weekend morning when he came to look at the plants in the terrace. He said it was not poetry because it didn't rhyme. The poem was an English translation. Something is always lost in translation and translating poetry from one language to another is probably one of the most difficult tasks. My husband who is also a poet and an ardent advocate of classical Arabic poetry maintains that if a verse does not rhyme it is not poetry. According to him, a poem should have "scales" and "notes," like music, occurring according to sets of sequencing rules to give it rhythm, beat, and cadence. He says that an error in sequence creates disharmony. In other words then, poetry and music follow coding sequence, just like the genetic DNA code. An error in DNA sequence results in a genetic abnormality or disease – a disharmony. Nevertheless, the image painted in the Chinese verse highly amused me.

Hajar is very much interested in the welfare of the plants in the terrace because they are "our plants, our garden," he says. Sometimes he frets that our plants don't get adequate sun in the winter months. When the roses don't bloom, he would ask. "Would you like roses? I'll cut some for you," and informing me that in the house garden the roses are blooming with "huge flowers."

Our bedroom, which is located on the second level of our house, opens into my study, which in turn opens to the veranda. Before we converted the veranda into a little garden I used to go walking about in the big house garden with a pair of scissors and a basket, cutting flowers. There are flowers, mainly roses. He likes roses. He loves to see flowers in bloom. Once, he told me, "A woman should be like a flower—soft and fragrant." When I told him that the rose, the most beautiful of flowers has thorns, he had replied, "Yes, but you don't see the thorns." He gave me once six potted roses and everyday he inspected them for signs of budding; and when they finally flowered, he was dismayed that all the roses bore white flowers. "I had hoped that at least one of them would bear red roses," he said, disappointed, but marveled at the statistical chance of them being all white. I was delighted at such random occurrence. He said that he had a lot of red roses but when he potted my roses they were not in bloom, so he had not known the colors. I replied that white roses were beautiful and that I liked them. The rose has long been a symbol of love and beauty: white signifying purity and innocence, red for love and passion. "In Greek legend" I said, "the rose was originally white. Aprrhodite, the goddess of beauty and love created the red rose. Running to comfort her lover Adonis who had been gored by a wild boar, she scratched herself on the thorns of a rose bush and her blood turned the white blooms red."

But Hajar's preoccupation in his garden is vegetables and fruit bearing trees. He makes rounds on his plants every evening. He grows lettuce, carrots, tomatoes, onions, cabbage, spinach and other boring vegetables and fruit trees. I used to always get insect bites in his garden so when we made a small study with a terrace for me and I acquired my own computer, I rarely walked about in the house garden anymore. But he says the real reason is because I would get lost in the big house garden because I have no sense of direction. I tell him that if he grew interesting plants such as tobacco, poppy, coca, khat and other plants that have enticed and beguiled humans throughout history, I would be encouraged to roam around his domain so I could eat or chew on the flowers of paradise.

"Ah, why should life all labor be?" wrote Alfred Tennyson in his beautiful poem, "The Lotos Eaters." The poem is based on the story of Odysseus and his sailors who, on returning home from Troy after ten years of war with the Trojans, encounter the lotos-eaters. They were a group of people who existed in a state of dreamy and languorous forgetfulness induced by eating the fruit of the lotus plant. In Greek legend, those who ate the fruit of the lotus forgot their friends and homes and lost all desire to return to their native land. I playfully encourage my husband to grow lotus. I would nibble on its honey sweet fruit and live in a state of lethargic bliss like the mild-eyed melancholy lotos-eaters: "There is sweet music here that softer falls / Than petals from blown roses on the grass . . . / Music that brings sweet sleep down from the blissful skies . . ./ How sweet it were, hearing the downward stream, / With half-shut eyes ever to seem / Falling asleep in a half-dream / To dream and dream, like yonder amber light . . . / To hear each other's whispered speech; / Eating the lotos day by day . . ."

Nibbling on lotus and dreaming . . . it sounds idyllic. Certain varieties of the lotus plant have powerful psychoactive properties (they alter the state of consciousness or awareness) when preparations are made from their roots. For this reason it was used by the monks and priests of ancient India and Egypt as a secret doorway to divine realities. The high priests of ancient Egypt may have used the Blue Lotus of the Nile to induce an ecstatic state to facilitate communion with the divine. It is not certain what specific lotus plant may have been referred to in the lotos-eaters of Greek legend but since the Egyptian civilization is older than Greek, and many Greek legends are derived from Egyptian mythology, it is very likely that the lotus of the Lotos-eaters was related to the Blue Lotus of the Nile.

Lotus flowers . . . I recall, long ago, a pretty red lotus flower in a pond outside the Cairo Museum in Egypt; my husband had snapped my picture by that pond with the red lotus. The museum was renovated and regretfully the pond was no longer there when I visited the museum again a few years ago. I have also seen white lotuses growing in ponds in my country. I remember a white lotus growing in the backyard of my childhood home, far back in the marshy section. I used to think how lovely the flower, rising magnificently on a tall stalk from a flat base of large, round leaves, and how magical the whiteness of its bloom. The lotus is native to South Asia, Australia and parts of the Middle East, particularly Egypt and Iran. Lotus is a water plant that grows in the mud of shallow ponds, lagoons, lakes, rivers, marshes, and flooded fields. Unlike other water lilies whose leaves and flowers rest on the surface of the water, the lotus leaves and flowers are elevated above the surface of the water. Its flower is graceful and exquisite, pure and clean, and fresh like morning dew.

I would like a lotus flower in my terrace, not to eat or nibble on but for the beauty and symbolism of its bloom. The lotus flower is the flower of spirituality. The flower represents purity, divine wisdom, and the individual's progress from the lowest to the highest form of consciousness. The flowers have been sacred in South Asia and the Middle East (ancient Egypt and Persia) for over five thousand years. The lotus flower features prominently in the art, architecture, mythology and religious literature of Hinduism, Buddhism, the ancient religion of Persia and ancient

Egypt. It became a common motif in these cultures and continued even with the advent of Islam. Lotus flowers are a common design on oriental carpets, textiles, architecture and feature in intricate patterns on perforated screens, tiles, and ceramics.

I desire to grow lotus in my terrace for the beauty and fragrance of its flower—and for what it stands for: purity and untarnished enlightenment amid ignorance. Perhaps its flower will remind me to be just like itself—receptive to light and beauty. The lotus flower will inspire me to strive through difficulties, to be the best that I could be, and to be always true to myself—to be "just like the lotus flower." The challenge is growing it in my terrace, in the desert, since it is a water plant. *Would it grow, would it flower,* I wonder. It has never been grown in Doha and I have been told that it won't grow here because of the climate. It seems though that nobody has tried. The lotus flower is exotic. Like me, the flower is foreign in this part of the world. But with tender loving care, it might survive and flourish, the way I did.

I read that lotus can be grown in a large round shallow pan filled with a few inches of aquatic soil and then covered with water, imitating the conditions in a pond. In my terrace, I shall try to grow the sublime lotus, protecting it from the scorching desert sun and minding the moonlight, wind, and dew. Hajar will help me, I know. If I succeed in growing the flower of spirituality in my terrace, its magnificent bloom might help me with my spiritual journey onwards, a journey that began long ago when I met my husband in another foreign land, when he penned a charming little poem for me:

> *Life is like an ocean I sailed through.*
> *I met so many ladies but who was who?*
> *I never loved Mary, I never loved Sue.*
> *I never loved any one before I met you.*

Rachel love, and love is true,
You are my love and my life too.

The poem—and the poet—conquered my heart. I entrusted my heart in his hand and his hand brought me to his land. And here I am, sitting in my study, watching the days and seasons pass, through the flowers in my terrace.

Love brought me . . . where life is like a dream, a place *east of the sun and west of the moon.*

Lightning Source UK Ltd.
Milton Keynes UK

171812UK00002B/2/P